S0-BDP-338

Population
and
Technological
Change

John Howland Rowe

Population and and Technological Change

A Study of Long-Term Trends

Ester Boserup

The University of Chicago Press

ESTER BOSERUP is a Danish economist writing in English. She has held administrative and research positions with the Danish government and with the United Nations. In addition to her many articles and chapter contributions, Boserup is the author of *Conditions of Agricultural Growth* and *Woman's Role in Economic Development*.

THE UNIVERSITY OF CHICAGO PRESS, CHICAGO 60637
BASIL BLACKWELL, PUBLISHER, OXFORD OX4 1JF

© 1981 by The University of Chicago
All rights reserved. Published 1981
Printed in the United States of America
85 84 83 82 81   5 4 3 2 1
Published in the United Kingdom with the title
Population and Technology.

The table on page 10 is reprinted with the permission of The Population Council from "Historical estimates of world population: An evaluation," by John D. Durand, *Population and Development Review* 3, no. 3 (September 1977): p. 259 (Table 2).

Library of Congress Cataloging in Publication Data

Boserup, Ester.
  Population and technological change.

  Includes index.
  1. Population.   2. Technological innovations.
I. Title.
HB871.B587   304.6'2   80-21116
ISBN 0-226-06673-8

CONTENTS

TABLES

PREFACE

We are living in a period of rapid population growth and fast techno-logical advance, and many scholars are studying the determinants of change in either population or technology. Since there are many deter-minants for each, contributions from many disciplines are needed to understand them.

It is widely, if not unanimously, agreed that the two phenomena are interrelated. Population change is one of the determinants of techno-logical change, and technological change is a determinant of demo-graphic change. I have selected this pair of determinants for investiga-tion, while ignoring others or mentioning them only occasionally. I chose this selective approach for analytical purposes; it does not imply that I believe factors other than the ones selected for systematic analysis are without importance. Partial models are sometimes more revealing than more comprehensive models, but it is important that the reader be aware of the difference.

I have once before—in *Conditions of Agricultural Growth*, which ap-peared in 1965—made a study of population and technology in which I used a selective approach. Although this new study is independent of the earlier one, it may be useful to clarify the difference of scope between them.

In both books, I focus on those types of technology which are related to population changes, while I ignore or only occasionally mention types which seem to me to have little, if any relationship to demographic changes. But while in my earlier book the focus was on agricultural technology, here I also include other population-linked technologies. I use a broad definition of technology, including, for instance, agricultural methods, sanitary methods, administrative techniques, and literacy.

Because I wanted to exclude nonagricultural technologies from my earlier book, I had to abstain from analysis of the effects of technological change on population change. I therefore discussed only the effects of population change, not its causes. This book deals with all types of population-linked technologies, and I have made an attempt to deal with both sides of the interrelationship.

The earlier book focused on agricultural societies, with only one brief chapter on the types of agricultural technologies which have been de-veloped in industrialized societies. This book has a broader scope. It deals briefly with preagricultural communities, and in much more detail with societies at early stages of industrialization. But no attempt is made to discuss the most recent technological innovations in the highly in-

dustrialized societies. The focus, when dealing with highly industrialized societies, is on their relationship with societies at lower technological levels. The internal problems of the highly industrialized societies
are outside the scope of the book.

If this book is broader in scope than the earlier one in several respects,
it is in one respect more narrow. Several chapters in my earlier book
focused on the effects of demographic and technological change on land
tenure and organization of society. To include a similar systematic analysis of the wider implications of demographic and technological change
in the present, more comprehensive, study would be a major task, since
I would have to deal with both sides of the interrelationship, taking into
account the repercussion of changes in organization on choice of technology and rates of population growth. Therefore, although I recognize
the importance of these problems, I have abstained from making more
than casual reference to them. I have chosen to deal with a partial model,
well aware of the weaknesses, but also of the strength, of partial models
compared with more comprehensive ones.

I have also abstained, as in my earlier book, from peeping into the
future. To be useful, forecasts of the future must be based on studies
of technologies still in the pipeline, and such are clearly outside the
scope of this work. Thus, this is a study of the past and the present
without any conclusions about the future. It is my hope that this con-
sideration of the past and of the general nature of the interrelationship
between technology and population can, however, help others undertake future forecasts.

Last, it should be said that this book is not a revision of the theory
I put forward in *The Conditions of Agricultural Growth*, but only an attempt
to broaden and deepen it. My earlier book provoked much comment
from scholars belonging to many disciplines. A number of them have
attempted to test the theory, either by reinvestigation of already existing
information, or by gathering new data. A sufficient number of these
studies have come out in support of my theory to make me confident
that I was on the right track and have nothing to regret, so far as the
theory is concerned. I owe much to the scholars who have supported
my views and provided me with encouragement to engage in this study
and with new studies on which I have drawn extensively. They, of
course, are not responsible for the use I have made of their material and
conclusions.

I should also express my thanks to many of the scholars who have
made critical comments on my earlier book. I have learned much from
the critical voices, although they did not convince me that my theory
is wrong. However, so many overlooked some of the reservations I

made myself, and quoted me for statements that I never made, that I have tried to be much more explicit in the present study, especially when I touch on subjects on which my opinions have been misinterpreted.

I want to express my gratitude to Robert McNetting, Douglass North, Vernon Ruttan, and Niels Holger Skou, who have read all or parts of the manuscript and made many valuable suggestions for improvement. Of course, they should not be presumed to share the views found in the volume or to have any responsibility for its errors and omissions. Finally, I am deeply indebted to Elisabeth Case, who edited the manuscript. Her thoughtful and skillful work has greatly improved the consistency, clarity, and style of the text.

I   The Framework

1 POPULATION SIZE AND TECHNOLOGICAL DEVELOPMENT

Human history can be viewed as a long series of technological changes. Just a few of the crucial ones are the discovery of the usefulness of fire at least 350 millennia ago, the appearance of food production more than 10 millennia ago, the construction of urban centers more than 5 millennia ago, the invention of mechanized large-scale industry a few centuries ago, and the invention of nuclear power a few decades ago.

Some inventions were made by chance, others after centuries of speculation and experiments aimed at solving particular problems. Except for the inventions of recent centuries, the circumstances in which they were made are seldom known; nor, often, do we know even the approximate time of the invention or the region in which it occurred.

Many of the inventions had important effects on the size and distribution of world population. The use of fire reduced mortality by providing better protection against wild animals and permitted settlement in areas with temperate and cold climates. Many later inventions also helped reduce mortality rates and promoted either decentralization or centralization of population. World population grew from very small numbers at the time when human beings began to use fire to more than four billion today; and the rate of growth accelerated as well, especially in recent centuries. This multiplication of world population would not have been possible without successive technological changes.

It is generally agreed that successive changes in technology had an important influence on population size, but opinions are divided concerning the type of technological change which had the greatest influence in different periods and in different regions. The opposite side of the interrelationship, the influence of population size on technology, has attracted less attention. The focus in historical research has been on original inventions rather than on transmission of techniques from region to region, and the influence of demographic factors on the invention of techniques is less obvious than is the influence of such factors on the transmission of techniques.

Yet societies have most often advanced technologically by introducing technologies already in use in other societies. If we want to study the causes of changing technology in various periods and parts of the world, it is more important to focus on the conditions for transmission of techniques than on the conditions for the appearance of inventions. It is, of course, a matter of choice where the line is drawn between a new invention and a technological adaptation of an existing technique to a new environment. The distinction between invention and transmission of technology becomes blurred if we use a definition of inventions broad enough to include minor adaptations of known technologies.

The speed with which major inventions have been transmitted from place to place varies enormously. During early stages of human history, some inventions seem to have been transmitted relatively quickly over huge distances. By contrast, other major inventions never moved from one people to its nearest neighbors, although contacts were frequent during many millennia. There are still some groups of people who have never introduced food production, and many more who have never constructed urban centers of their own. Much of the world population lives in areas still at early stages of the industrial revolution. It is more important to study the obstacles which prevent the transmission of technologies than to compare the number of inventions which have been made in different societies.

Demographic factors help to explain why some technologies fail to be transmitted in the wake of human contacts. Certain technologies are uneconomic or inapplicable in areas with a small and sparse population, others in areas where population density exceeds a certain level. A technology could be inapplicable for a small population because its use requires a large collective effort. Other technologies require the use of more space than is available in areas with a high population density. Large differences in population density between various areas have existed for many millennia, and the links between population size and the use of particular technologies must have significantly limited the possibilities for transmission. Thus, a technological invention might spread to distant areas with similar population size or density, but not to those areas in between with a different size or density.

Although demographic factors seem to have played a larger role in transmission than in invention of technology, they no doubt also provided some motivation for invention. In the twentieth century, nearly all invention is the result of demand-induced or cost-induced organized research, and there is usually correlation between the resources devoted to research within a given field and the speed of technological progress within that field. Thus, there is a link between the motivation for innovation and the amount of invention.

Such a link existed even before the time of organized scientific research. Most of the inventions in the early stages of the industrial revolution were not made by scientists, but by people with little or no education, who experimented to find new and better solutions to urgent problems.[1] Sometimes they succeeded after many years of vain efforts, which they would not have made had the problem confronting them been less urgent. Experiments to find new solutions to urgent problems no doubt have been made at all periods of human history, since the time of primitive hunters, but in early periods the chance of success was much smaller, and the period of trial before positive results were obtained much longer, than today. Even today, when large resources are invested in scientific research, the attempts at innovation within some fields continue to be unsuccessful. In other fields the time lag between discovery and practical application is often many decades. In past ages, when inventions were made by trial and error, few experiments were likely to succeed, and in case of success, this time lag may have been centuries rather than decades. Even so, it would seem that motivation had a strong influence on invention.

If it is agreed that many inventions—today as well as in the past— have been demand-induced, it becomes pertinent to ask to what extent this demand pull was in turn determined by demographic changes. Radical changes in the relation between human and natural resources occur in areas in which population multiplies. Shrinking supplies of land and other natural resources would provide motivation to invent better means of utilizing scarce resources or to discover substitutes for them. Moreover, population increase would make it possible to use methods that are inapplicable when population is smaller. Once these motivations led to invention or importation of technologies, the technological changes would then result in further population change, which in turn would induce still further technological change. In this way, an interlinked process of demographic and technological change would occur. Other areas would have little or no technological change because of stagnant populations, and would continue to have stagnant populations because of no technological change.

The interrelationship between population and technological change is a complicated one. Increasing population size may make life easier because there will be more people to share the burden of collective investments, but it may also make life more difficult because the ratio of natural resources to population decreases. At different periods and places, one or the other tendency may prevail. In some periods, a society with a growing population may be motivated to import new technologies by the desire to draw benefit from large collective investments. In other periods, the transmission of important new technologies may be a means to reduce or eliminate the disadvantages of a declining ratio of natural resources to population.

A growing population gradually exhausts certain types of natural resources, such as timber, virgin land, game, and fresh-water supplies,

and is forced to reduce its numbers by emigration or change its traditional use of resources and way of life. Increasing populations must
substitute resources such as labor for the natural resources which have
become scarce. They must invest labor in creation of amenities or equipment for which there was no need so long as the population was smaller.
Thus, the increase of population within an area provides an incentive
to replace natural resources by labor and capital.

Major migrations change the population-resource ratio and also the
ability to make collective investments. The area of immigration improves
its ability to make collective investments, but pays for it with a higher
population-resource ratio, while the area of emigration pays for a reduced pressure of population on resources with a reduced ability to
create—and maintain—collective investments. Therefore, major migrations of population are likely to be accompanied by important technological changes in all the areas affected by the migrations.

If it is agreed that, although many technologies are unrelated to population size, others are inapplicable or uneconomic in areas with either
a small or a large population, the next step is to ask whether it is feasible
to draw up the approximate limits for the population size which permits
or prevents the use of "population-linked" technologies. In the first part
of this study, an attempt is made to draw up such limits for different
techniques of food supply. The method used is cross-country comparison of recent data; the main purpose of the exercise is to throw light
on historical interrelations between population size and technology.

Part 2 discusses population size and technological levels in the ancient
world. Focus is on two major technological changes: the beginnings of
food production and the appearance of urbanization.[2] The early urbanized societies could function only by means of infrastructure investment
in construction and transport facilities. These investments could be undertaken only with a large labor force, since they employed human
muscle power mainly or exclusively. Therefore, in ancient times, high
population size and high technological levels went together.

Dependence upon a large labor force made the ancient urbanized
societies vulnerable to major demographic changes. Often technologically advanced societies reverted to a lower technological stage after
epidemics or wars reduced population. Meanwhile, low population
densities provided a handicap to urbanization in Western and Central
Europe. After the end of the first millennium A.D., however, population
densities in that region seem to have reached levels which permitted
widespread urbanization. Part 3 discusses the interrelations between
demographic trends and technological change in the period of preindustrial urbanization in Europe. It focuses on the increasing shortage

of forest areas for cutting timber and fuel wood and for producing the charcoal necessary to smelt iron ore. This shortage of forest areas provided motivation for some of the important technological changes during the industrial revolution.

Part 4 considers the centuries after 1750 when industrial technologies were transmitted from Western Europe to other parts of the world. Until then, areas with low population density were apparently unable to reach technological levels as high as areas with higher densities. The correlation between population density and technological level now became much less close, partly because improved transport enabled areas with sparse population to import labor, capital, and skills from Europe, and partly because some of the most densely populated parts of the world suffered from increasing strains due to a decreasing resource-population ratio.

After 1950, rates of population growth accelerated in most of the world because mortality but not fertility declined rapidly. The reasons are discussed in part 5. Rapid increases in world population were accompanied by rapid technological change. The process of interrelated demographic and technological change resulted in radical changes in the pattern of international trade and factor proportions.

2 REGIONAL DIFFERENCES IN POPULATION AND TECHNOLOGY

Differences in technological levels between countries pose a major problem to the international community today. There are also significant technological differences between ethnic groups within some countries where smaller or larger groups continue to apply primitive technologies abandoned by other inhabitants millennia ago.

If we compare the primitive technologies still used by some groups with the technologies applied in the large industrial centers, we find that the gap between the most advanced and the least advanced has been widening. But if we use a historical perspective to look at the differences between major regions, we find not only widening but also narrowing gaps, as well as shifts of technological leadership from one region to another.

East Africa[1] and Southeast Asia,[2] which have low technological levels today, seem to have been among the leaders at early stages of human history. At a later stage, North Africa and western Asia may have been ahead of others, and still later the leadership seems to have moved from west to east in Asia. Before Europe took over, after the middle of this millennium, China seems to have been the most advanced society.[3] In recent centuries, technological leadership has shifted frequently. It took only a few centuries for the United States to replace Europe, and less than a century for the Soviet Union and Japan to challenge the U.S. in certain fields. The history of technological development is a tale of both widening and narrowing technological gaps, and belies the idea that some peoples are or have been technological leaders because they were more "inventive" than others.

LONG-TERM TRENDS IN WORLD POPULATION

It was suggested in chapter 1 that differences in demographic trends may have contributed to the widening or narrowing of technological gaps between different peoples. During many millennia, regional differences in population size and density seem to have been very large, and before the industrial revolution there seems to have been a positive correlation between size and density of population and technological levels.

All such statements must, however, remain tentative because the evidence we have of population size in the past is limited. Most, but not all, countries have reliable population statistics today, but many took their first census after 1950, and only a few before the nineteenth century. Thus our information is based on estimates, many of which have a very large margin of error. It is true that China, Japan, and a few other countries began to make records of population size centuries ago, but nearly all this evidence is lost, and the surviving data are difficult to interpret. The same is true of earlier counts of households or fireplaces made in European countries.

Estimates are therefore based on indirect written evidence, such as tax records, registration of agricultural land, or information about the size of armies. Archeological research provides additional evidence; for instance, the number of burials and house sites, the amount of surface covered by buildings, and the distances between towns and villages. Archeological evidence of dietary habits combined with estimates of the numbers who could be nourished on that diet are also useful. Such calculations based on estimates of "carrying capacity" suffer, however, because they are estimates of maximum rather than actual population. It is unrealistic to assume that all populations were large enough to utilize the full capacity for food supply in the area in which they lived.

Before the Christian era, all we have are either "informed guesses" on the size of world population or more reliable estimates for small areas. However, for the beginning of the first century A.D. and for selected later periods, attempts have been made to compare, revise, and supplement existing estimates from many sources and to produce consolidated estimates of world population, broken down by regions. Recently, Durand[4] has produced such a comprehensive estimate of long-term trends in world population, based upon earlier estimates by Colin Clark[5] and predecessors. Durand's estimates are reproduced in table 2.1.

In the period covered by the table, i.e., between A.D. 1 and 1975, world population increased from some 300 million to around 4 billion. In this book, the figures for population in millions have been transformed into persons per square kilometer and expressed in density groups, as shown below. Each group has twice the density of the previous one.

Density	Density group	Persons per km²
Very sparse	1	0– 1
"	2	1– 2
"	3	2– 4
Sparse	4	4– 8
"	5	8– 16
Medium	6	16– 32
"	7	32– 64
Dense	8	64–128
"	9	128–256
Very dense	10	256–512

TABLE 2.1 POPULATION ESTIMATES FOR WORLD REGIONS (in millions)

Region	A.D. 1	1000	1500	1750	1900	1975
China	70–90	50–80	100–150	190–225	400–450	800–900
India, Pakistan, Bangladesh	50–100	50–100	75–150	160–200	285–295	740–765
Southwestern Asia	25–45	20–30	20–30	25–35	40–45	115–125
Japan	1–2	3–8	15–20	29–30	44–45	111
Remainder of Asia, exc USSR	8–20	10–25	15–30	35–55	110–125	435–460
Europe, exc USSR	30–40	30–40	60–70	120–135	295–300	470–475
USSR	5–10	6–15	10–18	30–40	130–135	255
Northern Africa	10–15	5–10	6–12	10–15	53–55	80–82
Remainder of Africa	15–30	20–40	30–60	50–80	90–120	315–335
North America	1–2	2–3	2–3	2–3	82–83	237
Central and South America	6–15	20–50	30–60	13–18	71–78	320–335
Oceania	1–2	1–2	1–2	2	6	21
Total	270–330	275–345	440–540	735–805	1650–1710	3950–4050

SOURCE: John Durand, "Historical Estimates of World Population: An Evaluation," *Population and Development Review* 3, no. 3 (New York, 1977).
NOTE: Because of the large margin of error, Durand gives "indifference ranges," i.e., limits within which he sees little ground for preference between the lower and the higher figure.

In 1975, the last year shown in table 2.1, the average population density in the world was around thirty persons per square kilometer. (Total territory is defined as total land area, except for areas permanently covered by ice.) This is close to the limit between our density groups 6 and 7 (thirty-two persons per square kilometer). Medium population density has therefore been defined as group 6–7 level in this book, with densities below 6 considered low, and densities above 7, high. (See appendix for a list of the countries in each density group.)

At the beginning of the period covered by table 2.1, average population density in the world is assumed to have been at group 3 level, i.e., less than four persons per square kilometer (see table 2.2). However, regional differences were very large: many regions had group 1 densities, i.e., less than one person per square kilometer, while India may already have had medium population density. Estimates of Indian population size, however, are even more uncertain than those for other regions.[6]

China and India, which seem to have had higher population densities than other regions, had large variations in density within their territories, and variations seem to have been the case also with Mesopotamia and Egypt.[7] Even within the extremely sparsely populated American continents, there seem to have been pockets of dense population around A.D. 1.[8] Those areas were seats of ancient urbanized societies, which were at high technological levels by the standard of the time.

TABLE 2.2 DENSITY OF POPULATION FOR WORLD REGIONS

Region	A.D. 1	1000	1500	1750	1900	1975
China	4–5	4	5	6	7	8
India, Pakistan, Bangladesh	5–6	5–6	6–7	7	8	9
Southwestern Asia	3–4	3–4	3–4	3–4	4–5	6
Japan	3–4	5–6	7	8	8	10
Remainder of Asia, exc USSR	2–3	2–3	3–4	4–5	6	8
Europe, exc USSR	4	4	5	6	7	8
USSR	1	1	1	2	4	5
Northern Africa	2–3	1–2	2	2–3	5	5
Remainder of Africa	1–2	1–2	2–3	3	3–4	5
North America	1	1	1	1	4	5
Central and South America	1	1–3	2–3	1	3	5–6
Oceania	1	1	1	1	1	3
Total	3	3	3–4	4	5	6

DATA SOURCE: Same as table 2.1 and UN statistics.

Within Europe also, variations in population density were large. Greece and Italy had medium population densities, while other parts of Europe were very sparsely populated. As late as the mid-eighteenth century, at the beginning of the industrial revolution, Europe, including European Russia, was still sparsely populated (see table 5.2). Even if Russia is excluded, Europe had only medium density at that time. High population densities for major regions are a recent phenomenon. At the time of the industrial revolution, all the regions listed in tables 2.1 and 2.2 except the small territory of Japan still had low or medium densities.

Large parts of the world continue to be sparsely populated today. Average population density in Oceania is at group 3 level. The Soviet Union, Africa, and North America are at group 5 level, and Latin America is just approaching group 6 level. Only east and south Asia and Europe are densely populated.

REGIONAL DIFFERENCES IN TECHNOLOGICAL LEVELS
Using counts of artifacts and selected traits, Carneiro has made interesting quantitative comparisons of technological and cultural levels in ancient societies and in certain contemporary communities.[9] Worldwide quantitative comparisons and long time series for many countries, however, must await the collection and analysis of further data. Attempts at measuring technological levels in quantitative terms are limited in this study to those for the present. Even these involve difficulties, and the results must be interpreted with caution.

Higher technological levels are reflected in higher production per head of population, and nearly all countries publish information about per capita production. These figures, however, are not suited for inter-country comparison of technological levels for a number of reasons. It is difficult to compare money incomes of countries with different price structures and degrees of monetization. Moreover, a country with a small population but a highly profitable industry, for instance, an oil industry, would appear to have a high technological level even though the majority of the population might use primitive technologies. Finally, use of per capita production figures would exclude all communist countries, which define national production in a way that makes comparison with other countries impossible.

To obtain a broad view of contemporary technological levels it is, therefore, necessary to combine a number of statistical series. These should include indicators of different types of technology, not only production, construction and transport, but also health technologies and availabilities of human skills. These indicators must be available for a large number of countries. These principles led to selection here of four indicators, out of seven for which figures are available, from a U.N. study for a period close to 1970.[10] These indicators are:

1. Energy consumption per capita in kilograms of coal equivalent, representing technological levels in production, construction, and transport.

2. Number of telephones per thousand inhabitants, representing levels of communication within the country.

3. Average life expectancy at birth, representing health technology and levels and quality of food supply per capita.

4. Literacy among persons aged fifteen years and over, representing levels of skills and know-how.

The indicators were ranked and given equal weight in a combined index, which was divided into five groups with twenty-six countries in each group. The average value of each indicator for each group is shown in table 2.3.[11] (The grouping of each country according to technological level around 1970 is shown in the appendix.)

Table 2.3 depicts the huge gap between the least developed countries in group I and the highly industrialized countries in group V. Average energy consumption in the first group is 50 kilos per capita, as against 5,000 kilos in group V; number of telephones is 2 per thousand persons in group I, and 280 in group V; adult literacy is 12 per cent as against 98 per cent; and life expectancy at birth is 41 years as against 72 years. However, the figures in table 2.3 do not support the widespread belief in a sharp contrast between a small number of countries with high technological levels and a very large group at very low technological levels. The wide gap between the first and the last group is filled in with

TABLE 2.3 TECHNOLOGICAL LEVELS AROUND 1970

Indicators	Technology Groups				
	I	II	III	IV	V
Per capita energy consumption in kilos of coal equivalent	50	205	445	1785	4910
Number of telephones per thousand persons	2	6	10	70	280
Life expectancy at birth	41	47	55	66	72
Percentage of literates 15 years old and over	12	29	46	80	98

DATA SOURCE: United Nations, *Developing Countries and Level of Development,* E/AC 54/L 81 Annex II (New York, 1975).

a large number of countries at intermediary stages of technological development. Countries in group IV are on average not much below those of group V, and those of group III are so high that the term medium-technology countries will be applied to groups III and IV taken together. The term low-technology countries will be used for groups I and II. (For the sake of brevity, groups I–IV will be called countries at lower technological levels, i.e., lower than the high-technology countries in group V.)

The use of a common term for groups I and II should not tempt us to overlook the large differences in technological levels between the least developed countries in group I and the other low-technology countries in group II. The energy consumption in group II is four times that of group I, number of telephones is three times as large, adult literacy is 30 per cent as against 12 per cent, and length of life 47 years as against 41 years. Although most countries had taken significant steps to introduce modern technologies by 1970, a minority still remained at largely preindustrial levels.

Table 2.4 shows regional differences in technological levels. The high-technology countries were still mainly European ones in 1970, but a minority of European countries were at medium technology levels. Nearly all countries in America and in the Arab region (i.e., all the countries of North Africa and west Asia, from Morocco in the west to Afghanistan in the east) were also at medium levels, with group IV countries predominating in Latin America and group III in the Arab region. But it should be noted that the figures refer to a period before the rise of oil prices started a process of radical change in technological levels in the Arab region. Technological levels in east and south Asia vary much more than those in other regions, but the majority of Asian countries, including the large countries in the Indian subcontinent, In-

TABLE 2.4 DISTRIBUTION OF COUNTRIES BY TECHNOLOGY GROUP

Region	Technology Group				
	I	II	III	IV	V
Europe	0	0	0	5	21
Oceania	0	0	1	1	2
America	1	1	8	13	2
Arab region[a]	1	2	11	3	0
East and South Asia	4	6	4	3	1
Africa[b]	20	17	2	1	0
Total number of countries	26	26	26	26	26

[a] Western Asia and North Africa.   [b] Excluding North Africa.
DATA SOURCE: Table 2.3.

TABLE 2.5 DISTRIBUTION OF COUNTRIES BY TECHNOLOGICAL LEVEL AND POPULATION DENSITY AROUND 1970

Density Group	Technology Group				
	I + II	III + IV	V	Unclassified	Total
1–5	26	13	7	15	61
6–7	18	21	3	2	44
≥8	8	20	16	3	47
Total	52	54	26	20	152

DATA SOURCE: Table 2.3, and also UN population statistics.
NOTE: In this and some of the later tables, Taiwan and Puerto Rico are included in technology group IV, since it is evident from their official statistics that they belonged to this group.

donesia, and probably China, were at low technological levels around 1970. Nevertheless, Asia was ahead of Africa. Africa is sparsely populated, and the large, low-technology countries in Asia are densely populated: although there no longer is the close correlation between high population density and high technological levels there seems to have been before the industrial revolution, the number of countries with a pronounced inverse relationship between density and technological level is relatively small, as can be seen from table 2.5. Only eight among the forty-four densely populated countries which could be classified by technology group were at low technological levels, and only seven among the sixty-one sparsely populated countries were high-technology countries.[12] The historical developments which have produced this picture will be discussed in later parts of this study. We shall look first at the relationship between population density and technologies of food supply today.

3 POPULATION DENSITY AND FOOD SUPPLY SYSTEMS

In this chapter I will attempt to establish a quantitative relationship between an area's population density and its predominating food supply system. A number of different food supply systems are in use in different parts of the world today. Systems such as hunting, pastoralism, and long-fallow agriculture can support only a sparse population. Unless they rely on imported food, densely populated areas must employ systems of intensive agriculture, such as annual cropping or multicropping. In other words, there is a positive correlation between intensity of food supply system and population density.

Food supply systems are of course dependent to some extent on climatic conditions. Cold climates may be suitable for hunting and pastoralism, but unsuitable for agriculture, and the same may be the case with desert areas. High population densities in such areas would require large imports of food, and are therefore unlikely. The close relationship which exists today between population density and food supply system is a result of two long-existing processes of adaptation. On the one hand, population density has adapted to the natural conditions for food production by migrations and difference in natural rates of population growth; on the other hand, food supply systems have adapted to changes in population density.[1] We shall look at this process of mutual adaptation in later parts of this study; here, by means of contemporary agricultural statistics, we study its results.

All the major systems of food supply, agricultural and nonagricultural, can make use of either primitive or high-technology equipment and other inputs. In some parts of the world, hunters use automatic rifles; in others, bow and arrow. Land preparation for intensive agriculture is done with hoes in some areas, with animal operated plows in others, and with tractors in still others. Fertilization for intensive agriculture is variously provided by chemical fertilizer, animal manure, or gathered vegetable matter. Following the lead of Theodore W. Schultz,[2] many experts focus on such differences in quality of inputs and classify agricultural systems as either "traditional" or "modern," without paying attention to the differences in fallow systems. However, if long-fallow systems, in which one crop is followed by twenty years of fallowing, and systems with short or no fallow are lumped together under the heading "traditional agriculture," the important relationship between demographic conditions and methods of food supply is overlooked. In

15

the analysis of food supply systems in this and later chapters, the basic classification will concern extensive and intensive systems and the different lengths of fallow; we shall distinguish the quality of inputs only when it is relevant.

ADJUSTMENT OF POPULATION DENSITIES FOR AGRICULTURAL ANALYSIS
In some countries, a large share of the national territory consists of arctic areas, unirrigable deserts, or mountains too steep for terracing or use as pastures. In such cases, it is misleading to use overall population densities for comparison of food supply systems, and many studies measure number of inhabitants per unit of arable land or agricultural land instead. Such a procedure eliminates the downward bias in the population density for countries with large deserts or arctic areas, but it produces a no less serious upward bias for many other countries by eliminating potentially cultivatable land,[3] including land unused for lack of infrastructure investment and investment in land clearing and other improvement; land which is covered by and classified as forest; land used for long-fallow agriculture, since areas are rarely classified as agricultural land if they have been fallow for more than two years;[4] land which belongs to pastoralists and is classified as "rough grazing"; and even land used for pastures for domestic animals, if arable and not agricultural area is used to calculate proportions.

In other words, it is necessary to eliminate unusable land for calculation of population densities, but not land which could be, but is not, part of the agricultural area. Most areas which should be eliminated according to this criterion are classified as "other areas" in international statistics of land use, but this classification also includes land which could be used for agriculture if population were larger.[5] Therefore, we have eliminated "other" land only if it is likely to be arctic or desert and accounts for such a large share of total territory that eliminating most of it would lift the country into a higher density group.

As a result of this admittedly very crude adjustment, a number of countries were lifted into a higher density group for the purpose of agricultural tables. In many cases, however, the density group remained the same, and only in one case did a country move two steps up in the density classification. This was Egypt, which moved from density group 6–7 to density group 10 and above. Many of the countries with large arctic or dry areas listed in the appendix are excluded from the tables in this chapter for lack of agricultural statistics or indicators for technological level.

Systems of Supply for Animal Food

Most people consume both animal and vegetable food, and we shall begin with the systems of supply for animal food. The following systems are in use in various parts of the world: hunting, i.e., killing wild animals; pastoralism, i.e., keeping herds and flocks on natural pastures; keeping domestic animals and birds, which gather their food in the fallows, pastures, or forests surrounding the villages or isolated farmsteads; intensive animal husbandry, in which animals and birds consume grains and other fodder, either produced for them in fields and meadows or imported from other areas. Sea, lake, and river fishing, i.e., catching "wild" fish; hatching "domesticated fish" in ponds or flooded paddy fields.

Fishing is often the predominant system of supply of nonvegetable food in densely populated islands and coastal areas. Other densely populated areas have either intensive animal husbandry, or large-scale imports of meat and fodder; alternatively, the population may live on a near vegetarian diet, since they cannot afford to use a large share of the land for natural pastures. The number of animals per head of population and the ratio of pasture land to arable land, both shown in table 3.1, are good indicators of the predominant system of food supply within an area.

TABLE 3.1 DISTRIBUTION OF COUNTRIES BY LIVESTOCK NUMBERS PER INHABITANT AND RATIO OF PASTURE TO ARABLE LAND, AROUND 1970

Density Group	Units of Small Livestock per Inhabitant[a]				
	0–1	1–2	2–4	≥4	Total
1–3	2	3	0	3	8
4–5	4	8	9	7	28
6–7	9	10	22	4	45
8–9	11	4	2	0	17
≥10	5	0	0	0	5
Total number of countries	31	25	33	14	103

	Ratio of Pasture to Arable Land[b]				
	0–0.5	0.5–2	2–10	≥10	Total
1–3	1	1	1	7	10
4–5	2	6	15	8	31
6–7	9	18	14	0	41
8–9	15	14	2	0	31
≥10	5	3	0	0	8
Total number of countries	32	42	32	15	121

[a] Includes only countries in technology groups I–IV.
[b] Includes countries at all technological levels.
DATA SOURCE: *UN World Economic Survey* (New York, 1973), vol. 1, table A-40 (livestock units per inhabitant); *FAO Production Yearbook* (Rome, 1972), table 1 (pasture and arable land).

If the ratio of pasture to arable land is very high—say, more than ten—
and the number of animals per head is also large, pastoralism predominates. If the ratio is low, less than two, not pastoralism but one of the
agricultural systems is predominant within the area. Only in sparsely
populated areas do we find ratios which point to pastoralism as the
predominant system in the country as a whole, though within a country
with higher population density there may be sparsely populated areas
in which pastoralism predominates. On the other hand, virtually all the
densely populated countries have low ratios of pasture to arable land,
and only two have more than two animals per head of population. There
are also several countries with low ratios and few animals and which
are sparsely populated. These are countries in which the predominant
system of supply for nonvegetable food is hunting or fishing.

Most of the calories contained in the fodder consumed by animals are
lost by the transformation to meat, milk, and other products for human
consumption. Pigs and poultry are more efficient transformers of fodder
to animal products than are cattle and other herbivorous animals, but
in all cases a large share of the calories is lost. Consequently, populations
in densely populated areas can have large numbers of animals and
consume large amounts of animal food per capita only if they can afford
large-scale imports of meat or fodder from other areas. Many densely
populated, highly industrialized countries do import large quantities of
animal food and fodder, but table 3.1 does not include highly industrialized countries. Therefore, virtually all densely populated countries
in the table have low numbers of animals per head of population, and
low per capita consumption of animal food. They use their land mainly
for supply of vegetable food.

SYSTEMS OF SUPPLY FOR VEGETABLE FOOD
The systems of supply for vegetable food are characterized by differences
in the frequency of cropping. The only nonagricultural system, that of
food gathering, can be viewed as a system of permanent fallow, in which
no crops are planted or sown. Only self-grown wild plants, roots, and
fruits are harvested. A population which uses an area only for gathering
is using that area very extensively; land use is a little more intensive if
the population uses the forest-fallow system and plants one or two
successive crops with intervals of 15–25 years fallow or more.

In table 3.2, the major systems of supply of vegetable food are ranked
according to intensity of land use, with the most extensive systems at
the top, and the most intensive at the bottom. The most intensive agricultural systems are annual cropping, in which a crop is sown or
planted each year, leaving only a few months for fallow, and multi-

TABLE 3.2 SYSTEMS OF SUPPLY FOR VEGETABLE FOOD

	System	Description	Frequency of Cropping
G	Gathering	Wild plants, roots, fruits and nuts are gathered	0%
FF	Forest-fallow	One or two crops followed by 15–25 years' fallow	0–10%
BF	Bush-fallow	Two or more crops followed by 8–10 years' fallow	10–40%
SF	Short-fallow	One or two crops followed by one or two years' fallow	40–80%
AC	Annual cropping	One crop each year with only a few months' fallow	80–100%
MC	Multicropping	Two or more crops in the same fields each year without any fallow	200–300%

NOTE: Frequency of cropping is average cultivated area as percentage of cultivated plus fallow area.

TABLE 3.3 FREQUENCY OF CROPPING AROUND 1960 IN 56 COUNTRIES

	Technology Group				
Density Group	I	II	III	IV	V
1–3	(35%)				73%
4–5	34		59%	50%	92
6–7	39	62%	61	66	91
8–9		86	82	95	95
≥10	(99)				99
(N)	8	5	16	11	16

DATA SOURCE: Joginder Kumar, *Population and Land in World Agriculture,* Population Monograph Series no. 12 (Berkeley: University of California, 1973), annex table 6.
NOTE: In this and the following tables, parentheses around a figure indicate that information was available for only one country.

cropping, in which the same piece of land bears more than one crop each year without ever being left in fallow. Total output of vegetable food in an area is of course many times larger if intensive rather than extensive systems are used.[6]

Let us now compare the percentages of cultivation characterizing the agricultural systems listed in table 3.2 with those derived from agricultural statistics. Such information is available in a study by Kumar, which contains ratios of cultivation to fallow around 1960 in fifty-six countries.[7] In table 3.3, this information has been arranged in the same density and technology groups used in the preceding chapter. The table shows that frequency of cropping is positively related to both population density

and technological level. The percentages are higher for countries with
high population density and high technology. Table 3.2 suggests that
if an area had a percentage above eighty, annual cropping or multicropping predominated. This means that annual cropping or multicropping predominates in densely populated countries at all technological levels. (Multicropping is not included in table 3.3. Therefore, the
highest feasible percentage is 100.) By contrast, countries with medium
and low population densities use different systems if their technological
levels are different. In technology group I the percentages for countries
with low and medium densities are below forty, implying that bush
fallow is the predominant system. In technology groups II to IV, all the
percentages are within the ranges typical for short-fallow systems. This
is also the case for high-technology countries with very low population
densities, but annual cropping predominates in high-technology countries in all other density groups. It is probably because of this predominance of annual cropping in high-technology countries that many experts have paid little attention to differences in frequency of cropping,
and to the relationship between population density and food supply
systems, when discussing agricultural problems in the Third World.

If we can rely on table 3.3, it is apparent that there is little long-fallow
agriculture in countries other than those in the lowest technology group.
It should, however, be noted that information about fallow is available
for only five of the twenty-six countries belonging to technology group
II, and only eight in technology group I. The lack of fallow statistics
probably means that countries with fallow periods longer than two years
provide no information about fallow because the international classification excludes such areas from the definition of fallow. Thus there is
good reason to assume that the distribution shown in table 3.4 is biased,
and that it is necessary to supplement the information provided in
national statistics with information provided in special studies covering
smaller areas.

TABLE 3.4 DISTRIBUTION OF FORTY COUNTRIES IN TECHNOLOGY GROUPS I–IV BY
AGRICULTURAL SYSTEM

Density Group	FF	BF	SF	AC	(N)
1–3	0	1	0	0	1
4–5	0	1	8	0	9
6–7	1	2	15	2	20
8–9	0	0	1	8	9
≥10	0	0	0	1	1
Total number of countries	1	4	24	11	40

DATA SOURCE: Same as table 3.3.

A study by Turner, Hanham, and Portararo[8] compares frequency of cropping and population densities in twenty-nine communities of tropical subsistence producers in many parts of the world. None of these communities used plows and plow animals. Table 3.5 is a rearrangement of this material in density groups. These communities have a positive relation between population density and frequency of cropping, and the table provides us with much more information about long-fallow systems than does table 3.3. Among the nine sparsely populated communities, all but one used long-fallow systems. The three communities in density groups 1–3 all used the forest-fallow system, while the bush-fallow system predominated in communities with density 4–5. Bush fallow was also the predominant system in nearly all the communities with medium population density, while most of the densely populated ones had short fallow. It is obvious that fallowing played a much larger role in these communities than is indicated in the countrywide statistics for the countries included in table 3.3, where lack of information about long-fallow systems makes for an upward bias in the percentages for frequency of cropping.

Neither table 3.3 nor table 3.5 accounts for multicropping, but some information about the use of this system is provided in a study by Dalrymple.[9] An inquiry was made in twenty-four countries which were expected to use the system. In table 3.6, the results are arranged in density groups. All but two of the countries studied (Japan and the U.S.) were at medium or low technological levels. It appears from the table that multicropping is the predominant system in countries with group 10 densities and above (5 out of the 7 listed in the appendix were studied). Some countries with 8–9 densities also have high percentages of multicropping. These are Asian countries with large regional differences in population density, and it is in the regions with the highest densities that multicropping is widespread. Eastern China, in which

TABLE 3.5 DISTRIBUTION OF COUNTRIES BY AGRICULTURAL SYSTEM: 29 TROPICAL COMMUNITIES

Density Group	FF	BF	SF	AC	Total
1–3	3	0	0	0	3
4–5	1	4	1	0	6
6–7	1	8	0	0	9
8–9	0	2	6	3	11
≥10	0	0	0	0	0
Total number of communities	5	14	7	3	29

DATA SOURCE: Turner, Hanham, and Portararo, "Population Pressure and Agricultural Intensity," *Annals of the Association of American Geographers* 67, no. 3 (September 1977): 386–87.

TABLE 3.6 DISTRIBUTION OF COUNTRIES BY USE OF MULTICROPPING AROUND 1970

Density Group	Area of Multicropping as Percentage of Arable Land					
	0–5	5–30	30–50	≥50	Total	(N)
1–3	0	0	0	0	0	15
4–5	2	0	0	0	2	31
6–7	5	3	0	0	8	42
8–9	2	3	4	0	9	35
≥10	0	0	1	4	5	7
Total number of countries	9	6	5	4	24	130

DATA SOURCE: Dana G. Dalrymple, *Survey of Multiple Cropping in Less Developed Nations* (Washington, D.C.: U.S. Department of Agriculture, 1971).

multicropping predominates, has river valleys with extremely dense population; the Indonesian island of Java also is characterized by dense population and predominance of multicropping. By contrast, the percentages were low in those countries with medium and low population density.

Since all systems of food supply, for animal and for vegetable food, are related to population density, the animal and vegetable systems are to some extent linked to each other. In sparsely populated areas with long-fallow systems, the extensive areas of fallow and other unused land provide natural fodder for herds and flocks of pastoralists or for wild animals which can be hunted. In densely populated areas, intensive agriculture leaves little fallow land for gathering of self-grown fodder. Moreover, use of inferior land for cultivation, improved in some cases by large investments of labor and capital, leaves little land for use by domestic animals. Therefore, annual cropping and multicropping are often associated with intensive animal husbandry based upon production or imports of fodder, while short-fallow agriculture in areas with medium population densities makes it possible to avoid fodder production and feed the animals on fallows and natural pasture land.

A summary of the conclusions reached above is presented in table 3.7. The table refers only to low-technology countries. By pairing domestic animals and intensive animal husbandry with particular vegetable systems, we arrive at a simplified classification of seven major systems found to predominate in low-technology areas within the range of population densities suggested for each system. The very low densities suggested for hunting and gathering seem to be generally agreed upon,[10] although no statistics are available. The densities suggested for pastoralism are derived from table 3.1, those for forest and bush fallow from table 3.5, those for short fallow from tables 3.3 and 3.5, those for annual cropping from table 3.3, and those for multicropping from table

TABLE 3.7 PAIRING OF POPULATION DENSITIES WITH FOOD SUPPLY SYSTEMS IN LOW-TECHNOLOGY COUNTRIES

Food Supply System	Density Group
Hunting and Gathering (HG)	1–3
Pastoralism (P)	1–3
Forest fallow (FF)	1–3
Bush fallow (BF)	4–5 and 6–7
Short fallow with domestic animals (SF)	6–7
Annual cropping with intensive animal husbandry (AC)	8–9
Multicropping with little animal food (MC)	≥10

TABLE 3.8 USE OF CHEMICAL FERTILIZER AROUND 1970 (kilos in fertilizer content per hectare of arable land)

Density Group	Technology Group				
	I	II	III	IV	V
1–3					22
4–5	(3)	5	16	19	210
6–7	1	6	44	37	206
8–9	1	24	47	89	224
≥10				247	575

DATA SOURCE: UNRISD, *Data Bank of Development Indicators* (Geneva, 1976), 1:56.
NOTE: Includes 81 countries.

3.6. It must be kept in mind that this pairing of densities and food supply systems relates only to "typical" low-technology areas, and that climatic and other factors account for deviations from these values.

TECHNOLOGICAL LEVEL AND FOOD SUPPLY SYSTEMS

It appears clear from the analysis in the preceding section that countries at high technological levels use much less fallowing than do countries at lower technological levels with similar population densities. The main explanation of the large differences is the much more widespread use of industrial chemicals in countries at higher technological levels. Countries in technology group I use virtually no fertilizer on food crops (small quantities are used for nonfood crops for export), while countries in group V with densities above group 1–3 level use hundreds of kilos per arable hectare, as can be seen from table 3.8. Only the most densely populated countries in technology group IV use quantities of chemical fertilizer which approach those used in technology group V.

Fallowing serves several purposes. Some of the most important ones are to prevent exhaustion of soil fertility, to reduce weed growth, and to limit the spread of plant disease. These purposes can also be served by use of chemical fertilizer, herbicides, and pesticides. In other words, industrial inputs can substitute for fallowing, and they do so in high-technology countries.

Chemical inputs, however, are not the only substitute for fallowing. Proliferation of weeds can be prevented by repeated weeding. Parasites can be removed by hand from individual plants subject to attack, or such plants can be removed. Soil fertility can be preserved by applying manure and night soil as well as vegetable matter found in forests and other uncultivated areas or at the bottom of rivers and lakes. Table 3.8 includes only chemical fertilizer, not composts made of other fertilizing matter. It can be seen from table 3.9 that as late as 1965, other than industrially made fertilizer accounted for the larger share of Chinese fertilizer consumption, and a large part of Japan's as well.

Use of such fertilizing matter, most of which is gathered by peasants and their families and placed in the fields, is the chief means of preserving soil fertility in densely populated areas in which the peasants are unable to use fallowing. Therefore, use of chemical fertilizer, is not a good indicator of fertilizer use; only if differences in population density are taken into account is it an indicator of technological levels in agriculture.

It was mentioned above that one of the purposes for which fallowing is used is to reduce the growth of troublesome weeds. Therefore, producers who use a plow to prepare the land before sowing or planting can better reduce the length of fallow periods than those who use only hand tools. The manure from draft animals may also help to reduce fallowing. The difficulties in reducing fallowing when no plows are used help to explain why the tropical communities with medium population densities in table 3.5 used long-fallow systems. These communities used neither plows nor draft animals.

Use of intensive agricultural systems with frequent cropping not only requires that the problems of fertilization and weed control be tackled

TABLE 3.9 USE OF FERTILIZER IN CHINA AND JAPAN (kilos in fertilizer content per hectare of arable land)

		Chemical Fertilizer	Other Fertilizer	Total Fertilizer
China	1957	3	112	115
	1965	18	117	135
Japan	1958	224	196	420
	1970	386		

DATA SOURCE: Shigeru Ishikawa, *Factors Affecting China's Agriculture in the Coming Decade* (Tokyo, 1967); Japan 1970 figures from UNRISD, *Data Bank for Development Indicators* (Geneva, 1976), vol. 1, table II, 18.

by one of the methods mentioned above, but also often necessitates regulating the water supply and leveling or terracing land, especially for the use of multicropping. Because the second and third crops must be grown outside the most favorable season, irrigation may be needed even in areas with a relatively humid climate. The extensive use of water control in areas with group 10 densities in which multicropping predominates can be seen from table 3.10. This table also shows that all countries with more than forty per cent of the arable land under irrigation around 1970 were densely populated countries. In contrast, nearly all sparsely populated countries have low percentages of their arable land under irrigation. This may seem surprising, since many of them have dry climates. The explanation is that the population in a sparsely populated country with dry climate can limit cultivation mainly to land near rivers and lakes, which receives natural humidity. The inhabitants may also be mainly pastoralists, whose herds and flocks may use dry land. Therefore, the populations in these sparsely populated countries have been able to avoid investments in the irrigation facilities needed in densely populated countries with similar climatic conditions.[11]

Like fertilization and weed control, water control can be effected either by industrial inputs or by labor-intensive operations. With primitive or mechanized equipment, ground water can be lifted or surface water gathered from rivers and lakes and transferred to the fields, and land can be terraced to prevent erosion. The relationship between use of mechanized draft power, population density, and technological level is shown in table 3.11. Erosion of hillsides used for cultivation can also be prevented by a forest-fallow system, and fallowing is sometimes used to preserve humidity in land which is too dry to bear a crop each year. In humid areas, draining facilities are likely to be needed for intensive agriculture, and many densely populated European countries have

TABLE 3.10 DISTRIBUTION OF COUNTRIES BY PERCENTAGE OF IRRIGATED LAND AROUND 1970

Density Group	Percentage of Arable Land Equipped with Irrigation Facilities				
	0–5%	5–20%	20–40%	≥40%	Total
1–3	4	1	0	0	5
4–5	17	5	2	0	24
6–7	24	10	3	0	37
8–9	10	14	6	3	33
≥10	1	3	1	3	8
Total number of countries	56	33	12	6	107

DATA SOURCE: FAO, *Production Yearbook* (Rome, 1972), table 1.

TABLE 3.11 NUMBER OF MALE AGRICULTURAL WORKERS PER TRACTOR UNIT

Density Group	Technology Group				
	I	II	III	IV	V
1–3	11000	560		(20)	
4–5	30000	1260	100	60	
6–7	24000	2860	240	150	(1)
8–9	(7000)	2980	2230	70	7
≥10			(300)	(51000)	(45)

DATA SOURCE: *UN Implementation of the International Development Strategy* (New York, 1973), vol. 1, table II,18.
NOTE: Includes 69 countries, only selected countries for technology group V.

draining facilities. However, such facilities are not covered by statistics, which include areas equipped with draining facilities only if these are part of irrigation facilities. This explains why the percentages for water control are low in many densely populated countries.

In other words, there are three different ways to deal with the problems of soil fertility, weeds, water control, and erosion: (1) fallowing, as in sparsely populated countries; (2) industrial inputs, as in high-technology countries; and (3) labor-intensive practices, as in densely populated countries at low technological levels.

POPULATION DENSITY AND OUTPUT OF LAND AND LABOR
Densely populated countries use a larger share of their territory for food production, as shown in table 3.12, and also use it more intensively than sparsely populated countries. Gross output per unit of land used for crops and pasture is much higher, as can be seen from table 3.13, which is based on data for output of land and labor computed by Hayami and Ruttan.[12] Since countries at higher technological levels have better statistics table 3.13 includes mostly countries in technology groups III to V; India is the only low-technology country included. In each technology group, output per hectare can be seen to rise with increasing population density, with the most densely populated countries having more than ten times the output of the most sparsely populated countries within the same technology group. There are also differences in output per hectare between technology groups with similar densities, depending on use of industrial and scientific inputs or imported fodder, but these differences appear to be smaller than those between density groups.

The area per male agricultural worker tends to be larger in high-technology countries, because they use better equipment and purchased

TABLE 3.12 DISTRIBUTION OF COUNTRIES BY AVAILABILITY OF ARABLE LAND AROUND 1970

Density group[a]	Arable Land[b] as Percentage of Total Territory					
	0–5	5–10	10–20	20–40	≥40	Total
1–3	11	3	1	0	0	15
4–5	16	9	3	2	0	30
6–7	3	6	20	11	1	41
8–9	0	1	4	19	11	35
≥10	0	0	3	5	1	9
Total number of countries	30	19	31	37	13	130

	Hectares of Arable Land per Inhabitant					
	0–0.1	0.2–0.4	0.5–0.8	0.9–1.6	≥1.7	Total
1–3	1	2	2	1	4	10
4–5	2	14	7	6	4	33
6–7	0	17	16	8	0	41
8–9	9	20	7	0	0	36
≥10	10	0	0	0	0	10
Total number of countries	22	53	32	15	8	130

[a] Unadjusted densities. [b] Arable land is land under crops plus land classified as fallow.
DATA SOURCE: FAO Production Yearbook (Rome, 1972), table 1.

TABLE 3.13 ANNUAL OUTPUT OF LAND AND LABOR AROUND 1965

	Technology Group									
Density Group	I	II	III	IV	V	I	II	III	IV	V
	Number of Countries[a]					Average Output per Hectare[b]				
1–3	0	0	0	0	2					0.5
4–5	0	0	1–2	4	2			0.3	0.4	1.8
6–7	0	0	2	3	4			0.6	0.4	2.1
8–9	0	1	2	3–4	8		(1.2)	2.2	1.8	3.0
≥10	0	0	1	1	3			(7.8)	(11.9)	7.6
	Area per Worker[c]					Average Output per Worker				
1–3					240					120
4–5			(18)	48	57			(11)	(19)	102
6–7			15	23	28			9	9	58
8–9		(2)	2	11	13		(2)	5	20	39
≥10			(0.6)	(0.7)	6			(5)	(8)	46

[a] 39 countries for output per hectare and 37 for output per worker. [b] Gross output converted to wheat units, but excluding fodder and other inputs produced and consumed in agricultural enterprises. Hectares include arable land and pasture. [c] Workers include only male, adult workers.
DATA SOURCE: Yujiro Hayami and Vernon W. Ruttan, *Agricultural Development: An International Perspective* (Baltimore, Johns Hopkins University Press, 1971), p. 732.

inputs instead of labor inputs. But the differences between technology groups seem to be smaller than those between density groups. However, if we compare output per male worker in density groups at similar technological levels, the smaller area of land per male worker in the densely populated countries is compensated for by the higher output per hectare. Therefore, differences in output per worker are relatively small between density groups, and output per worker tends to be lower in densely populated countries than in sparsely populated ones at similar technological levels.

It is important to note that while the figures in the table refer to annual output per adult male worker, work hours are not of equal length, and work days per year are more numerous when intensive systems are used than when extensive can be applied. Moreover, there are large differences in the extent to which women and children participate in agricultural work in different countries.[13] Therefore, differences in output per unit of labor input are likely to deviate considerably from the differences per male worker shown in the table. We shall return to differences in labor input in later chapters.

II   Population and Technology in the Ancient World

4 FROM FOOD GATHERING TO AGRICULTURE

Chapter 3 focused on the relationship between population density and food supply systems today. We saw that densely populated areas have intensive systems of agriculture, while areas with sparse population have extensive systems. This correlation between population density and intensity of the food supply system is the result of a long historical process of change of both population size and technologies of food production. Population densities have adapted to differences in natural conditions for food production, partly by migration and partly by differences in rates of natural population growth. Technologies of food supply have adapted to changes in population density.

In this and subsequent chapters, we shall study this process of interrelated changes in population and technology. The approach will be a selective one, with focus on certain periods and regions. We begin with the prehistoric change from the system of hunting and gathering to agriculture.

ADAPTATIONS TO POPULATION INCREASE AMONG HUNTER-GATHERERS

Little is known about the prehistoric change from food gathering to food production, and although new information on prehistoric populations and the technology they used is steadily being obtained by archeological research, we still have to rely on speculation more than on facts. Until fairly recently, the generally agreed upon theory about the origin of food production reflected the view of eighteenth-century European economists on the interrelationship between demographic and technological change. The rate of population increase was accelerating in Europe, and social scientists became interested in demographic problems. In a later chapter, we shall discuss this theory in relation to the demographic and technological changes in the period when it was first brought forward; here we are concerned with the validity of applying it to technological change in prehistoric times.

Malthusian theory considered the emergence of agriculture to be the result of the fortunate invention of food production techniques some ten millennia ago, and the increase of world population in the following period to be an adaptation to the increase in the world's carrying capacity obtained by this technological innovation. It was assumed that, before the invention of food production, prehistoric populations lived in a state of permanent semistarvation, because their fertility was high and their numbers tended to outgrow the supply of wild animals and other wild food. According to this view, only the invention of food production saved humanity—for a time—from the plight of chronic malnutrition.

A radical improvement in nutrition due to the invention of agriculture was thought to have caused a shift from stagnant population to rapid growth, as agricultural populations and agricultural methods invaded more and more of the world.[1] In recent years, however, increasing numbers of archeologists, anthropologists, and demographers have questioned the idea that chronic malnutrition was the fate of prehistoric populations, and have suggested other explanations for the slow rates of population growth in prehistory.

Our direct knowledge of the composition of the diet of prehistoric populations is improving due to a reorientation of archeological research, away from monumental structures, artifacts, and ceramic chronologies, and toward prehistoric subsistence systems.[2] But we have very little evidence of the state of nutrition before the appearance of food production. However, information about technologies used in historic times or today and apparently resembling those of prehistoric peoples can supplement the direct evidence and be used to interpret it.

Anthropologists count about twenty-seven main groups of hunter-gatherers living today.[3] Intensive collaboration between scholars studying these peoples and scholars specializing in prehistoric archeology has resulted in a revision of the traditional ideas about the conditions of life in prehistoric times.[4] There is no denying that intermittent starvation may have been the lot of some prehistoric peoples, but there is little reason to believe that lack of food was a more frequent and widespread phenomenon among hunter-gatherers than among food-producing populations.

The idea that the food situation of prehistoric populations was more precarious before than after the beginning of agriculture was based on the belief that hunter-gatherers lived exclusively or predominantly from the results of large animal hunts. In older literature, prehistoric man is usually depicted as a hunter. In most cases, however, he was probably also a gatherer of vegetable food, or women and children gathered vegetable food and caught small animals while the adult men hunted large animals. Studies of primitive hunters living today, leaving aside peoples living in arctic areas, have revealed that members of communities considered as hunters derive only 20–40 per cent of their calories from hunting.[5] Their remaining calories come mainly from vegetable food, together with fish and shellfish. It seems likely that prehistoric hunters consumed more nuts, fruits, and other vegetable food than is usually assumed. It is true that archeologists have found accumulations of large bones and shells as evidence of the subsistence activities of prehistoric populations, and it is understandable that they should classify the peoples who have left these remains as hunters or consumers of shellfish. However, bones and shells would be the most durable and spectacular remains from a mixed diet. The peoples who left them may not have starved when they were unsuccessful in their hunt; they may have varied the composition of their diet and consumed more of other types of food.[6] The ability of human beings to digest a large variety of food items is one of the main explanations of their survival and gradual spread across the earth.

Studies of gatherers living today show that they know their habitat well and exploit it in a systematic way.[7] This evidence is in sharp contrast to the earlier notion of prehistoric hunter-gatherers confined to a catch-as-catch-can existence, "dashing all over the place trying to capture or collect any edible plant or animal in sight."[8] Moreover, many of today's hunter-gatherers spend only a small amount of time on subsistence activities. For instance, among the bushmen of the Kalahari, women who do the food gathering use only two or three days per week to provide the necessary calories, and there are no seasonal hunger periods.[9] There are other examples as well of food-gathering peoples who obtain the necessary food with a small input of labor.[10]

If food-gathering peoples living today can obtain sufficient food by means of a relatively small input of time in systematic food gathering in a territory which they know well, it seems likely that most of the food-gathering peoples in prehistoric times could have done so. We must remember that today most gatherers live in marginal areas, in which unfavorable climate, poor soil, or both, limit the supply of wild food. In prehistoric times most food-gathering populations lived in fertile areas with favorable climate, those that today feed dense agricultural and urban populations. It seems realistic to assume that they were able to find sufficient wild food as long as population densities were low.

Of course, resources of a particular type of wild food do not increase in step with population increase, unlike the supply of produced food. But a group of prehistoric hunter-gatherers had several ways to avoid being reduced to starvation as a result of population growth.[11] If the wild animals and plants usually consumed fell into short supply, because the group increased in size or for other reasons, the group could adapt to this situation by consuming types of food it had been leaving ungathered and unhunted, or migration, or control of fertility, or technological change.

It is well established by archeological research that some prehistoric hunters changed their diet in response to increasing population pressure on resources of wild food.[12] Archeologists classify the last period before the introduction of food production as the period of "broad spectrum," during which many types of food were eaten. Apparently, some peoples in different parts of the world responded to growing population pressure in the preagricultural period by broadening their diet to include more and more items.

The tendency to react to population increase by migration has been observed in groups of hunter-gatherers living today. Usually, such people live together in small groups of 25–50 persons. If numbers increase beyond that size, they split up the group and some move to a neighboring area. A similar behavior was probably a frequently used means of adaptation when groups of prehistoric peoples increased in numbers.[13] The result would be that food-gathering populations gradually came to inhabit a larger and larger area.

Populations which continue to spread over a larger area must sooner or later move into another climatic zone, whether they ascend or descend mountain slopes or move horizontally. Such moves would necessitate adding new types of food to the diet, to replace those which were unavailable in the new environment. Thus, the adoption of new kinds of food could be the result of, as well as an alternative to, migration.

Some hunter-gatherers living today restrict the size of their families by infanticide, induced abortion, and other means. Limitation of offspring may occur for reasons which are unconnected to problems of food supply, for instance, children with special characteristics may be killed because they are believed to bring ill luck.[14] But restriction of births may also be a deliberate means to keep family size relatively low, because more spacing of births is desired or there is a fear of food shortage. Many anthropologists assume that prehistoric populations kept their numbers down by large-scale use of infanticide and abortion.[15] We shall return to this hypothesis later in this chapter.

Many different types of inventions made in the hunter-gatherer period served to increase the supply of food. One example is processing by fire, another the use of grindstones. Both techniques made it possible to broaden the diet to include cereals and other items which must be processed to be edible. These innovations preceded the change from gathering to production of cereals.[16] Population increase may have had no relation to the invention of the grindstone, but it probably had some influence on the later diffusion of the technique from one human group to another.

A third type of technological change which served to increase the supply of food was improvement of weapons and methods to catch wild animals, birds, and fish. Improvement of hunting techniques in response to population growth would, however, provide only temporary relief if it meant overtaxing the hunted species. A fourth type of innovation, domestication of herbivorous and other animals, would provide more lasting relief, since the animals were thereby protected against nonhuman foes and slaughtering was made selective.[17]

Shifting from gathering wild plants to crop production serves to increase the supply of food. For a population of hunter-gatherers, who have gathered, processed, and consumed wild cereals or tubers, a shift to food production requires only one additional operation, that of sowing or planting, and no new tools if a simple long-fallow type of agriculture is adopted. To sow or plant the species usually consumed is easy for people who are familiar with these plants because they are gathering them.[18] Prehistoric food gatherers, who were using fire for preparation of food and for many other purposes, could hardly fail to observe that the plants they were eating proliferated if some seeds were left in the ashes from their fires. Thus, if they found it difficult to gather enough wild plants, they might sow or plant some of the gathered seeds or tubers in ashes from a fire lit for other purposes. If they did so, they had invented the most simple system of long-fallow agriculture.

No new tools were needed to shift from gathering to this type of agriculture. Some food-gathering peoples use sticks to dig up wild roots, and similar types of digging sticks are used by peoples who apply long-fallow techniques on scorched land. No weeding and fertilization are needed for this type of agriculture, provided that cultivation is shifted to another burned plot after a few crops have been taken in the old one, and that the deserted plots are left unused for many years.

The idea that food gathering and long-fallow agriculture are closely associated is supported not only by the use of digging sticks in both systems, but also by similarity in sex distribution of work. As was mentioned above, today food gathering is often done by women, and in populations using long-fallow techniques women are most often the ones who plant, sow, and harvest. The role of adult men is limited to tree felling, while protection of crops against wild animals and birds is the task of children.[19] Thus, there are several reasons to believe that early shifts from gathering to agriculture may have involved long-fallow methods. In some cases, pollen analysis shows that early agriculture went together with burning of vegetation.

RESTRICTIONS ON POPULATION GROWTH IN PREHISTORIC TIMES
If the step from gathering wild plants to their cultivation by long-fallow methods is not a difficult one, there is little reason to believe that the prehistoric shift to food production was preceded by a period of acute

population pressure on the supply of wild food. And if the peoples who lived in the period preceding the appearance of food production were not starving, the effect of this technological change upon rates of population growth may have been much less revolutionary than was assumed by the Malthusian school.

This school assumed that the introduction of food production meant a big improvement in diet. But the shift from a varied diet obtained by hunting and gathering to a diet consisting mainly of cultivated cereals and tubers is likely to have resulted in a deterioration of nutritional levels.[20] People consuming a varied diet of wild foods were probably less exposed to hunger in years of bad climatic conditions than agricultural peoples heavily dependent upon the harvest of one or a few crops, especialy if those crops were imported from elsewhere or were not indigenous to the region in which they were cultivated and consumed.[21] It is well known that agricultural populations may be decimated by famines in years of unfavorable harvest, while famine seems to be less frequent among hunter-gatherers.

Even if we give up the idea that prehistoric peoples lived in a state of permanent semistarvation, which kept their numbers from increasing, it is not difficult to understand that the growth of world population should remain very low in that period. Violent death was probably frequent, until weapons against man-eating animals were invented. Analysis of prehistoric skeletons, our best source of information about the causes of death in prehistoric times, indicates that life was short and frequently ended violently.[22]

Moreover, various diseases may have taken a heavy toll of human life. The revolutionary decline of mortality which followed the introduction of new health techniques in nonindustrialized societies in recent decades underlines the importance of disease in explaining the low rates of population growth in earlier periods. It is necessary to revise our ideas about population trends in prehistoric periods in the light of this new evidence. The idea that populations without access to modern health technology would grow rapidly if they had sufficient supplies of food now appears unrealistic. The "normal" rate of growth for prehistoric populations is likely to have been not rapid, but very slow.

Little is known about the diseases which ravaged humanity in prehistoric times,[23] but prehistoric skeletons from certain regions provide evidence that malaria existed. This is an important discovery, since recent experience gained by the use of chemicals against malaria-carrying mosquitoes reveals that this disease has been a major killer, especially of infants, in many parts of the world. Before mosquitoes developed resistance against the chemicals, mortality rates declined spectacularly in those areas in which the disease had been epidemic. It has also been revealed that malaria contributes to low fertility.

Evidence not only of malaria, but also of malnutrition has been discovered by studying some prehistoric skeletons, but the material which has been found and analyzed so far is too small to allow reasonably firm conclusions about causes of death. The skeletons provide more evidence about the approximate age of death. A little more than three hundred skeletons of adult persons (i.e., aged fifteen years or more) from Europe and Africa dating from before 8000 B.C. revealed an average age of death of around thirty years.[24] Numbers of male and female skeletons were nearly equal, but the estimated age of death was thirty-three years for adult men and less than twenty-eight years for adult women. This difference in age of death implies that mortality related to pregnancy and childbirth was high.

Admittedly, this evidence is very limited, but it may be taken as a rough guide to longevity for those members of prehistoric communities who managed to survive the difficult years of childhood. Here we have a clue to the question of why world population remained so low until recently. Prehistoric women probably became fertile around age sixteen; if on average they died before the age of twenty-eight, they had less than twelve years in which to give birth. How many girls were they likely to bear within that period, and how many of these were likely to reach adult age? Unfortunately, skeletons cannot be used to derive rates of infant and child mortality, because bones of children are less durable than those of adults. But the number of live children born per woman would depend on the incidence of sterility, the number of involuntary and induced abortions, and the spacing of children. Let us look at what we know about these conditions and practices in other societies with primitive health conditions.

Usually, sterility affects only a small percentage of women, say around five per cent, but today some populations in sparsely populated areas have much higher percentages of sterile women, defined as women who have reached age forty-five without having borne a child, although they have had opportunity to conceive. In many areas of central Africa, as much as twenty per cent of the women never bear any children, and in some districts the rate is fifty per cent.[25] These high rates are due to endemic disease. Both venereal disease and malaria may cause sterility. Sterility is also widespread today in some sparsely populated areas of Asia, including Tibet,[26] apparently due to venereal disease. It is possible that not only high mortality, but also high rates of sterility, reduced the rates of population growth among some prehistoric populations.

The intervals between births vary widely in societies that are not using deliberate birth control. The length of the period of breast-feeding, together with involuntary abortion, seems to be the most important factor influencing the time interval between births. Unless they were breast-fed for a long time, infants probably had little chance of survival in groups of prehistoric hunter-gatherers, and continued breast-feeding for years may have contributed to a wide spacing of births in many, or perhaps all, prehistoric populations.[27] Mobile populations subsisting by hunting and gathering have a special motive for spacing children, because small children have to be carried on hunting and food-gathering expeditions.[28] Mobility thus may have induced both low birthrates and exposure or killing of infants. Moreover, the long walks carrying babies may have resulted in high rates of abortion.

Some anthropologists have made estimates of the likely number of children born alive to women belonging to prehistoric groups of hunter-gatherers. One estimate[29] is that a women could have 4.7 live births within a fertile period of thirteen years, if the interval between births was twenty-two months, sterility twelve per cent, and involuntary abortion twelve per cent. If fifty per cent were girls, and fifty per cent of these died before they reached adulthood, the annual rate of population growth would be a little above 0.7 per cent. Since this is much above the likely long-term rates of growth at those times, the conclusion is that a large share of the potential offspring was removed by means of induced abortion and infanticide.

However, the positive growth rate could easily become negative, if the assumptions mentioned above were less optimistic. A distance between one birth and the beginning of the next pregnancy of only thirteen months is on the low side for populations with long periods of breast-feeding; prehistoric populations are also likely to have had higher rates of child mortality than are assumed in the estimate above. If a population with high child mortality and high female mortality in the reproductive years also had wide spacing of births, it seems likely that a generation of women would often fail to produce a similar number of adult daughters. In that case, declining numbers in some populations in some periods would slow the long-term trend of growing world population.

The belief that all prehistoric hunter-gatherers limited population growth by induced abortion and infanticide is probably as unrealistic as the earlier belief in uncontrolled breeding. It was suggested above that prehistoric populations had a choice between adapting population to resources by means of fertility control and adapting resources to population by means of changes in consumption patterns, migration, or technological change. The peoples who chose the first alternative and killed the population surplus—or the surplus of girls—in periods of natural population increase would probably never become so numerous that they had to introduce food production. They might end up subservient to another people with increasing population, or they might continue as hunter-gatherers in inaccessible areas. The extent of fertility control observable among hunter-gatherers today may be misleading as a guide to understanding the customs of prehistoric hunter-gatherers. It seems likely that peoples who adapted resources to population instead of population to resources were the ones who ceased to be hunter-gatherers long ago.

In periods for which there is better evidence of demographic trends, there has been wide diversity in growth rates of population, both between different peoples and regions and between different periods in the history of a given people. There is little reason to believe that there was less diversity in demographic trends in the hunter-gatherer period, and the idea that all prehistoric hunter-gatherers stabilized their populations at a level somewhat below the assumed "carrying capacity" of the territory seems unconvincing. It seems much more likely that many prehistoric peoples had long periods with negative rates of population growth and gradually disappeared, and that others with low positive rates took over their territories. Probably the peoples with increasing populations sometimes hastened the decline of the others by killing the remaining ones when they had become too few to defend themselves efficiently.

If the idea of diversified population trends among groups of hunter-gatherers is accepted, it may be suggested that those who first changed from gathering to food production were likely to be ones who did not practice fertility control and who had earlier adapted to increasing population by changing both consumption patterns and technology. For such peoples, the shift to food production—by invention or by transfer of techniques—would be just one more technological change, which did not necessarily affect the rates at which their populations were growing.

Diffusion of the Techniques of Food Production

If we abandon the unrealistic assumption that world population in the prehistoric period of hunting and gathering was stabilized at or somewhat below the ceiling set by the capacity for hunting and gathering, we may make the assumption that some of the peoples who subsisted by hunting and gathering were slowly increasing in numbers and that they adapted to increasing population density by migration, changes in consumption patterns, and technological change. Viewed in this perspective, the shift to food production in more and more areas appears as part of this process of adaptation to an increase in world population.

It is known from radio carbon data that some 9–10 millennia ago food was produced in western and eastern Asia, in Mesoamerica, and in Oceania. It seems likely that the appearance of food production based on different crops in such widely dispersed areas was the result of independent "inventions" rather than transfer of techniques. These changes probably were promoted by increasing pressure of population on resources of wild food.[30] It seems unlikely that food production appeared in an area before increase of population or climatic change made it more difficult to gather enough wild food than to plant and harvest crops. Philip E. Smith[31] suggests that the availability of wild food was the reason why the apparently easy step from gathering to production of food occurred at a relatively late stage of human history.

In western Asia and Mesoamerica, the shift from gathering to production occurred very slowly.[32] A village in western Asia occupied during the period 7500–5500 B.C. provides evidence of very slow population growth and of a very slow shift from reliance mainly on gathered food to reliance mainly on cultivated crops. At the beginning of the period, wild legumes were a major food item, but during the two millennia the village existed, supplies gradually declined and were replaced by grains of cultivated cereals together with weeds and plants typical of fallowed agricultural land. This slow change from gathering to cultivation seems to indicate that the population only reluctantly, and in step with population increase, abandoned the techniques of food gathering for those of food production.

Direct evidence of prehistoric change from gathering to agriculture is rare, but since the diffusion of food production was a slow affair, there is much evidence of such change in later periods. The evidence throws light on the relationship between this technological change and demographic conditions and supports the hypothesis that the change occurs in response to increasing population pressure on wild food resources. It seems to be normal behavior to continue with food gathering as long as possible. Long after a local group has changed from gathering to production of basic crops, its members continue to obtain a part of their food supply by gathering. Even today, the inhabitants of sparsely populated areas, and even some densely populated ones, gather many types of fruits and other vegetable food and hunt wild animals when available.

Hunting and gathering seem never to be given up as long as there is any wild food available in an area, and agricultural advisers sometimes complain that these activities are so popular that the local population neglect their crops in order to engage in them. In many areas, hunting and gathering contribute significantly to the calorie and protein intake of agricultural populations. Usually this food is underestimated or forgotten in calculations of food supply and nutritional levels, and therefore many estimates of deficiencies in nutritional levels in sparsely populated areas are misleading.

In the millennia after food production began in some regions, crops and techniques of production were transferred from early centers of food production to other areas. The diffusion of wheat and barley from western Asia followed a peculiar route. In the millennia after 8000 B.C., these crops appeared in northern India, China, and Europe, while many areas located much nearer to the primary center continued to base their subsistence upon hunting and gathering or pastoralism. It is pertinent to ask whether differences in population densities provide a clue to this pattern of distribution.

Contrary to what was believed earlier, it now seems that migration of agricultural populations from the primary center in western Asia played little if any role in the diffusion of crops from region to region. It is now the prevalent view that the crops migrated on their own.[33] It is, then, more likely that new crops and methods spread because increasing population density created the need for a change of subsistence system.

However, for more than nine millennia after the "invention" of food production, most of the occupied territory of the world continued to be peopled by hunters, gatherers, and pastoralists. As late as A.D. 1500, hunter-gatherers seem to have occupied most of North America, large portions of South America and Africa, and all of Australia.[34] It can be seen from table 2.2 that in all these regions average population densities were still at group 1–3 levels around A.D. 1500. Later, when the rate of world population growth accelerated, and mass migration took place from one continent to another, the areas which had enough wild food became fewer and fewer. Except for the twenty-seven major groups which exist today, the hunter-gatherers changed to crop production or pastoralism if they survived the invasions of agricultural peoples or pastoralists.

The extremely slow diffusion of the techniques of food production and the preference, in sparsely populated areas, for hunting and gathering as subsidiary activities seem to indicate that agriculture is not a preferred technique under all demographic conditions. It seems that production of crops is preferred only when a certain population density is exceeded and wild food falls into scarce supply. In other words, it indeed seems plausible that increasing population density promotes a

change of food supply technology, while areas with stagnation or decline
of population are much less likely to adopt this type of change.

It should be added that one source of food supply—fish, whales, and
other seafood—is still at the "gathering" stage all over the world, except
for a few very densely populated areas in which fish are hatched in
ponds and flooded paddy fields. However, the rapid increase of world
population in recent decades, together with the improvement of fishing
technology, has induced international negotiations for control of "gathering" in the oceans, the last major reservoir for food gathering.

5 TECHNOLOGICAL CHANGE IN ANCIENT AGRICULTURE

In many parts of the world, there seems to have been little change in population density or technology in the millennia between the appearance of food production and the Christian era. At the end of this period, the world was still very sparsely populated, and the overall population density in most continents is assumed to have been at group 1 level (table 2.2). The regions with this density seem mostly to have been inhabited by hunters, gatherers, or peoples who subsisted by pastoralism or forest fallow.

In some areas, however, this period brought vast technological changes. In a number of areas in the eastern hemisphere, and in a few in America, population multiplied many times, and gradually hunting and gathering were replaced by less extensive subsistence systems. Later, with further increase of population density, these systems were replaced by systems of intensive agriculture. It is important to note that the multiplication of population in the ancient world bore no resemblance to the recent explosive increases. Mortality was high, and estimates for long-term rates of natural growth point to annual growth rates of 0.1–0.2 per cent in areas with growing population.[1] These rates correspond to a doubling of population in 350–700 years. Thus, ancient populations had ample time to adapt to population increase by development or imports of new systems of food supply, and by improvement of the quality of inputs.

In chapter 3, a distinction was made among the qualities of inputs used in an agricultural system. A similar distinction can be made for agriculture in the ancient world. All the major systems of food supply discussed in chapter 3 were developed before the Christian era; the quality of inputs[2] used, however, varied widely. In a number of areas in the eastern hemisphere, intensive systems replaced extensive ones in step with increases of population densities; simultaneously, introduction of animal draft power, iron tools, and water control by flow irrigation improved the quality of inputs. In areas with population increase in the western hemisphere, on the other hand, there was little or no improvement in the quality of inputs.[3]

Some experts on ancient development, including Childe[4] and Wittfogel,[5] have focused on the quality of agricultural inputs and interpreted the changes in ancient societies in terms of invention of new technologies. The other side of the picture, that of increasing intensity of land use in step with population increase, was overlooked by these experts but has been brought into focus by Adams's study of long-term changes in land use in Mesopotamia[6] and by later studies of long-term changes in ancient land use.[7] We shall look at the long-term changes in agriculture in some of the areas covered by these studies. First we shall discuss the characteristic features of ancient agricultural development in more general terms.

TYPES OF LABOR INPUTS IN EXTENSIVE AND INTENSIVE SYSTEMS

Although ancient agriculture used other sources of energy to supplement human labor, it relied mainly on labor inputs for all types of agricultural operations. The extensive systems of food supply could be practiced with very few operations, while the intensive systems, the only ones that could be used in densely populated areas, required a large number of current operations and considerable labor investment. It is useful to review these operations, in order to get an idea of the problems which had to be solved if population increase were to encourage intensification of food supply systems.

Table 5.1 provides a synopsis of the agricultural operations needed for each of the major systems of food supply discussed in chapter 3. All these systems predate the Christian era and have been in use in some parts of the world since their invention. Therefore, the synopsis can serve as a reference not only in this chapter, but also in later chapters which deal with agricultural changes in more recent periods.

Table 5.1 lists each of the major systems with two variations for bush fallow, one extensive and another intensive. It is assumed that pastoralists use forest fallow to supply vegetable food and that forest-fallow cultivators derive animal food from hunting, while extensive bush fallow goes together with pastoralism, and intensive bush fallow with domestic animals. Both short-fallow and annual cultivators are assumed to use plows, while multicroppers are assumed not to do so. The last line in the table shows the population densities which went together with each of these systems in countries which were at low technological levels in 1970 (cf. table 3.7). The range of figures in columns 5–7 reflect climatic and other natural differences. In the column for multicropping, repetition of an operation for a second crop is treated as a second operation.

Some of the operations listed in the table are heavy work, others light work; some, like guarding animals, occupy a large number of hours throughout the year, while others are limited to a short season. The table therefore is a poor substitute for a real account of labor input in different systems of agriculture, but it does give a picture of the large additional effort required if increasing population density induces a

TABLE 5.1 NUMBER OF OPERATIONS NEEDED FOR DIFFERENT FOOD SUPPLY SYSTEMS

	HG	P with FF	FF with H	BF with P	BF with domest. animals	SF with plow	AC with plow	MC without plow
Current operations								
Harvesting	1	1	1	1	1	1	1	2–3
Chasing prey	1	0	1	0	0	0	0	0
Guarding animals	0	1	0	1	1	1	1	0
Clearing for long fallow	0	1	1	1	1	0	0	0
Sowing or planting	0	1	1	1	1	1	1	2–3
Soil preparation	0	0	0	1	1	1	1	2–3
Gather fertilizer	0	0	0	0	1	0	1	2–3
Weeding	0	0	0	1	1	0–1	0–1	2–3
Watering crops	0	0	0	0	0–1	0–1	0–1	1–3
Scaring wild animals	0	1	1	1	1	1	0	0
Feeding domestic animals	0	0	0	0	1	1	1	0
Producing fodder	0	0	0	0	0	0	1	0
Repair of irrigation	0	0	0	0	0–1	0–1	0–1	1–3
Total current operations	2	5	5	7	9–11	6–9	7–10	12–21
Labor investments								
Complete clearing of land	0	0	0	0	0	1	1	1
Training of draft animals	0	0	0	0	0	1	1	0
Leveling or terracing	0	0	0	0	0–1	1	1	1
Bunds, wells, canals	0	0	0	0	0–1	0–1	0–1	1
Draining	0	0	0	0	0–1	0–1	0–1	1
Total labor investments	0	0	0	0	0–3	3–5	3–5	4
All operations	2	5	5	7	9–14	9–14	10–15	16–25
Density group	1–3	1–3	1–3	4–5	6–7	6–7	8–9	≥10

population to move from left to right in the table. While two types of operations are sufficient for hunting and gathering, pastoralism and forest fallow require five, and we saw in chapter 4 that many preindustrial populations seem to have preferred the easier system if wild food was sufficient to feed them.

If population density in a primitive group increased to group 4–5 level and induced a change to extensive bush fallow, there would be additional work with soil preparation and weeding. If it increased to group 6–7 level and stimulated a shift to intensive bush fallow, new current operations would need to be added, and probably labor investment would become necessary. In chapter 3, the need for labor-intensive operations in intensive agricultural systems was mentioned. Different types of such investments are listed in table 5.1 as well. The largest increase in number of operations would occur if population density reached group 10 level and widespread multicropping was introduced. Additional investment in water control would probably be needed when crops had to be grown outside the most favorable season. Fertilization would become an acute problem, partly because much more fertilizer would be needed and partly because there would be little wasteland left in which fertilizer could be gathered; long walks to distant mountain regions would be needed or manure crops would have to be grown in some of the fields. And all these operations would have to be repeated, thus eliminating off-season periods of leisure or nonagricultural work.

The whole process of intensification of agriculture can be seen by reading table 5.1 from left to right. It may be viewed as a gradual shift from gathering to production of more and more items, accompanied by the addition of new inputs, which themselves would first be gathered and later produced. At the first stage of this process, food would be gathered. Later, it would be produced, but with few inputs except for liberal use of land as fallow. At a later stage, new types of inputs would be gathered, substituting for fallow and natural water supply. Fertilizing matter, water, and fodder would be the most important of these inputs. Finally, labor investments would be made in order to create facilities for production of these inputs, and labor would be spent on the production. Thus, it is a far more complicated and labor-consuming process to produce food using intensive supply systems than extensive ones. The idea that underemployment increases and an "agricultural labor surplus" is created when population pressure on land increases is based upon insufficient insight into the true nature of the process of agricultural intensification.[8]

SOURCES OF ENERGY SUPPLY FOR ANCIENT AGRICULTURE

The need for new labor-intensive operations, induced by population pressure, provided motivation for efforts to avoid or reduce the increasing work burden by improvement of equipment and use of such non-human sources of energy as were available to the populations of the ancient world. Cultivators in some parts of the world reduced their labor input in agriculture by using "high-level technologies." The most important such technologies were water power for flow irrigation, animal draft power, iron tools, and fire for land clearing and for improvement of hunting and pastoralism. These are still the predominant agricultural technologies in countries at low technological levels, and they are of course far more efficient than wooden digging sticks, hoes with celts of stone, and buckets for head transport of irrigation water—the technologies used in "low-technology areas" of the ancient world.

While Wittfogel[9] focused his analysis of ancient agriculture on the use of flow irrigation, others, including Childe,[10] attached great importance to the use of iron, especially for plowshares. Felling trees with stone axes takes much longer than with iron axes. But use of nonhuman power could reduce the work burden even more than could the change from wood, stone, or clay tools to metal tools. If long-fallow cultivators equipped with stone tools set fire to the forest vegetation at the end of the dry season, leaving the half-burned trees on the ground, clearing a plot might take less time than clearing by means of iron axes without the use of fire. Fire was the most efficient technology which prehistoric populations possessed, and the conditions for and consequences of use of fire provide an important clue to the understanding of the development of food supply systems in the ancient world.

Use of Fire
Pollen research has shown that prehistoric populations made extensive use of fire. Burning forest vegetation saves labor: setting fire to forested areas facilitates hunting; setting fire to grassy land improves conditions for pastoralism; as already mentioned, burning plots aids long-fallow agriculture. But hunter-gatherers and long-fallow cultivators living in forested areas today also derive much they need from the forest. Vegetable food is gathered or grown, and animal food is obtained by hunting. Tools and dwellings are made of forest products. Wood and other forest products are burned to supply heat for cooking and body warmth, and to provide protection against enemies. If the forest thinned out and disappeared because of population increase or because fires escaped control and burned large areas, radical changes must have ensued in prehistoric times.

The area of forest per head of population is, of course, a function of the population density. Japan, which today has a population density at group 10 level, has only 0.25 hectare of forest per inhabitant, although forest occupies seventy per cent of the whole territory. By contrast, Gabon, with a similar share of forest in total territory but with population density at group 2 level, has more than 40 hectares of forest per inhabitant. Because of the multiple uses of forest in preindustrial societies, this link between population density and the area of forest per head is extremely important, and we shall come back to it in later chapters. Here let us note that in the course of history, the forest area per head has been reduced, partly because of the increase of world population and partly by absolute reduction of the forested area.

The population living in an area may reduce or eliminate the area of forest by four different means: setting fires which escape control; keeping large herds and flocks that reduce the forest by their grazing and browsing; shortening fallow periods (i.e., changing to the bush-fallow system); felling forest in order to provide grazing for animals or per-

manent fields (i.e., shifting to pastoralism, short-fallow, or annual cropping). It is apparent from this list that if a population gradually moved
from the left to the right in table 5.1, not only were many more operations
required, but the possibilities for saving labor by burning forest land
and pasture land were reduced. In other words, the use of fire would
be prevented at the very time it was likely to be more needed than ever.

Fire is most efficient in dry climates, but it is also most destructive.
Although much savanna and desert land antedates occupation by man,
human occupation has contributed to transform forested land into savannas, and savannas into deserts.[11] Many dry areas were made still
drier, in prehistoric times or later, when fires or tree felling to expand
the fields reduced the forest cover. When forest became scarce or fallow
periods became short, or both, fire as a means to reduce the labor input
in agriculture had to be given up. Input of human muscle power per
unit of food production must have increased sharply, thus enhancing
the need to introduce other labor-saving devices. In humid areas, forests
are more likely to have survived until the land was needed for expansion
of the fields, but in the dry areas they probably disappeared long before
the land was needed for agriculture—that is, when population densities
were still low.

Use of Animal Draft Power

Plows drawn by animals are not very efficient in areas in which fallow
periods are so long that clearing can be done by fire. Unburned parts
of the natural vegetation obstruct attempts to plow the fallows for cultivation. Nor is the plow necessary so long as grassy weeds are sup-
pressed, during long-fallow periods, under forest cover. But if increasing
population density forces the use of shorter fallow, and grassy weeds
proliferate in the fallow, a wooden plow drawn by an ox is a more
efficient tool for preparation of the soil than digging sticks or hoes.
When fallow became so short that it was grassy, fire was no longer
efficient for land clearing because it left the roots of the grasses undis-
turbed. So, at the stage when fire became inefficient, animal-operated
plows became more efficient than before.[12] Moreover, the demand for
fertilization, which arose with shortening of fallow, could be met at least
partly by introduction of draft animals; the droppings helped to fertilize
the soil, either directly or by being mixed into composts and spread in
the fields.

With higher population densities, a larger share of the area had to be
used for fields, perhaps requiring draining or irrigation. Plows were
well suited to work in heavy waterlogged land and to draw furrows for
irrigation. Therefore, when population pressure on land necessitated

use of land with too much or too little water, there was motivation for introducing plow techniques or improving the plow, for instance, by adding mulboards which turned the soil.[13] Draft animals could also be used to carry water to the fields and to lift water from rivers or wells. In other words, introduction of plow techniques at a certain level of population density helps to expand the area under cultivation by putting more difficult land into use, and to intensify land use by shortening fallow. In both cases, the introduction or improvement of the plow is a means of adapting to increasing population density.

Table 5.1 indicates that if the plow is introduced at the intensive bush-fallow or short-fallow stage of the process of agricultural intensification when population densities are at group 6–7 levels, the number of current operations will be reduced.[14] The need for annual clearing, gathering of fertilizer, and weeding will disappear or become less urgent. More-over, human labor is saved if plows rather than hoes are used to prepare the soil. In many cases, however, reductions in current labor input must be paid for by additional labor investments, before the land is suitable for plowing. It might be necessary to clear the land of stumps, roots, and stones, to level the land, or to terrace it. Labor must also be invested in training draft animals. Thus, introduction of plowing requires much additional work in the initial period, and labor-saving effects are felt only when the investments are completed.

Use of plow techniques has a lower and an upper limit, depending on population densities. The advantage is largest at medium densities, when use of fire has been abandoned and there are still sufficient areas of fallow and pasture in which domestic animals can gather their fodder. If population becomes dense, even agriculture with plows becomes labor intensive. Fertilization and fodder become acute problems, when annual cropping or multicropping is applied, and there is little if any fallow and natural pasture for draft animals and other domestic animals.

Draft animals fed on produced fodder are not an efficient source of energy supply. The mechanical energy supplied by them is probably only some 3–5 per cent of the energy contained in the fodder they consume.[15] This rate of conversion is no disadvantage if they can feed on fallow and natural pastures unneeded for other purposes. But if labor investments would be needed to transform meadows and other waste-land into fodder-producing areas, then this additional labor might well outweigh the labor saving obtained by using draft animals instead of human muscle power for land preparation. For this reason, it is assumed in table 5.1 that multicropping is performed without use of the plow.

Water Power for Flow Irrigation

Besides fire and animal draft power, flow irrigation was used by many ancient populations as a substitute for human muscle power. Flow irrigation is labor saving because the power of running water is used to irrigate the fields. If the river carries silt, the burden of gathering fertilizer and spreading it in the fields can also be avoided. Flow irrigation occurs naturally along many rivers and lakes by overflow during the rainy season. From an early date, many populations living along river banks helped to spread the water inland by providing obstacles to the natural flow of the river. A single family or a small community living on the bank of a river could provide small-scale flow irrigation in this way. Large-scale flow irrigation systems involving damming large rivers and building canals to spread the water over a large area could be used only by peoples who had become numerous enough to provide the very large labor force required for the initial investment as well as the upkeep and repair.[16]

The silt carried by rivers is topsoil. In many regions, destruction of topsoil at the upper run of a river serves to fertilize areas at the lower run. If mountain areas are deprived of their topsoil by erosion caused by overgrazing, misuse of fire for pastoralism, or too intensive long-fallow cultivation, the river banks at the lower run of the river may become suitable for intensive cultivation, or easily made so by human-built flow irrigation. In other words, population pressure in a mountain region, by inducing cultivation of mountain slopes and overgrazing of mountain pastures, helps to create those "natural conditions" which permit the use of intensive agriculture in broad valleys at the lower run of the rivers. This type of development seems to have occurred in ancient Mesopotamia.

AGRICULTURAL DEVELOPMENT IN MESOPOTAMIA

As we saw in chapter 4, evidence of food production in Mesopotamia (i.e., the Mesopotamian plain and the mountains and plateaus surrounding it) dates from the eighth millennium B.C. During the following eight millennia, there was repeated multiplication of population in this area. A number of shifts took place, from more extensive to more intensive systems of food supply, accompanied by improvements in the quality of inputs.

Around 8000 B.C. there was only a small population in the Zagros mountains above the Mesopotamian plain, and this population was in the process of changing from hunting and gathering to pasturing of goats and sheep and crop production. The broad river valleys below the mountain range seem to have been empty or nearly empty at that time.[17]

Some 7–8 millennia later, these broad plains were occupied by a large and dense population. In the first millennium B.C., population density in the plains seems to have reached group 8–9 levels. This dense population used intensive systems of agriculture based upon flow irrigation; multicropping was also introduced.[18] Fields were prepared by plows with mulboards and iron shares, drawn by oxen. The irrigation system used waterwheels for lifting water to fields located above the major river, which provided the water.[19] Thus over a period of some eight thousand years, Mesopotamia became densely populated and passed through the series of food supply systems we have been discussing. Gradually, the population changed from primitive food gatherers to people who applied the most sophisticated systems of food production existing in the ancient world.

The first part of the story of long-term development of Mesopotamian agriculture was told by Smith and Young in a study of development of population and agriculture in greater Mesopotamia between 8000 B.C. and 4000 B.C.[20] The authors measured growth of population by comparing information about early village sites revealed by a large number of diggings and other archeological research. During the period covered by Smith and Young's study, agriculture, which began in the mountain slopes, gradually spread downward to the plain as population multiplied. But not all of the increase migrated to new land. Part remained and intensified the land surrounding the villages. Intensification seems to have consisted in shortening fallow, and, at a later stage, in investment in water control.

Smith and Young suggest that the agricultural system in use in prehistoric villages may be identified by means of implements discovered by the diggings. They concede, however, that identification is a difficult task, since wooden tools have disappeared and only tools or parts of tools of stone and iron are found. In Mesopotamia, no tools were found in the oldest villages, and the authors suggest that agriculture in this region began with long-fallow methods and wooden digging sticks. In some sites, stones were found that could have been used as weights for digging sticks. By contrast to the older sites, some of the newer ones contained stones that resembled celts for hoes. The continued increase of population may have made it necessary to use shorter periods of fallow, involving more intensive land preparation and weed control.

Flow irrigation is a characteristic feature of Mesopotamian agriculture, as already mentioned. Small-scale flow irrigation seems to have appeared at an early date, apparently in response to population pressure in the mountains. The first traces of irrigation in the mountains date from around 5000 B.C. and refer to an area where increasing population density is well documented. For a long time, irrigation seems to have been conducted on a small scale, consisting of periodic cleaning and perhaps straightening of clogged natural water courses leading from the mountains into the plains. Later, when increasing population pressure in the mountains pushed an overspill of population down to the dry land in the plain, irrigation was expanded and the methods were improved.[21]

Not only flow irrigation, but also animal draft power was used from an early date in Mesopotamia. Smith and Young[22] have shown that some late village sites in the mountains have no celts for hoes, and they suggest that hoes may have been replaced by wooden scratch plows (plows without mulboards, which can be used in land which has been imperfectly cleared), which have disappeared without leaving traces. Introduction of plow techniques was facilitated by the importation of oxen in addition to the goats and sheep which were kept during the whole period covered by their study. These oxen could be used to draw scratch plows.

The continuing increase of population is proved by the multiplication of villages and sites and by the remains of ancient irrigation canals.[23] Such evidence can better be used to measure changes in density than absolute densities. Therefore, estimates of population densities are rare for most regions. An estimate is available for the Sumerian plain in the third millennium B.C.,[24] however, and this information makes it possible to compare the population density and the system of agriculture in that period. According to this estimate, the Sumerian part of the Mesopotamian plain had some 500,000 inhabitants, or around 20 persons per square kilometer, corresponding to density group 6. The Sumerians used short fallow with animal draft power, and medium population density corresponds to the results of our investigation of the links between population density and agricultural systems in low-technology countries in chapter 3.

In his study of Sumerian land use, Adams underlines that most early sites (around 4000 B.C.) were widely dispersed at considerable distances from each other,[25] and if the estimate of population is correct, only ten per cent of the territory was used for cultivation in the third millennium B.C. This information corresponds well to what was found to be typical for countries with group 6–7 densities in chapter 3, in which the arable range was 10–20 per cent of the territory (see table 3.12). The Sumerian fields were irrigated because the climate was so dry, and the large areas which were unused for fields were used for grazing draft and other animals belonging to cultivators and pastoralists. The irrigated land in third-millennium Sumeria seems to have been around 0.6 hectares per inhabitant.[26] The fields were fertilized by droppings from draft animals and silt carried by water from the river. This figure of 0.6 should be compared with those in table 3.12, which show that most countries have less than half a hectare of arable land per inhabitant today, and only a small share of this is irrigated. Unless the estimate for Sumeria is far off the mark, the early Sumerians had plentiful agricultural resources.

But between the third and the first millennia B.C., population in Mesopotamia multiplied further. Gradually the dry spaces between the irrigated areas were filled in with irrigation facilities, and a system of lateral canals was built, leading inland from the main waterways. The steadily increasing labor force transformed the landscape. Swamps and sandbanks at the mouths of rivers were transformed into fields by draining the swamps, controlling the floods, and leading water to the rainless deserts by artificial canals.[27] When population continued to increase, the upper part of the rivers also was irrigated, though Adams's studies have shown that the potential for irrigation was never fully utilized.[28]

When increasing demand for food, the consequence of population growth, created the need to irrigate land located above the major river, the problem of lifting large amounts of water became acute. Already around 2000 B.C. a device for this purpose, the shaduf, was in use in western Asia. Two millennia later, the waterwheel, probably invented in India, was used in Mesopotamia to lift water from the rivers to canals. Waterwheels were operated by men or animals, or set in motion by the flow of the main river or canal. These innovations served not only to expand irrigation, but also to remove surplus water and transform marshes into fields.[29]

Thus, the development of irrigated agriculture in Mesopotamia, from early interference with the natural course of small streams to spectacular systems of organized large-scale irrigation in the large river basins, was slow and gradual.[30] Small-scale irrigation started around 5000 B.C., and it was not until four millennia later that large river valleys became covered by flow irrigation. The period of change was so long because the Mesopotamian population was growing at low annual rates. It only very gradually needed the large amounts of food produced by the system or became large enough to make the investments, maintain and repair them, and cultivate the large plains.

SPECIAL FEATURES OF AMERICAN AGRICULTURE

Mesopotamia was not the only area in which population increase was accompanied by intensification of food supply systems and by improvement of inputs. Several river basins in the eastern hemisphere developed intensive systems of flow irrigation with use of draft animals and iron.

In other regions, especially in the western hemisphere, population increase was accompanied by intensification of food supply systems, but little if any improvement in the quality of inputs, as pointed out by Sanders.[31] One of these areas, Mesoamerica, was a center for development of maize production. There is evidence of cultivation of maize · in this area around 7000 B.C., i.e., only one millennium after the first proved cultivation of crops in Mesopotamia. Before the Europeans arrived around A.D. 1500, population densities in core areas of Mesoamerica were as high as those prevailing in Mesopotamia and other technologically advanced areas in the eastern hemisphere. There are interesting similarities and differences between the development in Mesoamerica and that in Mesopotamia, as shown by Adams in a comparative study of these two regions.[32]

Development in Mesoamerica was delayed, compared with Mesopotamia, by much more than the thousand years separating the first evidence of agriculture in these two regions. This delay seems related to a very slow shift of consumption from gathered food to maize.[33] Maize may have been difficult to domesticate,[34] or perhaps population growth was so slow that the population for millennia after the introduction of agriculture could continue to rely mainly on consumption of gathered and hunted food. In any case, population density in the whole of the Mesoamerican region seems to have remained very low until the first millennium B.C., but in the last 2–3 millennia before the Spanish conquest, population probably increased by some 0.1 per cent annually, on average.[35] When the Spaniards arrived, average density was probably around group 5 level, but there were high densities in some parts of the region, as already mentioned.

The area in southern Mesoamerica inhabited by the Mayas is mainly tropical lowland with little need and few possibilities for flow irrigation. Today the lowlands are sparsely populated, and the predominant system of agriculture is an extensive bush-fallow system. The ratio of cultivation to fallow is approximately 1:4.[36] It was long taken for granted that the bush-fallow system was the only one ever in use in that area. But archeological research has revealed the existence of a period of high population densities, up to group 9 level in some areas.[37] These densities could not possibly have been sustained by means of extensive bush fallow, even though the natural fertility of the soil is high.[38]

Further archeological research has revealed that a number of intensive agricultural techniques were in use in the peak period of population density, toward the end of the first millennium A.D. As population density increased, the inhabitants of Mesoamerica developed—or imported—many ingenious techniques of intensive agriculture. In some parts of the Maya region, ancient terraces and walled fields, now abandoned, are witness to intensive cultivation. Elevated and walled fields are known from other areas. Large amounts of labor must have gone into creating such fields, with ditches or canals around them for draining off surplus water in the wet season, and perhaps for irrigating in the dry seasons, if multicropping was used by the Mayas as Turner suggests.[39]

Moreover, the location of the major centers near lowland swamps and lakes seems to indicate that the Mayas may also have used a system of artificial islands.[40] Intensively cultivated islands were created in shallow lakes in the platau in the northern part of Mesoamerica when high population density was reached; similar techniques were probably used by the Mayas. In addition, they may have relied to some extent on consumption of nuts from ramon trees cultivated around their dwellings.[41] After an abrupt decline of population in the last centuries before A.D. 1000, the Mayas seem to have given up intensive methods. Investments made in the period of peak population were abandoned, and it was then that extensive bush fallow became the predominant agricultural system.

By contrast to the Maya region, the relatively dry northern part of Mesoamerica had some rivers suitable for flow irrigation. Increasing population density in this area resulted in shortening of fallow, irrigation efforts, and terracing of hillsides. Small-scale irrigation developed first, but gradually, especially in the last centuries before the Spanish conquest when population reached its peak in the northern area, irrigation came to cover more valleys and the systems were expanded.[42] However, because the rivers were much smaller, construction could not compare with the massive systems of dams and dikes in the large irrigated areas of the eastern hemisphere, nor could terracing in Mesoamerica compete with the impressive terraces for flow irrigation in the Andean region.[43]

The major problem in Mesoamerican agriculture was not irrigation, however—most of the northern region has enough rain for one crop, and part of the southern region has a humid tropical climate. The major problem, when population density became high, was low labor productivity due to unavailability of plow techniques and iron. Even today, when steel tools are available, this area is seriously handicapped by troublesome weeds, particularly grasses.[44] The Mayas applied extensive bush fallow to combat these weeds. When population density in Mesoamerica was too high to use long-fallow methods, plows with animal draft power were badly needed, but this technique was not introduced in the western hemisphere until the Spanish conquest more than eight millennia after the appearance of agriculture. Until then, the inhabitants had to rely on human muscle power for eradication of weeds when they abandoned the forest-fallow system.

It was not because the American Indians were less "inventive" than the inhabitants of the eastern hemisphere that they never introduced plow techniques. It was rather that the western hemisphere had no animals to draw a plow. Except for the llamas used to carry burdens in the Andean region, large animals suitable for domestication became extinct in America long before the period here considered. Therefore, land preparation and the fight against weeds, as well as all other agricultural operations, had to be performed without the help of animals. Moreover, the lack of draft animals and other large domestic animals meant that fields could not be fertilized by their droppings. And because of the topography in Mesoamerica, only a small share of the cultivated area could benefit from fertilization by silt carried by flow irrigation. Thus the problem of fertilization must have been acute, except for those northern parts which benefited from volcanic soil.

The western hemisphere was further handicapped because techniques of metal production lagged far behind those in the eastern hemisphere. Iron plowshares and other iron tools existed from an early date in Mesopotamia and other technologically advanced areas of the eastern hemisphere, but iron technology was first introduced in the western hemisphere around A.D. 1500. Until then, the American Indians were confined not only to the use of human muscle power without the help of animals, but to human muscle power aided by tools made only of wood and hardened clay.[45] Preparation of land for crops, the fight against weeds, and all the types of heavy labor investment necessary for the intensive agricultural systems of pre-Columbian America were performed by human beings with very primitive tools. Under these conditions, output per labor hour in crop production must have been very low in the areas with high population densities.

DEVELOPMENT OF ANCIENT EUROPEAN AGRICULTURE
Conditions for food production were much more favorable in Europe than in Mesoamerica. Located in the eastern hemisphere and in frequent contact with western Asia and North Africa, Europe had the opportunity to import crops, domestic animals, and methods of cultivation from technological leaders. There is archeological evidence for cultivation of crops in Europe in the sixth millennium B.C., and in the fifth millennium, agricultural settlements spread from southeastern Europe to Central Europe and northwestern Europe. Pollen analysis and settlement patterns reveal that the agricultural system was forest fallow with use of fire for land clearing.[46]

Archeological research also has revealed four core areas in different parts of Europe, all apparently with long-fallow systems. There is also evidence of population increase accompanied by some intensification of the agricultural system. Fallow seems to have been shortened to bush fallow, and the forest was thinned out and reduced in size.[47] The European response to increasing population was a shift to a more intensive system of agriculture, i.e., from forest fallow to bush fallow, and also dispersal of population by migration.

Migration appears to have played a larger role in Europe, and intensification of agriculture a smaller role, than in Mesopotamia and Mesoamerica with their mountains, deserts, and oceans. The European continent is a large open area with good conditions for agriculture nearly everywhere. The temperate, humid climate permits the growth of one crop per year without irrigation; most of the territory consists of large plains or gently sloping hillsides; and surface water for drinking and other purposes is available nearly everywhere. So when population increased, it was easy for the population to disperse without any need to adopt other types of food or change the way of life.

If ease of migration induced the population surplus to move to hitherto unoccupied or more sparsely populated areas, the remaining population could continue to apply extensive systems of food supply. Carneiro[48] has drawn attention to the tendency of populations in "noncircumscribed" areas to choose migration as a means to preserve the easy but primitive long-fallow systems. His theory helps to explain the paradox that in spite of the possibility for imports of techniques from Asia, agriculture developed much more slowly in Europe than in the advanced regions of Asia.

In the course of time, the spread of population to new areas and the change from forest fallow to bush fallow caused a reduction of the forested area and an increase of open grassy land. This land seems to have invited occupation by pastoral peoples with their herds, perhaps immigrants from Asia.[49] The thinning out of forests and proliferation of grasses also provided motivation for introduction of the scratch plow from Asia. Oxen from the herds were used as draft power. There is substantial evidence for use of the scratch plow over a wide area of Europe by the middle of the second millennium B.C., and some signs of its existence still earlier.[50] The scratch plow was probably used in areas in which population increase led to change from long forest fallow to somewhat shorter fallow periods in more grassy land. In addition to improved food crops and plow techniques, Europe imported iron technology from Asia in the second or first millennium B.C. Thus, in quality of inputs, Europe was several millennia ahead of Mesoamerica. But compared with Mesopotamia it was far behind. Mesopotamia already was using a much more efficient type of plow in its permanent fields when Europe imported the scratch plow for use in its bush-fallow system.

Owing to the better possibilities for scattering of population in Europe compared with other areas, no part of Europe reached high population densities, i.e., group 8 or higher, before the Christian era. Table 5.2 presents available estimates of population size in various parts of Europe, expressed in density groups. According to these estimates, around A.D. 1 Greece and Italy had the highest densities, but even these were only group 6–7 (medium), and all areas north of the Alps were sparsely populated. Table 5.2 indicates that Spain, France, and the Low Countries had group 4–5 densities, and most other parts of Europe group 1–3 densities. The average density of Europe including European Russia seems to have been at group 3 level. This information should be compared with the results of the cross-country analysis, in chapter 3, of food supply systems in low-technology countries. In that, population densities at group 1–3 level were identified with hunting-gathering, pastoralism, and forest fallow; densities at group 4–5 levels, with bush fallow; and densities of 6–7, with short-fallow systems in areas with access to plows and draft animals.

This linkage between population densities and food supply systems corresponds remarkably well to what is known about population den-

TABLE 5.2 DENSITY GROUPS OF EUROPEAN COUNTRIES, A.D. 1–1970

	A.D. 1	500	1000	1340[b]	1500	1750	1900	1970
Greece	6–7[a]	7	7	7	7			8
Italy	6–7	5	5–6	7	6–7	7–8	8	9
Spain	5	4	5	6	5–6	6	7	8
France	4–5	5	5	7	6	7	8	8
Germany	3–4	5	5	6–7	6–7	7	8–9	9
Low Countries	5				6–7	7–8	9	10
British Isles	2–4	2–3	5	6	5–6	6–7	9	9
Scandinavia					1–2	3	5	6
Poland			4	5	4–5	5–6		8
Hungary		4	5–6	6	5–6			8
European Russia			1	2	2	2	3–4	5	5
Total Europe	3	2–3	3	4	4	5	7–8	8

[a] The range of density groups indicates either that there is some doubt about the size of the territory to which the estimate refers, or that there are substantial differences between estimates given in the sources quoted below.   [b] I.e., before the Black Death.

DATA SOURCES: Reinhard, Armengaud, and Dupaquier, *Histoire générale de la population mondiale* (Paris, 1968); Carlo Cipolla, ed., *Fontana Economic History of Europe* (Glasgow: Collins, 1972—), vols. 1–3.

sities and food supply systems in various parts of Europe at the beginning of the Roman Empire. Those parts which seem to have had group 1–3 densities seem to have been inhabited largely by pastoralists and people using forest fallow. In his history of ancient Europe, Piggott concludes that on the eve of the Roman conquest, food supply systems north of the Alps ranged from true pastoral nomadism on the steppes of Russia, to modified forms of pastoralism among the German tribes and in Ireland, to sedentary villages in France, Central Europe, and England.[51]

In sharp contrast, Greece and Italy had group 6–7 densities and short-fallow systems. The short-fallow system in Greece during the first millennium B.C. seems to have been similar to the three-course rotation system used 1–2 millennia later in Western Europe,[52] when population densities seem to have reached levels similar to those of Greece in the first millennium B.C. (cf. table 5.2). In Italy, one rotation of crop and fallow per year seems to have been predominant in the Roman period. Classical authors—for instance, the Greek geographer Strabo—noted the important difference between the more developed systems of food supply in Greece and Italy and the primitive systems used north of the Alps.[53]

It should also be noted that population densities and food supply systems in ancient Greece and Italy resembled those of Sumeria in the third millennium B.C. Like prehistoric Sumeria, classical Greece and Italy had densities around group 6–7 levels and agricultural systems with permanent fields plowed by oxen. They had less irrigation than Sumeria, because the winter rain saved Mediterranean Europe from the need to invest large amounts of labor in irrigation facilities. However, some irrigation facilities were built in the Roman period in both southern Italy[54] and southern France. Population density in Provence in southern France is assumed to have been at group 6 level in the Roman period,[55] and the summer climate is dry.

REGIONAL DIFFERENCES IN LABOR INPUT IN FOOD PRODUCTION

In the preceding sections of this chapter, the distinction was made between three different types of agricultural development in the ancient world and in pre-Columbian America. In the first type, represented by Mesopotamia, multiplication of population went together with introduction of intensive agriculture and with qualitative improvement of inputs. In the second type, for which the Maya region of Mesoamerica provides a clear example, multiplication of population also went with intensification of agriculture, but without any significant improvement of inputs. In the third type, represented by Europe north of the Alps, multiplication of population went with improvement of the quality of inputs, but without introduction of intensive agriculture, because the population avoided high densities and settled new areas instead. At the time of the Roman Empire, nearly all of Europe north of the Alps still had long-fallow systems and pastoralism.

Owing to these differences in development of agriculture, per capita input of labor in food production must also have been different. To provide a framework for analysis of these differences, we may look back to table 5.1. We find that a change from extensive to more intensive systems of food supply requires a steady increase in the number of necessary operations. Some of the operations tend to become more onerous when agriculture becomes intensive; others that are relatively light work, such as protection of crops against wild animals and supervision of herds, become less needed as population density increases. One would therefore expect that per capita input of human energy in food production would increase when growing populations change from extensive to intensive systems of food supply.

However, we must also take account of changes in the quality of inputs. Earlier in this chapter we concluded that one type of nonhuman energy, fire, facilitated the use of extensive systems but was inapplicable in intensive agriculture. This conclusion supports the expectation that human labor input in food production increases when extensive systems are replaced by intensive agriculture. On the other hand, some of the peoples who adopted intensive agriculture in the ancient world also introduced animal muscle power and water power for flow irrigation and got access to metal tools. Such inputs would, of course, serve to reduce per capita input of human labor compared with that of people who use intensive agriculture without them. In areas of the type for which Mesopotamia served as example, two opposing tendencies were at work when population density increased: a tendency for human labor input per capita to increase because of the intensification of agriculture and abandonment of fire; and a tendency for it to decline due to introduction of new types of nonhuman energy and better quality tools.

The differences in development are illustrated by table 5.3. The layout of this table corresponds to that of table 3.13, in which differences in technological levels were shown horizontally and differences in population density vertically. However, in table 3.13 the differences in technological levels referred to 1965. In table 5.3, the reference is to technologies used in the ancient world and in pre-Columbian America. Thus, in table 5.3, "low technological level" stands for human muscle power unaided by iron, draft animals, and water power; "medium technological level," for iron and animal draft power for scratch plows;[56] and

TABLE 5.3 POPULATION DENSITY AND FOOD SUPPLY SYSTEMS IN THE ANCIENT WORLD AND IN PRE-COLUMBIAN AMERICA

Density Group	Technological Levels					
	Low		Medium		High	
	Area	System	Area	System	Area	System
1–3	Most of Europe North of Alps[a]	P + FF				
4–5			Parts of Europe North of Alps[b]	BF		
6–7			Greece and Italy	SF		
8–9	Maya Region	AC + MC?	Northern Mesoamerica[c]	AC + MC	Southern Italy Mesopotamia	AC + MC AC + MC

[a] Extensive use of fire. [b] Some use of fire.
[c] No iron and animal draft power, but flow irrigation.

"high technological level," for plows with mulboard and iron shares, and for water power for flow irrigation. It should be noted that one technology, that of fire, is available only in the upper part of the table.

When Mesopotamia, Mesoamerica, and Europe introduced agriculture, they had low population densities and used fire extensively, as shown in the upper left of the table. Later the Maya area moved steeply downward to the lower left, while Mesopotamia moved both downward and to the right, and ended up in the lower right corner. Europe did not reach the bottom of the table in ancient times, and most of Europe either remained in the upper left or introduced medium technological levels, as population became less sparse or reached medium densities.

The table can be used to throw some light on the question of the causal connection between population growth and agricultural changes in the ancient world. Take the Maya region: it seems obvious that per capita labor input in food production must have become greater, and output per unit of labor lower, than that of any other area represented in the table. In this case, increasing and high population density would not be due to improved nutrition and good nutritional levels. The agricultural changes must have been an adaptation to increasing and high population density and not the cause of the demographic trends.

The case is less clear for Mesopotamia, which moved both downward and to the right. However, as Adams underlines: "For all the renowned productivity of Mesopotamian agriculture, the attainment of even the bare margin of subsistence was always precarious."[57] It is also worth noting that the Mesopotamian system of agriculture resembled the systems of flow irrigation which were until recently in use in some densely populated regions of China and India. It is well known that output of labor in these areas was very low, and so were nutritional levels. Is there any reason to assume that conditions were better two millennia ago in Mesopotamia, which had similar population densities?

Let us now turn to Europe. It had no flow irrigation, but it did not need it, because the climate was humid and population densities low. Use of the scratch plow rather than the more sophisticated Mesopotamian plow probably reflected a desire to preserve long-fallow agriculture and avoid the heavy labor investment in complete clearing of land. All parts of Europe must have produced food with a much lower per capita labor input than the Mayas. It is less clear how Europe compared with Mesopotamia. It seems likely, however, that Europe was nutritionally the better off. In other words, it seems fairly obvious that we should look for other explanations than poor nutritional levels to explain the low population density in most of Europe at the time of the Roman Empire.

6 POPULATION SIZE AND URBANIZATION

Chapters 4 and 5 dealt with the relationship between population size and technologies of food supply in prehistoric and ancient societies. In this and the following chapter, the focus will be on demographic trends and the apparently related development of an urban sector in some societies.

Ancient urban centers were clustered around temples or palaces, and often fortified and surrounded by walls. The urban societies in both hemispheres were stratified, with large differences in living standards and status. Stratification was not, however, a sufficient cause for the appearance of urbanization. Archeological and historical evidence proves that stratification appeared long before urbanization, and that stratified societies can exist for millennia without ever developing urban centers. Many peoples living today have not reached the urban stage, but have stratified societies with considerable differences in wealth and influence among various families.

The process of stratification seems to be closely related to the changes in subsistence system when population density in a region gradually increases. Anthropologists have noted that peoples who today subsist by hunting and gathering usually live in small, flexible, unstratified groups, which individual families can leave or join as they desire.[1] But at the stage of pastoralism, there are large differences in the size of the herds belonging to different families, and corresponding differences in prestige and authority. Moreover, it is well known that from antiquity pastoral peoples have had strong military organizations and powerful chiefs, and sometimes large numbers of slaves.[2]

Among pastoral peoples and peoples who subsist by long-fallow agriculture, all members of the tribe or the local group have free access to pasture and cleared plots on all land dominated by their own people. This system persists as long as population is so small that there is abundant land for grazing and cultivation. However, when increasing population size creates a shortage of land or water, this system of common or tribal ownership usually breaks down, as in recent times in Africa. Individual families then obtain permanent rights in the land they have been using, or the local chief or a foreign conqueror transforms a duty to assign land or water to individual families into a right to obtain an income from it himself.[3] It seems likely that this process, which has happened so often in history, also took place in prehistoric societies which developed early urbanization. Many early towns in Mesopotamia and elsewhere housed not only military chiefs and religious leaders and their followers and servants, but also a landlord class that disposed of land by sale. However, the ruling class in Mexican towns seems to have been heads of lineages whose land had never been private property.[4]

Agricultural changes are not the only ones that promote economic and social stratification in societies in which population continues to increase. The fortifications and large temples in ancient towns are indications that military power and religious ceremony provided motivation for urban concentration. Such physical structures also are related to population size and density. Carneiro has emphasized that when local groups become larger, and fill the empty land between them with additional villages, conflict is likely to break out.[5] When pastures are transformed into arable land because of increasing population density, conflicts are unavoidable between cultivating and pastoral tribes living in the same region. In some areas, fortified villages preceded fortified towns,[6] and the appearance of walled towns in Sumeria has been explained as a defense against pastoral tribes or other enemies.[7]

Increasing population density may not only create tension between different tribes; it may also promote internal conflict in individual groups or villages when opportunities for migration are reduced. These internal and external conflicts enhance the power of chiefs and military leaders. Religious leaders are also likely to get more authority and power under such circumstances.[8] Thus, when the size and density of population are increasing, the social system is likely to become hierarchized and more complex through the interplay of several factors.

AGRICULTURAL SURPLUS AND URBANIZATION
The factors mentioned above may explain why a scattered population of agricultural producers concentrated their dwellings in a small area surrounded by walls and including one or more temples. But before large urban settlements with a majority of nonagricultural population can appear, other conditions must be fullfilled. Thus it is generally agreed that there must be an agricultural surplus large enough to feed the nonagricultural population. Why did it become possible to produce a large agricultural surplus in some areas, like Mesopotamia, earlier than in other regions?

More than one answer has been suggested. One explanation stresses the high fertility of the soil in the large river valleys in Mesopotamia, Egypt, northern India, and eastern China, which all had early urbanization. Another explanation links the appearance of urban centers to technological levels in agriculture. It is underlined that there is evidence in these regions of early use of animal-drawn plows, iron tools, and flow irrigation. These technologies, which were at advanced levels according to the standard of those times, may have raised output per worker in agriculture so much that urban centers could appear. It is not to be denied that fertile land with annual deposits of silt and use of high-quality inputs in agriculture facilitated early urbanization in the large river valleys. But many other fertile areas did not have early urbanization, and areas which used high-quality inputs did not necessarily have higher output per worker than areas in which more primitive methods were used. These two explanations were accepted because the focus in earlier research concerning ancient agriculture was on Asia and Egypt. The evidence from Mesoamerica and Europe indicates that there is something wrong with these theories. Europe north of the Alps used better quality inputs in agriculture than Mesoamerica, and had fertile and well-watered soil. Yet large urban centers appeared in Mesoamerica more than a thousand years before they grew up north of the Alps.

The two explanations of early urbanization miss the crucial point because they focus on agricultural surplus per worker rather than on total surplus. Even the best technologies available to the ancient world, when used on the best land, did not allow one agricultural family to supply many nonagricultural families. It was the number of food-producing families on which the size of the surplus for urban consumption primarily depended. The size of the population available to supply an urban center was far more important than how much food could be delivered or sold per agricultural worker. Thus, whether urban centers with large nonagricultural populations could appear depended primarily upon demographic factors, i.e., size and density of population in that area.[9] Fertility of land and agricultural technology were secondary factors; the prime condition for early urbanization was a sufficiently large and dense population.

If fire could be used for land clearing, it was probably easier to produce the necessary food for a family by extensive long-fallow methods than by intensive agriculture. The inhabitants of Mesoamerica must have been better able to produce more than their own needs before the urban period, when population was small and could use long-fallow techniques, than later, when population became many times larger and the urban populations were supported by intensive agriculture with stone age tools. However, peoples who use extensive long-fallow systems must live widely scattered in a thinly populated area, the non-food-producing members living together with the food producers in small scattered villages with a few hundred inhabitants or less, rather than in urban centers.[10]

In chapter 5 we concluded that it is open to doubt if Mesopotamia were ahead of barbarian Europe with respect to labor productivity in agriculture, in spite of its silt-laden rivers and advanced agricultural technology. Mesopotamia had to use a large share of its labor input in agriculture on upkeep and maintenance of a flow irrigation system, which barbarian Europe did not need because of its more humid climate and lower population densities. Thus it was the large population rather than high output per worker which allowed early urbanization in river valleys in Asia and Egypt. The large population size explains both that there was sufficient labor and sufficient demand for food to have large-scale irrigation, and that large-scale urbanization could appear. But in the Maya region of Mesoamerica, large-scale urbanization could appear without flow irrigation. If a large and densely settled population produces a large total output within a restricted area, urbanization can appear even if labor productivity in agriculture is very low and the surplus delivered per family for urban consumption very small.

Do we know anything about the size of the surplus per agricultural family which could be available for feeding urban, non-food-producing families in the ancient world? The best means to get some idea of this is to look at the available information concerning crop shares and taxation of agriculture in ancient urbanized societies. The available information about crop shares paid by peasants to landlords or other authorities shows that in irrigated areas these could be up to one-third of the harvest, or even more.[11] But this tells us little about the share available for urban use, because a large part would have fed men and animals doing the work necessary for the functioning of the irrigation network and other rural infrastructure. Levies on local producers designed for consumption outside the area were much smaller. For instance, the basic rates for tribute payments from the provinces to Rome were 5–10 per cent of the crop, though Caesar once levied twelve per cent as a penalty.[12] It is true that in the centuries after A.D. 1 rates increased, but we have no examples of rates above twenty per cent, and of course not all these supplies would have reached Rome for consumption. This information supports the suggestion made by Kingsley Davis that rarely would more than one-tenth of total agricultural output in a region which supplied an urban center be available to the nonagricultural population of that center.[13] Small urban centers with a population of some two thousand nonagricultural persons including nonworking family members would require a population of at least twenty thousand in the food-supplying area. Urban centers in the hundred-thousand-size group—which some ancient societies had—must have required a total population of a million or more.

The Importance of Transport Technology

Urbanization required that population reach certain minimums in terms of size and density. In addition, the distance which food could be transported depended upon the level of transport technology. If population density was low, the supplies to a center of given size would have to be transported over longer distances than if a dense agricultural population surrounded it.

The sources of energy for transport purposes in ancient urbanized societies were the same as those used in agriculture. Humans and animals carried food and other products; flowing water moved boats downstream; wind power could be used to move boats and ships against the current as well as with it. It is important to note that the most efficient sources of energy available to the ancient societies, water and wind, could be used for transport only by water. Both of these sources of energy were used for transport long before they came into use in agriculture. Wind power to move sailing boats was in use in the fourth millennium b.c. in Sumeria, and downstream flotation much earlier. Also, wheeled wagons drawn by animals were in use in Mesopotamia in the fourth millennium.[14] Besides these means of transport, pack animals, human porterage, and wheelbarrows were available. Information brought together by Colin Clark indicates that pack animals are not much more efficient than human porterage, when the need to provide fodder is taken into account.[15] Even wheeled transport on roads was inefficient in the ancient societies, because of the primitive techniques of wagon building and harnessing animals; it was, however, more efficient than porterage, except for mountain areas.

Transport with animals as draft power was dependent upon building and maintenance of roads, which required a large labor force. Therefore, like other major investments in economic and social infrastructure, road building was feasible only when undertaken as obligatory labor by a dense rural population in the agricultural off-season, or as military investment by a large empire which could organize large works in sparsely populated areas. Even if they had knowledge of the technologies of road building, construction of wagons, and harnessing animals, populations in sparsely populated areas could not dispose of sufficient labor to provide the infrastructure necessary for the use of these technologies, or the volume of traffic to make investment in roads worthwhile. Therefore, densely populated areas, in which wheeled transport with animal power could be used, had better possibilities for transporting food surpluses to urban centers than regions with sparse population, in which it was necessary to use pack animals or human porters. The importance of infrastructure investment, especially transport facilities, is emphasized by all economic historians, but it is often overlooked that such facilities require a certain density of population. Urbanization requires the availability of transport, but the availability of transport is related to population density.

Areas with navigable rivers or access to large lakes or sea transport could better develop urbanization than areas with similar population density having only land transport. However, densely populated areas had an advantage even in water transport. Only in densely populated areas could a river be made navigable by canalization, because of the large labor force and volume of traffic required. More than a million men and women are said to have been mobilized for the construction of the imperial canal in China in the sixth century A.D.,[16] an investment which made long-distance bulk transport of food and other products possible. When densely populated areas were crisscrossed by irrigation canals, these could be used for local transport of food. Thus, while a sparsely populated area would at best have water transport up and downstream on a navigable river, a densely populated area might have a dense network of canals and roads, which allowed one or more urban centers to draw on food surpluses produced by the whole agricultural population in the surrounding area.

We can get some idea of the limits to urbanization in ancient societies due to sparse population and poor transport facilities, by means of a tabulation of the population size of a food-producing area under different assumptions about the feasible transport distance from the central town. Such a tabulation is made in table 6.1. It can be seen from the table that if food transports are limited to a distance of 7–8 kilometers from the center, areas with less than group 8 density cannot become urbanized. If population density is at group 6–7 level, there would be only 4–8 thousand persons, including nonworking family members, to

TABLE 6.1 TRANSPORT DISTANCES AND POPULATION (population in thousands)

Density Group	Transport Distance			
	7–8 km	15 km	30 km	60 km
1			2	8
2		1	4	17
3		2	8	34
4	1	4	17	68
5	2	8	34	136
6	4	17	68	271
7	8	34	136	543
8	17	68	271	1086
9	34	136	543	2172
10	68	271	1086	4344

supply the center with food. Such a population size could not supply food to more than a few hundred families, and a center with so small a nonagricultural population hardly deserves the title of urban center. Only areas of at least group 8 density could have become urbanized. This population density corresponds to that suggested by Sanders and Price as the minimum for urbanization with primitive means of transport.[17]

The study by Sanders and Price contains information about several cases of early urbanization. One relates to twenty or thirty small city-states with an average of around seventeen thousand inhabitants, including nonagricultural and agricultural population. These city-states were scattered over an area of twenty-five thousand square kilometers in the Sumerian part of the Mesopotamian plain in the third millennium B.C. As mentioned in chapter 5, the whole of the Sumerian plain had only group 6 density in this period. However, because of the dry climate, the fields were irrigated, and the irrigated area of each city-state accounted for some hundred square kilometers. If that area was a circular one surrounding the center, no crops would have needed to be transported more than 5–6 kilometers. Under the more realistic assumption that the irrigated fields were strips along the rivers, the maximum necessary distance for food transports would have been longer, but transport could have been made partly by boat. In any case, population density was high in the area which supplied food to the centers, and a large share of the plain was empty.

Another example in the Sanders and Price study refers to early urbanization in the western hemisphere. On the Peruvian coast, archeological research has revealed sites of twenty or thirty small concentrated settlements. The total area is not given, so the overall density cannot be derived. One of the settlements seems to have housed some twenty-five thousand persons, and food crops seem to have been grown on 170 square kilometers of irrigated land. The area used for food crops would thus have been around 0.6 hectares per person, a relationship which seems to have been fairly typical for the coastal area, and which is similar to the ratio for Sumeria mentioned in chapter 5. If a town was in the center of a circular area of irrigated land, the maximum distance for food transports would have been 7–8 kilometers, or a little longer than in the Sumerian city-states.

There are no estimates for the ratio between food-producing and non-food-producing families in any of these societies, but it seems unlikely that the size of the non-food-producing population, including nonactive family members, can have been more than 2–3 thousand persons per urban center. In Sumeria and on the Peruvian coast, the whole nonagricultural population may have been some fifty thousand persons. However, it is important to note that because of the small distances over which food could be transported, the nonagricultural population had to live scattered in many small towns surrounded by fields. Concentration in one or a few large cities was possible only later, with more dense population and better transport facilities.

If food transport over 15 kilometers in all directions from the center were feasible, a center could draw its food supplies from an area of 700 square kilometers, compared with less than 200 with 7–8 kilometer transports. But it seems unlikely that food transports over 15 kilometers were feasible at that time, except for centers located in the delta of a major river with water transport in many directions. Even at a late date, in much more technologically advanced societies than the ones mentioned above, distances for food transports on land were short. In the classical period in Greece and Rome, wheeled wagons were used but road transport was too inefficient for long distances. Peasant transports moved no more than 7–8 kilometers, and crops produced for sale by large farmers had to be grown within 15 kilometers from a town, army camp, or similar market to be worth producing.[18] As late as the eighteenth century in Europe, food probably was not transported more than 15 kilometers in typical cases.[19] Thus the solutions to the urbanization problem portrayed in the upper right of table 6.1, ones combining low population densities and long transport distances, did not exist in ancient societies.

ORGANIZATION OF TRANSPORT TO LARGE CITIES

Two to three millennia after the appearance of urbanization in Sumeria, the Mesopotamian plain housed large cities in the hundred-thousand-size group. By contrast to the small early centers, these must have had a predominantly nonagricultural population. They must, then, have been within reach of an agricultural population of a million or more. In the millennia following the appearance of urbanization, population increase in Mesopotamia was accommodated by filling the empty spaces between the irrigated areas with canals, as mentioned in chapter 5. An increasing population of food producers could produce increasing total surpluses of food for urban consumption, thus allowing a corresponding increase in total nonagricultural population. The network of watercourses on which food could be transported was also extended and linked together, making long-distance transport to large centers possible. Thus, part of the urban growth in large centers was obtained by concentration of the population, and the growth of large centers was accompanied by reduction of population in smaller urban centers or by their complete abandonment.[20]

We have seen that with group 6 density and 7–8 kilometer transport distance in the Sumerian plain, only small, dispersed urban centers could appear. But with the extension and linking together of the canal system, the area from which food could be supplied to a center grew rapidly. If in addition the size and density of the agricultural population increased, the change would have been dramatic. Table 6.1 indicates that with group 8 density and 30 kilometer transport distance, a quarter of a million people could supply a center housing a non-food-producing population of some thirty thousand. With group 9 density and 60 kilometer transport distance, an agricultural population of two million would be able to supply a large city.

There is little reason to assume that changes in output per worker occupied in food production contributed significantly to the increase of urbanization in Mesopotamia between the fourth and first millennia b.c. It is impossible to tell whether declining output per worker with continuing expansion of the network, or increasing output per worker due to improvement of technology, was predominant in this period. But in any case, the huge increase in total food surplus for urban use must have been due mainly to the large increase in the number of producers who could supply the urban centers, partly because the population grew in rural areas, and partly because food surpluses could be transported over greater distances.

A similar development favored the growth of large cities in Egypt, India, and China. The Mesoamerican region, however, especially the Maya region, was handicapped by having few possibilities for water transport. In chapter 5, we discussed handicaps to agriculture in Mesoamerica due to the absence of animals for draft power, the limited possibilities for using flow irrigation, and the primitive tools. All these factors of course also provided serious handicaps for transportation. Regions in the western hemisphere with population densities high enough to make road building feasible could not develop wheeled transport despite paved roads because of the lack of animals to draw a wagon. Mesoamerica did not even have pack animals. Except for boat transport on the available lakes and rivers, and perhaps some canals,[21] all food and other products had to be carried on human back or head.

In spite of these handicaps, increasing population densities brought urbanization in Mesoamerica. Sanders has shown the close connections.[22] All the major urban centers were located in the areas with the highest population densities and developed, as in Mesopotamia, after a period of population increase, due either to natural population growth or to immigration from a neighboring area. Northern Mesoamerica had somewhat better possibilities for water transport than the Maya region, and developed larger and earlier centers. Around A.D. 1, when population density in the northern basin of Mesoamerica seems to have been at group 7 level, the largest center is estimated to have had some forty-five thousand inhabitants. This is a high figure compared with what one might expect by looking at table 6.1, but it is assumed that agricultural families from the neighborhood were living in the center. Moreover, Sanders underlines the crucial importance which the chain of lakes in the basin undoubtedly had for development of urbanization in this part of Mesoamerica.

Around A.D. 700, population density in the basin seems to have reached group 8 level, and the largest urban center seems to have exceeded one hundred thousand. Around A.D. 1500, density was at group 9 level, and there were two large and many smaller centers, the largest being the Aztec capital located in the middle of the lakes. Compared with this development, urbanization in the south was much more dispersed. None of the southern centers ever approached the size of the largest northern ones, although population densities in the south also reached group 9 level in some areas. Ruins have been found of a large number of Maya centers, but none reached the hundred-thousand size. Tikal, apparently the largest, seems to have had a population of 30–50 thousand, and it was not so concentrated a settlement as the large centers in the north. Archeological research has revealed that Tikal resembled a gigantic cluster of hamlets, with intervening areas of light settlement which may have been used for intensive cultivation by agricultural families living within the urbanized area.[23]

The American Indians made up for their material handicaps by a high level of organizational skills, or "administrative technology." When the Spanish arrived in Mesoamerica, messages were being moved by foot three hundred miles a day, by a relay system with a station every ten kilometers.[24] Transports of food were handled by professional merchants, who used slaves of foreign origin, probably prisoners of war, for porterage. The tribute delivered from conquered peoples to the Aztec capital also was carried by slaves.[25]

The ability of the inhabitants of Mesoamerica to develop large-scale urbanization in spite of serious handicaps in agriculture and transport serves to underline the crucial importance of the only condition for large-scale urbanization they shared with areas in the eastern hemisphere, that of high population density. Although the large margin of error in population estimates for ancient societies makes it hazardous to draw any conclusion from them, it would seem that areas provided with a plurality of small urban centers had medium population density and that areas which housed urban centers in the hundred-thousand-size group were densely populated. But of course urbanization would not necessarily have appeared in areas in which such densities were reached.

Two special cases should be mentioned, in which the relationship between population density and urbanization was different from the one suggested above. One relates to small, isolated centers, which Sanders rightly put in a different category from other centers.[26] Such centers existed in sparsely populated Beluchistan, on the transit route between the urbanized societies in western Asia and those of northern India.[27] They also existed on the transit route between Mesoamerica and the Inca empire in the Andean area of South America.[28] In some parts of Europe as well, such isolated trading towns existed long before a home-based urbanization could appear. The other case is that of imperial Rome, which became a very large city at a time when average population density in Italy seems to have been at group 7 level.[29] How did Rome solve its problem of food production and food transport?

First, it is important to note that the pattern of small-scale urbanization in Mediterranean Europe seems similar to that in the areas mentioned earlier. We saw in chapter 5 that in the last millennium B.C., Greece and Italy reached medium population density, and a network of small urban centers appeared. These city-states used animal draft power in agriculture and for road transport. Moreover, as underlined by Finley, the Mediterranean towns used water transport for food supplies.[30] In its early days, Rome imported food from the Naples region on small boats that went up the Tiber to the town.

Second, by the time urban centers in Mediterranean Europe grew large, they could depend on food supplies from long distances, because other urbanized societies had already made great technological progress in construction of ships and shipping. At the time of the Roman Empire, it was cheaper to take a shipload of cereals from one end of the Mediterranean to the other than to cart it one hundred kilometers by road.[31] When Athens grew large, it got food supplies from the Black Sea by boat, and when the Roman port of Ostia was built, mass shipments of cereals from distant shores of the Mediterranean could be delivered as tribute or sold as food surpluses in Rome. Italian agriculture specialized in wine and meat, the latter delivered by overland transport of walking herds and flocks.

Rome could obtain these large shipments of food because there were other urbanized societies to produce and export it. In these societies, production and transport of food surpluses had already developed to supply the urban centers. By conquering these centers, located in areas with high or medium population densities, Rome was able to rely on food imports. When Rome became a large city, transport technology by sea had improved so much that a large consumer center did not need to be located in a densely populated area if it had a port to receive and unload bulk shipments of food. It was necessary, however, that the area which *exported* the food have a population density high enough to make mass transport of food to an export harbor feasible.

Within the Roman Empire, population densities and degree of urbanization were correlated. The food deliveries to Rome came from the areas with the highest population densities. The Nile valley had early urbanization and probably group 9 density in the Roman period; Syria, with considerable urbanization, seems to have had group 7 density. In contrast, Europe north of the Alps had only group 3–5 densities and little or no urbanization other than the colonial centers built by the Romans. The fortified Celtic settlements seem not to have deserved the title of urban centers.[32]

The densely populated Nile valley could not only deliver large food surpluses to Rome, but also feed the large city of Alexandria. Syria and other urbanized areas in the Mediterranean also contributed to feed the imperial capital. By contrast, sparsely populated Europe north of the Alps supplied only local Roman army camps at a few kilometers' distance from the producer, and some of the Roman colonial centers even got supplies from Rome by sea and river transport.[33]

LOW POPULATION DENSITY AS OBSTACLE TO URBANIZATION
At the time of the ancient empires, most of the world, including large parts of Europe, a large part of Asia, and nearly all of Africa, America, and Oceania had population densities at group 1–3 levels. The upper part of table 6.1 indicates that no urbanization was possible at such densities if transport technology was primitive. In this period, world population was so small that no more than a few areas had population enough to become urbanized.

It may be objected that the minimum density for urbanization could have been reached in many more areas since all that was needed was for more peoples to give up pastoralism and long-fallow agriculture and concentrate in areas which they could supply with irrigation facilities. This is, in fact, the way in which Wittfogel seems to assume that the ancient urbanized societies emerged.[34] But Adams has demonstrated that Wittfogel's assumptions are unrealistic,[35] and they contrast with all we know about the likely behavior of peoples who subsist by means of extensive systems of food supply.

Because of the rapid increase of population in nonindustrialized societies in recent times, there has been much opportunity to observe the behavior of pastoralists and peoples subsisting by long-fallow systems when population density increases in their usual habitat. Pastoralists seem to be well aware that their diet is more savory and their burden of daily work lighter than those of cultivators. Therefore, they are unwilling to shift to food production with animal husbandry if they have any possibility of migrating to a more sparsely populated area. It seems reasonable to assume that pastoralists in ancient times had a similar attitude in similar situations.

Like the pastoralists, people who use long-fallow techniques often move to more sparsely populated areas when population increase prevents fallow periods of the length to which they are accustomed.[36] To avoid additional work with weeding, fertilization, watering, and the other investments needed for intensive land use, they migrate to areas where it is still possible to clear land for long-fallow agriculture. Today there are few such areas left, but in ancient times the possibilities for avoiding intensification by migration were much better. But as long as there was room enough for migration of this type, the migrants and the ones that remained behind could avoid intensification of agriculture. The migrations meant that the area of emigration failed to reach the minimum density needed for urbanization. Mesoamerica and Mesopotamia could become urbanized at an early date because part of the population increase in the areas of original settlement did not migrate, but remained and intensified agriculture.

Migration to more sparsely populated areas promoted the diffusion of new subsistence techniques from more advanced areas. The migrants probably continued their own subsistence system in the new area, while the indigenous population had to adopt the new techniques if the immigration raised population density to levels which prevented use of their customary methods. If instead of adopting the technology of the migrants, they chose to move away to an even more undeveloped area, the process of diffusion of new subsistence techniques would continue, until few if any hunter-gatherers were left in the whole region or long-fallow systems became more intensive. In other words, it seems likely that migrations at the preurban stage reduced regional differences in population density and technological levels and delayed further technological change in the areas which were most ahead of other areas. In a large continent, such a process of dispersal of population could cause a long delay in urbanization, provided that rates of population growth were low. This situation may help to explain the long delay of urbanization in Europe, as already suggested, and also why urbanization was even more delayed in most of Africa and America.

7 CHARACTERISTIC FEATURES OF ANCIENT URBANIZATION

We have seen in previous chapters that there were two important linkages between population density and technological levels in ancient societies. The first was between population size and the amount and quality of infrastructure. A large population could undertake large-scale investment in canals, roads, and irrigation facilities, which would not be feasible for a smaller population. Therefore, increase in density of population by natural increase or by immigration was a precondition for use of more advanced technologies. The second link was that between population size and natural resources. When population density increased within a region, the amount of natural resources, both per head and sometimes in absolute amounts, was reduced. Therefore, technologies such as extensive subsistence systems could no longer be used when population density exceeded a certain level. Thus technological change was needed either to economize the use of natural resources, or to make it possible to use substitutes for them. As we saw in chapter 6, the disadvantageous changes resulting from an increasing ratio of population to natural resources could also induce migration to areas with lower population density. In that case, opportunities to benefit from more and better infrastructure were lost and urbanization was delayed. In this chapter, we shall focus on some cases in which population density increased and urbanization appeared, and we shall study the effects of these changes in infrastructure and in the population-resource ratio.

We have already discussed the effects relating to agriculture and transport. We have seen that in some areas, of which Mesopotamia served as example, the declining ratio of land to population resulted not only in intensification of agriculture, but also in changes in energy supply for agriculture. Other areas abandoned fire as a means of intensifying agriculture, without introducing other types of nonhuman energy. We have also seen that increasing population density and urbanization went together with improvement of rural infrastructure, either by construction of transport facilities and irrigation facilities as in Mesopotamia, or by improvements of organization ("administrative technology") as in Mesoamerica. These improvements in infrastructure made large-scale urbanization possible. But at the same time they were themselves the result of urbanization. Large cities were the result of a long process of small-scale urbanization, marked by improved rural and administrative infrastructure.

Urbanization meant that a number of new problems had to be solved by the intellectual elite. The new center had to be constructed and enlarged, and since construction activities were labor intensive, a large labor force had to be organized and managed. Materials for the construction had to be provided and food supplies for the labor force and other non-food producers organized. The elite met their many new demands by pooling their knowledge, skills, and administrative abilities. Cross-fertilization of ideas and systematic specialized training were possible because the elite now could live together in the urban center instead of being isolated in scattered villages, as formerly. An elite unburdened by daily toil existed before urbanization; the new feature was that such an elite could live together.

Urbanization was accompanied by rapid progress in the technology of large-scale construction, transport, and agriculture, as mentioned earlier. The advance in nonmaterial fields was even more important. Childe has emphasized that the needs of the urban centers called for organizational and administrative abilities that could be developed only in large urbanized societies.[1] The need to organize the urban economies and to keep accounts led to some of the most important inventions in the history of humanity, those of written language and numbers. Writing in Sumeria was first used to keep economic records within the temples.[2] Literacy is an urban skill, developed in response to demands that existed only in urbanized societies. Rural populations all over the world continued to be illiterate until recently, and even today many school leavers in rural areas lose the skill for lack of need for it in their daily lives.

Like literacy and numbers, sciences such as mathematics and astronomy evolved in the urbanized societies. Many innovations, however, occurred by diffusion of technology and science from one urbanized society to another, rather than by invention. Contacts seem to have been close between Sumeria, Egypt, and the Indus valley. The presence of imported goods in tombs, ruins, and refuse heaps reveals that already before 2500 B.C. a network of trade linked the Nile and the Mesopotamian rivers in the west, the Oxus in central Asia, and the Indus valley in India. In the words of Childe, "Three civilizations were pooling their cultural capital."[3]

Other urban societies in the eastern hemisphere developed later and could benefit from transfer of technology and science from the pioneers. The urbanized societies in America, on the other hand, had little if any contact with the eastern hemisphere. This lack of contact helps to explain the more primitive techniques in pre-Columbian America, compared with the urbanized societies in the eastern hemisphere.

SUPPLY OF MATERIALS AND ENERGY FOR THE URBAN ECONOMIES

It was mentioned above that since large urban centers were located in densely populated areas, they paid for their advantages in infrastructure and skills by an unfavorable ratio of natural resources to population compared with that of sparsely populated areas. We have discussed agricultural aspects of this problem. Another extremely important aspect of the link between high population density and large-scale urbanization is the problem of supplying wood for construction and heat.

During a large part of human history, wood was not only the predominant type of fuel, but also the predominant material for house building and other construction, and for tools and other equipment. Until the industrial revolution, nearly all boats and ships, carts, and other means of transport were of wood, and so were most bridges and fortifications. A population without easy access to wood faced great difficulties unless it developed substitutes. Europe had wooden churches before it replaced them with churches of natural stone and baked bricks, and many of the early urbanized societies probably also had a "Wooden Age." Natural stone was much more difficult to handle with primitive tools than was wood, and some alluvial areas had no natural stones which could be used for construction. Unbaked clay was another substitute used for dwellings, but it was unsuitable for large buildings, except when combined with timber.

But many ancient urbanized societies were located in areas in which wood was in short supply. Even where a humid climate favored forest regeneration after felling, the area of forest per head was small because of the dense population. Some ancient centers had no nearby forest, for climatic reasons or because it had been used up. Societies with a shortage of forest products developed various methods to economize on timber.[4] A comparison of rural housing in various parts of the world with differing access to forest shows clearly that wood and other forest products were preferred in unindustrialized societies, if available. Wooden houses predominate in forested areas; areas with less abundant supplies of wood use a combination of timber and clay; and areas very short in wood use adobe, unless natural stone is easily accessible.

Baked bricks are durable and easy to handle. Hardening clay by fire is an ancient art, first used for pottery. However, while constructions of wood, stone, and adobe can be produced by human muscle power without any other energy, baked bricks need large quantities of wood for the necessary fires. Thus, the best substitute for timber known to the ancient world would be in short supply when it was most needed. Therefore, ancient societies reserved baked bricks for their most urgent needs: military construction, bridges, aqueducts, temples, and palaces and tombs for the rulers. Thus, in spite of efforts to economize on timber and fuel wood, the demands of the construction industry and the need for fuel no doubt contributed to progressive deforestation. As a result of deforestation in the catchment areas, the rivers silted up and caused disturbance, and sometimes abandonment, of irrigated land.[5]

Technically, metals, especially iron, are excellent substitutes for wood in nearly all uses, except fuel. The art of iron production was known in the ancient societies of the eastern hemisphere. However, iron suffered from the same fault as baked bricks; it could not substitute for wood unless large amounts of wood were available for its production. Charcoal was used for smelting ore, but on the eve of the industrial revolution some four hectares of good forest were required to produce the charcoal for one ton of iron.[6] Probably even more were required in the time of the ancient urbanized societies. Therefore, iron production was limited to areas with sufficient forested land. Such areas would usually be far from the densely populated urbanized areas, and transport difficulties set a narrow limit to metal supplies in ancient societies. Under these circumstances, metal was reserved for the most important uses, mainly for weapons and armories. Agriculture, crafts, and manufacturing for civil use continued to apply wood. Iron plowshares were in use in large holdings in ancient Mesopotamia, but ordinary peasants in Asia continued to use small wooden plows.

Many ancient urban centers were forced to transport the necessary supplies of timber, stone, and metals over long distances. Mesopotamia and Egypt got timber supplies from Lebanon. The need to handle long-distance transports of heavy materials induced investment in transport facilities and improvement of transport equipment. It was for good reasons that the early urban centers in Sumeria were preoccupied with the problem of more efficient means of transport than human porterage, pack animals, and boats driven by human muscle power. They succeeded so well that before 3000 B.C. they were able to use wheeled animal-operated vehicles and boats driven by wind power. Thus, a relatively short time after the appearance of urbanization, animal power was applied to a new purpose, that of wheeled traffic on roads, and an important new source of energy, wind power, was used for transport purposes.

To reduce the risk involved in obtaining vital supplies from distant areas, efforts were made to obtain military control over access roads and areas of supply. Wheeled traffic was used for military transport in Mesopotamia a millennium before it came into extensive use for ordinary transport of goods. Roads and bridges were built for use by the armies, and the military sector was a major promoter of technological change. Some highways built for military purposes by the ancient empires ran over thousands of kilometers, and in China and Peru not only urban centers, but the frontiers of the territory, were protected by massive walls. Military demand provided the main motive for metal production and mining. Workshops were created in which skilled artisans produced weapons and other military equipment.[7] The first factories in the ancient world were often producing for the military sector.

METHODS OF DEALING WITH LABOR SHORTAGE

Ancient urbanized societies needed labor for such constructions as fortifications, roads, canals, temples, palaces, royal tombs and other monuments, dwellings, public granaries or markets, and aqueducts. In addition, and as a supplement to these activities, a large labor force was needed in mining and transport and for urban crafts and services. A many times larger labor force was needed to supply all these workers and their nonworking family members with food. Last but not least, manpower was needed to man the army. All these activities used labor-intensive techniques. Human muscle was the predominant source of power, although it was sometimes helped by animals, water power, and wind power. There were three kinds of labor supply available for non-food production in the ancient urbanized societies: slave labor, wage labor, and labor services performed by peasants. All three seem to have been used in most if not all ancient urbanized societies, but in widely different proportions. We shall look at the possible reasons for these differences.

An important clue is provided by the seasonality of agricultural work. In the off-season, the large agricultural work force could do other work without endangering food supplies. Such a mobilization of peasant labor would make the scope for expansion of nonagricultural activities several times larger than if full-time labor had to be used.

It was suggested in chapter 6 that the share of the total labor force which could be used in urban areas for purposes other than food production was seldom more than ten per cent. But if all or most of the peasant population could be mobilized in the off-season, it would become possible to have ten per cent full-time workers, plus an additional 80–90 per cent during perhaps one-third of the year. The result for the year as a whole would be nearly 40 per cent of the work force performing nonagricultural work. The suggestion that peasant labor could be mobilized for nonagricultural activities one-third of the year is not pure guesswork. Temple building in Mesopotamia went on for four months each year and was performed by peasants as labor service. The Inca empire built its impressive network of paved roads by means of peasants, who came with their food and tools to build roads in the off-season. Mesoamerica also relied mainly on labor services.[8]

The extent to which peasant labor could be used depended upon the length of the off-season and the amount of off-seasonal maintenance needed by the farms. Digging and cleaning of irrigation canals were obligatory labor for everybody in Sumeria, Egypt, Peru, and, probably, India and China.[9]

It is obvious that there must have been competition for peasant labor between the irrigation system, monumental construction in the urban centers, and road building and other investment in transport. Before their population density became very high, the Mayas may have benefited from their reliance on rain-fed crops rather than flow irrigation. This reliance helps to explain their extensive construction activities, done with equipment much poorer than that of Mesopotamia. However, we have seen that with increasing population density and increasing intensity of agriculture, additional operations become necessary. Many of these would occupy periods which before had been free of work with food production. It might become more and more difficult to use labor for nonagricultural purposes without endangering food production. This may help to explain why temple construction among the Mayas seems to have faded out when population densities became high, and why the Mesopotamians allowed their irrigation systems to silt up and decay.[10]

What alternatives did rulers of urban societies have if labor services were—or became—insufficient to meet the demand? They could conquer additional areas settled with peasants, or they could capture slaves to replace or supplement peasant labor services. These two measures often went together, because expansion of the urban population by importing slaves required additions to the peasant population to feed them. (However, the ratio would be less than ten to one, since most slaves were adults in working ages.) Usually slaves were prisoners of war. In Mesopotamia, war between independent city-states was an important source of slave labor, and in Rome the amount of building activity seems to have been determined chiefly by the availability of slave labor.[11] A victorious war in which many prisoners were taken was often followed by a building boom in Rome. The army became an important part of the civilian economy because war was the means to obtain labor for expansion of the urban economy. Slaves were used to liberate free citizens for service in the army, or were themselves used to man the army if sufficient free labor were unavailable. Societies which could afford a professional army were in a far better position than those which could afford only an army of peasants and had to interrupt the war for agricultural needs to avoid famine.

Kingsley Davis underlines that societies which base expansion of the economy on slave labor by prisoners of war and on tribute payment and labor services imposed on subjugated peasant populations must become militarily aggressive.[12] The goal then is to dominate and conquer as many of the neighboring peoples as possible, to use them either for obligatory works in the off-season or as slave labor. However, as long as transport techniques prevented transport of food over more than a few kilometers, neighboring urban centers enjoyed a natural protection, because they could not be used as regular suppliers of food and labor services. The growth of each center would be limited by the capacity for food supply of the restricted area in short distance from the center. This was the period of small, independent urban centers, each surrounded by an area of intensive agriculture. Later, population increase together with improved organization and transport technology made long-distance supplies possible. It became possible to tap conquered areas for their labor and their food supplies by destroying neighboring urban centers, killing the urban population, or transferring it as slaves to the metropolis of the conqueror.[13] Skilled and highly educated slaves seem to have been much appreciated, if we can judge from the prices paid in Rome.[14] The vanquished peasant population would become a source of tribute and labor services. This "imperial" period of the ancient urbanized societies is characterized by urban concentration, with disappearance of some centers and appearance of new and much larger ones. Both Adams and Sanders have described this phenomenon as a characteristic feature in the areas they studied.[15] Once the small centers were swallowed by larger ones, warfare continued between the large metropoles over the right to dominate the areas that separated them.

By contrast to Mesopotamia[16] and Mesoamerica, Greece and Rome based their urban economies mainly on slave labor and free wage labor, often performed by liberated slaves. Because they fed their populations by long-distance food imports, Athens and Rome could afford to use much more full-time labor, either slaves or free workers, than could urban economies which had to produce their food supplies in the neighborhood. Wage labor was of considerable importance in Rome, which taxed its provinces and colonies in money and kind. Rome could keep a standing, salaried army. During the republic, free citizens were made available for the army by use of slaves for manual labor,[17] but during the empire, the army came to consist nearly exclusively of non-Italians.

In peacetime, the army was used for construction works like fortresses, frontier works, and imperial highways.[18]

The urbanized economies, both city-states and empires, conducted wars among themselves and with tribal populations living as long-fallow cultivators and pastoralists at their perimeters. Members of these populations were brought to the urban centers as slaves or went there voluntarily, attracted by the possibility for recruitment to the army or wage employment. In such cases, the population remaining in the tribal areas was likely to become stagnant or decline, given the low rates of natural population growth. Thus, the tribal people could continue to live scattered and to use the easy extensive systems of food supply. They could not adopt the new, advanced technologies of the urban areas, since these could be used only when population was dense enough to afford the necessary infrastructure investment. Therefore, the period of ancient urbanization was one of widening technological gaps between urbanized and technologically advanced peoples, and technologically backward people living in sparsely populated areas. The urbanized, more densely populated areas increased their advantage in both population density and technological levels by skimming off the population surplus in surrounding areas by means of forced or voluntary migration to the urban centers and their immediate neighborhood. The other areas stagnated in population and in technological levels. The effect of migration in the urban period thus tended to be opposite to that of the preurban period, when migration went from more densely populated to more sparsely populated areas and reduced the differences in density and technological levels between different areas.

Thus, if we focus only on what happened in the urbanized economies, we observe a picture of rapid acceleration of technology in the urban period. But it should not be forgotten that this affected only a small part of the world. In most parts, changes in both population and technology were very slow or opposite to those of the urban centers. Moreover, many urbanized societies had temporary or lasting periods of regression.

CAUSES AND EFFECTS OF HIGH MORTALITY

Because the ancient urbanized economies relied upon slave labor, tribute, and labor services obtained through war and conquest, they seem nearly always to have been at war, as aggressors when they were strong, or as defenders when they were weak. Wars between different urban centers, as well as attacks on the urban centers by nomads and other tribal populations, often ended in sacking towns and cities. Residents were slaughtered, and the economic chaos that followed further raised mortality.[19] Moreover, besieged towns, besieging armies, and other military camps all were breeding grounds for disease. Epidemics followed in the wake of war, and sometimes death and disorganization were so general that one of the parties in the war disappeared completely. When wars prevented work in the fields and disrupted irrigation systems, famine followed. Famine also resulted from expropriation by the enemy of the peasants' seeds, animals, and labor, and from expropriation or destruction of urban granaries.

Even in peacetime, urban mortality seems to have been high. The ancient towns and cities were fertile breeding grounds for epidemics and other disease, especially when the population was squeezed within city walls under unsanitary conditions. The walls may have saved lives by making attack and conquest more difficult, but they may have cost more lives by epidemics and other disease, in peacetime and in war. Because of low natural rates of growth, the urban centers seem to have depended upon a steady inflow of forced or voluntary immigrants to prevent decline of population.

On top of high natural mortality for adults and children, there was infanticide and induced abortion. Studies of classical literature have revealed that a number of abortion methods were employed.[20] The ffect of some of them was probably to kill not only the fetus, but also the mother, thus reinforcing the demographic effects. Infanticide, apparently practiced mainly on girls, also had a double demographic effect.[21] A Greek author advised parents to "raise every son, even if you are poor, but expose every daughter, even if you are rich."[22] In imperial Rome, the government tried to counteract parents' desire to limit family size by introducing children's allowances as an encouragement to larger families. The outcome of this early example of a conflict between a pronatalist government keen on expansion of both the labor force and the army, and restrictive parent attitudes, was not a success for the government: the amounts offered as allowances were small and it is doubtful that they had much effect.[23]

But the breakdown of the Roman Empire was not a result of mass suicide through family limitation. The epidemic diseases brought in from other continents were much more important causes of Roman decay. McNeill has strongly underlined the importance of exposure to new diseases, against which the population had not yet had time to develop resistance.[24] New contacts occurred in war and in the course of long-distance trade and other expeditions to provide necessary materials and labor or luxury goods. In the first centuries A.D., many firm contacts were established between east and south Asia and the Mediterranean area. Caravan transports began to plow the silk road between China and the Roman Empire, and seafaring traffic was handled partly by Asian and partly by Greek ships. McNeill suggests that this contact resulted in catastrophic epidemics, which ravaged the Roman world in the first millennium A.D., and that the new mortal diseases are likely to have been measles and smallpox.[25] After the middle of the first millennium, bubonic plague, arriving from Asia or Africa, caused another demographic catastrophe.

These epidemics bore a great share of the responsibility for the decline and breakdown of the western part of the Roman urbanized economy. While urbanization survived the onslaughts of disease in the more densely populated eastern empire, the reduced populations in the western part were unable to keep up the infrastructure necessary for the urbanized economy. The combined result of depopulation and the breakdown of the transport network of the empire—roads as well as river traffic—was a long period of urban decay in Italy and in the sparsely populated west. The urban centers shrank to a fraction of their previous population, partly because of the epidemics, but probably also because the breakdown of the supply system forced them to stay at a size within the capacity of the immediate neighborhood to feed. Thus, even in regions in which there is little evidence of decline of the number and size of rural settlements or of cultivated area, the centers lost population on a large scale.[26] In Rome itself, around A.D. 600 the average age of death for adults, according to tombstone data, was down to 30–31 years for women and 35–36 years for men.[27] These are only slightly higher than the ages revealed by skeletons from the prehistoric period mentioned in chapter 4.

The depopulation and breakdown of the urbanized economy as a result of the onslaught of new diseases had even more dramatic effects in America than in Europe. Epidemics of smallpox, measles, and typhoid fever followed the arrival of the Spanish, killing the majority of the Indian population. When the conquerors tried to supplement the shrinking Indian labor force by imports of slave labor from Africa, the Indian population was further reduced by malaria and yellow fever brought by the slaves.[28]

The reduction of the Indian population in the urbanized societies of Latin America brought on ruralization and a return to extensive subsistence systems. The reduced, impoverished, or ruined centers could not support a rural and urban infrastructure, and the use of intensive systems of agriculture was no longer needed when population became much smaller. In the plateau in northern Mesoamerica, formerly irrigated and intensively cultivated terraces became pastures for cattle and sheep imported by the Spanish settlers.[29] There was neither labor to cultivate this land, nor demand for the food which could be grown on it. Fields which the Indians had cultivated intensively with hoes became more extensively cultivated with plows and animals imported from Spain. This change reduced crop yields by half, but it reduced the input of labor even more.

In southern Mesoamerica, the Mayas abandoned their elevated fields and terraced land and returned to long-fallow techniques. In all parts of Mesoamerica, the result of decline of population was return from annual cropping and multicropping to pastoralism, long fallow, and short fallow. Mining activities declined, as did the urban centers. The urbanized Indian cultures were eradicated, and the Indians remained a rural population for centuries following. The Indian administrators, priests, merchants, and skilled artisans were killed, or they converted to a rural life as agriculturists or pastoralists, if they could get animals.[30] If irrigation survived, the administration of the network passed from the state to local councils of water commissioners.[31]

None of the ancient urbanized societies seems to have avoided demographic catastrophes caused by epidemics or wars. In western Asia and North Africa, too, these catastrophes caused a reversal of the upward trends in population density. It can be seen from table 2.1 that as late as 1750, i.e., on the eve of the industrial revolution in Europe, population density in western Asia and North Africa was apparently similar to that in Roman times, nearly two millennia earlier.

However, the demographic setbacks in various regions occurred in different periods and for different reasons. When epidemics hit the Roman Empire, population was increasing in America and Mesopotamia. The major demographic catastrophe in Mesopotamia occurred six centuries later, and was caused not by an epidemic but by warfare, disorganization, and decay of the irrigation system.[32] Urban centers which based their economy on systems of flow irrigation were particularly vulnerable to war damage. When the irrigation system became damaged as a result of hostilities, agricultural output was sharply reduced, and the urban center, or perhaps the whole area, declined in population through emigration, famine, or both.

Even a moderate amount of damage to the irrigation system, or just lack of proper cleaning of the canals due to labor shortage, could produce poisonous swamps of stagnant water. Malaria, likely to have been a great killer in many areas, is known to have made the neighborhood of Rome uninhabitable in the period of the decline of the empire. Warfare destroyed the irrigation facilities, and the region remained empty for nearly two millennia. The last years of the Roman Empire and the twelfth and thirteenth century were periods in which urban economies were brought down by attacks from nomads.[33] Deliberate slaughter by nomads perhaps caused fewer deaths than the malaria which may have resulted from the destruction or disruption of flow irrigation systems by the nomads.

NUMERICAL STRENGTH AND TECHNOLOGICAL LEADERSHIP OF CHINA

In the beginning of this chapter, two linkages between population size and technological levels were identified. A large population has advantages from the point of view of infrastructure investment, but disadvantages from the point of view of ratio of natural resources to population. The discussion of the apparent causes of decay in the ancient urbanized societies has provided us with examples of both these linkages. In a number of cases, population reductions resulted in decay of the infrastructure necessary for urbanization, and in a consequent relapse into ruralism. Changes in resource-population ratios also played a role in the decay and breakdown of the densely settled urbanized regions. The efforts to maintain irrigation systems became insufficient, probably owing to labor shortage, as the systems were enlarged and made more complicated in step with the population increase, and as extension of cultivation and pasturing of larger herds and flocks caused erosion in catchment areas. Strains on peasant labor seem to have become overwhelming, owing to the combined demands of current operations and expansion, repair, and upkeep of investments. Investments were neglected, the armies grew too small, and the strength of one densely populated empire after another was undermined.

A development of this type seems to have contributed to the decay in Mesopotamia. It may also have motivated the Mayas to stop temple building and abandon the most densely populated part of their territory, more than half a millennium before the arrival of the Spanish, although the abandonment of the Maya core area could also have been flight from a mortal epidemic, perhaps due to new contacts. In northern Mexico there were also signs of stress. Possibilities for further expansion of irrigation were not utilized, probably because there already were excessive strains on peasant labor. Failure to invest in expansion of the network seems to have been the cause of a famine in the century preceding the Spanish conquest.[34]

The urbanized societies in east and south Asia suffered repeated demographic setbacks similar to those in the Western world. The earliest example of an urban economy relapsing into ruralism is that of the societies in the Indus valley, which disappeared after Aryan pastoralists invaded them in the middle of the second millennium B.C. Urbanization apparently appeared in China later than in India, western Asia, or Egypt. China, too, suffered from demographic setbacks, due to wars and epidemics. China, however, had the numerical strength to repair and rebuild its economic infrastructure and avoid relapse into ruralism, at least in the central parts. In his great study of Chinese technology, Needham makes an interesting comparison between the development of transport facilities in the Chinese and Roman empires in the first centuries A.D.[35] Both empires had an impressive network of roads, of about the same lengths. After the third century A.D., the road networks in both empires fell into decay for lack of upkeep. In sparsely populated Europe, the result was a return to ruralism. Transport facilities in the densely populated parts of the Chinese empire, however, improved in the following centuries. An immense network of navigable rivers and artificial canals was created. A large volume of traffic could be handled on this network more easily than on roads. In some regions, each little village and nearly every farmhouse were served by a canal.

China's transport network was built and rebuilt by means of labor services imposed on the huge peasant population. Millions of workers were mobilized for canal building, and in the first and second millennia A.D., a thousand-kilometer-long canal for transport of food was constructed. The invention of sluice gates resulted in improved water transport, and the method of harnessing animals made land transport more efficient as well. In Europe, land transport was inefficient, and neither the size and density of the rural population nor the potential volume of traffic was sufficient to allow canal building. Only in the last centuries before the industrial revolution did canal building begin in Europe, and the canals were small and primitive compared with the much earlier Chinese ones.[36]

In the centuries between A.D. 500 and A.D. 1000, hardly any urban centers were left in Europe north of the Alps; the Italian towns were small, mostly in the 5–6 thousand size.[37] By contrast, China, in which urbanization survived, made great strides in development of new technology, bypassing other urbanized economies. The development of foreign trade between India and China indicates that in the first centuries A.D., China was ahead of India even in textile technology. In spite of the high level of skills reached in Indian textile production, the Indian upper class at that time preferred fabrics imported from China.[38]

Another of the many fields in which China was far ahead was health technology. Already in the first millennium B.C., it had manuals concerned with protection of life. One of these suggested that government staff should include sanitation officials and sanitation police to remove rotting corpses of men and animals; organized street sweeping was also recommended. The importance of pure drinking water and periodic cleaning of wells was recognized.[39] This understanding of the roots of disease may have contributed to China's numerical strength, although it did not prevent decimation by epidemics. Around A.D. 1500, when China was the uncontested technological leader on a world scale, its population is assumed to have been 100–150 million (table 2.1), and population density was high in the core area of the empire.

But in the following two hundred and fifty years, as population seems to have risen to 200 million or more, China began to lag behind Europe in technological development. Had this change something to do with demographic trends? Did the high and increasing population density in China create stress on natural resources, while Europe was still at a stage of demographic development at which increasing density was a positive factor? We shall come back to the last part of this question in part 3. As for the first part, only gradually is enough information becoming available to treat it adequately. But we can now point to some signs of stress due to population pressure on natural resources in China in the period before the industrial revolution in Europe. One concerns energy supply. Needham reports that deforestation due to increasing population pressure and to demands for charcoal for the metallurgical industry caused fuel shortage and serious erosion.[40] China was far ahead of others in use of coal and production of cast iron. China used coal as fuel long before Europe, and, at least until the thirteenth century, seems to have remained the largest consumer of coal in the world. Cast iron was produced from the first century B.C., i.e., one and half millennia before Europe, and coal was used for smelting of iron ore at least from the fourth century A.D.[41] When deforestation caused a shortage of fuel wood, coal was used as a substitute. But the crucial problem with coal is the cost of transport. Coal unlike fuel wood is not available around every town and village. Therefore, use of coal on a large scale was never a practical proposition, except for localities linked to coalfields by good bulk transport. Thus, before the railway age, a watercourse had to link the coal consumer to the coal mine to make it feasible to utilize the mine. Rich coalfields, like those in the middle of the Indian continent, could become important only after the building of railways.

The other signs of stress concern increasing intensity of agriculture. Lack of forested areas causes not only lack of fuel wood but also stress on food supplies to urban areas. In a densely populated area deprived of forest, the peasants lack areas in which to gather vegetable matter for fertilizer when they are forced to abandon fallow. The scarcity of fertilizer in China became so acute that long-distance transports of night soil from the towns to the villages became necessary, as did extremely labor intensive digging of river silts. In the eleventh century, China introduced multicropping, based upon imports of early-maturing seeds from Java and Southeast Asia.[42] With increasing population density, multicropping probably spread more and more, as it is doing today. Multicropping eliminated the off-seasons which had been available for investments, repair of investments, and other purposes for which labor services by the peasants were used. When Lossing Buck made his study of Chinese agriculture in the first half of this century, the working seasons lasted nearly all year.[43] The unavailability of peasant labor for investments and repairs probably contributed to the increasing problems with flood damage to the ill-maintained irrigation system.

The strain on labor resources in China and other densely populated urbanized economies motivated labor-saving inventions. Many ancient economies of course dealt with labor shortage by using warfare as a means to provide labor; but this does not mean that nothing was done in these societies to save labor by means of technological change. We have already mentioned agricultural inventions, like plow techniques with flow irrigation, which were labor saving compared with alternatives like hoeing and lifting water by muscle power. Shadufs and waterwheels were introduced to lift water, and wind power replaced the labor of oarsmen when the wind was favorable. The use of water power and wind power for milling and other industrial work are old Asian inventions,[44] and a spinning wheel was in use in China in the eleventh century, some two centuries before this technology appeared in Europe.[45] Although later it lagged behind, China was much more than two centuries in advance of Europe in technology during this period. Needham enumerates twenty-six important Chinese inventions which later were adopted in Europe as part of the prelude to the industrial revolution.[46] His tabulation reveals that the average time lag between use of these technologies in China and in Europe was nine centuries, which tells us something about the technological inventiveness of China and the backwardness of Europe in the post-Roman period of demographic collapse.

III The Role of Demographic Factors in European Development

8 FOOD SUPPLY AND LABOR SHORTAGE

At the end of part 2, we noted the striking contrast between the backwardness of Europe and the advanced technological level of China in the first millennium A.D. We shall look now at some of the factors which helped Europe to pick up and then take the lead in technology during the industrial revolution. There can be no doubt that demographic trends played a major part in this development. Western and Central Europe were prevented by low population densities from urbanizing in the same periods as Mesopotamia, Mesoamerica, and Mediterranean Europe. Toward the end of the first millennium A.D., however, following a long period of slow increase, population reached medium density in a number of areas, and a large number of small urban centers appeared. Moreover, this urbanization started a period of rapid technological change.

The analysis of ancient urbanized economies in part 2 focused on the major problems of food supplies, raw material supplies, transport technology, and the methods used to deal with labor shortage. These problems came to be of major importance in Europe as well, and the following chapters will focus upon the way in which they were handled there. This chapter concerns problems of food supply and labor shortage; chapter 9, problems of raw material supply; and chapter 10, the period after 1750, when Europe had both its industrial revolution and its period of "demographic transition," in which first mortality and later fertility declined.

FIVE CENTURIES OF POPULATION INCREASE, 850–1350

If urbanization in Mediterranean Europe was late compared with Mesopotamia and Egypt, it was early compared with sparsely populated Western and Central Europe. A period of nearly two millennia separated the appearance of the small city-states in Greece and Italy from the appearance of small city-states north of the Alps. There, they appeared first during the long period of population increase which began toward the end of the first millennium A.D. and lasted until the onslaught of the Black Death in the mid-fourteenth century. During that period, the population of most of Western and Central Europe increased from group 4–5 levels, or lower, to group 6–7 levels, as can be seen in table 5.2. In Western and Central Europe, as elsewhere, urbanization was delayed as long as population densities were low, but appeared when a long period of slow population growth raised densities to medium levels.

The possible causes of the population increase between the ninth and the fourteenth centuries have been widely discussed. This discussion often is related to a theory shared by most economic historians, according to which stagnant population should be the normal pattern in preindustrial societies, and sustained population growth an abnormal feature calling for a special explanation. But this theory is not supported by factual evidence. There were many periods with prolonged population increase in the centuries and millennia preceding the industrial revolution; Mesopotamia and Mesoamerica provide two examples. A third is ancient Europe, which seems to have had gradually increasing population in the millennia preceding the Christian era. Therefore, instead of asking why the European population increased between the ninth and fourteenth centuries, we perhaps had better ask why it failed to increase, and instead declined, in the periods before and after.

If the question is posed in this way, it is not difficult to answer. There can be little doubt that the decline and stagnation of population in most of the first millennium A.D. was due to the ravages of major epidemics. As mentioned already, these seem to have been so severe because new types of disease appeared, against which the populations had not developed resistance.[1] The American demographic catastrophe after contacts with the Europeans around A.D. 1500 demonstrates how much new contacts could affect population trends in a region. In the first millennium A.D., new contacts were brought about by the migrations of tribal populations both within Europe and between Asia and Europe, as well as by general increases in sea traffic. In most of Europe, five centuries of population growth preceded the Black Death, which is assumed to have reduced the population of France from 17 to 10 million[2] and to have caused reductions of that order of magnitude in other parts of Europe as well. In the centuries before the industrial revolution (and even after), epidemics continued to decimate the population of Europe. From the mid-fourteenth to the mid-seventeenth century, only nineteen years have no evidence of pestilence in France.[3]

It has been suggested that the epidemics, and especially the Black Death, struck so hard because the previous period of population growth resulted in overpopulation, poor nutrition, and, therefore, little resistance to disease. The history of the Black Death, however, does not indicate significant differences in its virulence between prosperous and poor areas. The areas which fared best were areas of dry and healthy climate, like Spain and Anatolia, while humid areas with a prosperous population were hit much harder.[4] Most of the epidemics came to Europe from Asia, and it has also been suggested that the fluctuations in the Chinese population coincide roughly with the contractions and expansions which occurred in Europe.[5] If this is true, it supports the idea that shifting incidences of worldwide epidemics rather than nutritional conditions in Europe provide the main explanation of European population trends. It also supports the idea that the period between the ninth and fourteenth centuries was one of return to a "normal" pattern of slow growth after the abnormal disturbances of the preceding period.

The period from mid-fourteenth to the mid-eighteenth century again brought demographic setbacks, due to major epidemics. However, in this period, it seems that not only changes in mortality, but also changes in fertility, occurred. Apparently, it became customary to marry later than before; if so, the average number of births per woman would have fallen.[6] We shall come back to this change in chapter 14, which will focus on the relationship between technological development and fertility.

AGRICULTURAL TECHNOLOGY AND URBANIZATION
Population increases between the ninth and fourteenth centuries resulted in dramatic changes in the agricultural system. In earlier chapters, a distinction was made between change to a more intensive system under population pressure, and change in the quality of inputs, which sometimes but not always accompanied a change of system. In ancient Europe, changes of both types occurred. In the Roman time, parts of Western and Central Europe arrived at population densities of group 4–5 levels accompanied by long-fallow agriculture and medium-level technology with scratch plows (see table 5.3). Archeological evidence from Germany[7] and Denmark[8] has revealed that before the Roman period, unorganized cultivation of scattered plots was already being replaced by a system of organized forest-fallow or bush-fallow rotation. Villages moved after several decades in one location but later reoccupied it, when forest had taken over the abandoned fields. In later centuries when the European population multiplied, this system of semipermanent villages with long-fallow agriculture was replaced by permanent villages with short-fallow agriculture.

The new system, which spread in the period between the ninth and fourteenth centuries, was a three-course rotation of all the fields in a village, in which two cereal crops were followed by one year of fallow. The stubble and fallow were utilized for supervised grazing by domestic animals belonging to all the villagers.[9] Stubble-grazing animals fertilized the fields with their droppings, helping to compensate for loss of soil fertility by shorter fallowing, and for loss of natural pastures due to expansion of the cultivated area. Even so, it is possible that crop yields were lower than they had been under the long-fallow system, and it is likely that there was some shift of diet from animal to vegetable food as population continued to increase. When the Black Death later reduced population densities, an opposite shift to less vegetable food took place, as arable fields, made superfluous by the decline of population, returned to pasture.

However, European agriculture not only moves down and up the vertical axis in table 5.3; it also moves to the right on the horizontal axis. When a shift to short fallow took place, scratch plows were replaced by plows with mulboards, and a new type of harness, introduced from Asia, made it feasible to use horses for plowing. Lynn White has suggested that the technological changes in European agriculture began in the sixth century A.D. and were the main cause of the later multiplication of the European population.[10] In other words, he assumes that an improved quality of inputs caused a shift to the right on the horizontal axis in table 5.3, promoting a population increase.

Wailes's critical study of the existing evidence concerning the equipment used in European agriculture in this period shows that there is little evidence for this assumption, and that no precise dating is possible for the technological changes.[11] Since the innovations were transfers of inventions made earlier in different parts of Asia, they might have been imported at any time. Moreover, the crucial date is not when somebody in Europe first experimented with the use of improved plows, but when conditions were ripe for their diffusion on a large scale, i.e., when the population increase before and after A.D. 1000 made it necessary to change from long fallow to short fallow. This change has often been described as introduction of short fallow by settlement of hitherto unoccupied areas, but usually the areas had been used before for either long fallow or for pastoralism.[12]

The period between the ninth and fourteenth centuries brought not only important agricultural changes, but also urbanization, as already mentioned. Short-fallow systems and urbanization appeared in regions of Western and Central Europe in which overall population densities seem to have reached group 6–7 levels. These levels seem to be the ones at which these features appear in preindustrial societies. There is a pronounced tendency for short-fallow agriculture and urbanization to appear together. Usually permanent investments in land become necessary when short fallow replaces long-fallow systems; these promote a shift of tenure.[13] Long-fallow cultivators and pastoralists who do not need to make permanent investments in land have tribal tenure systems, with members of the tribe having the right to use land for long-fallow cultivation, pasture, and other purposes. However, when population density in an area becomes so high that agricultural systems requiring permanent investments in land or in water supply are introduced, the tribal tenure system is replaced by one which grants secure tenure to the person who either organizes the investment or carries it out with family labor. The change from tribal to peasant-and-landlord tenure and creation of permanent villages facilitate investments in rural infrastructure and encourage production and transfer of surpluses for urban use. Moreover, urbanization is facilitated, if improved equipment makes it possible to expand short-fallow agriculture at the same time that population increase enlarges the labor force. By imposing taxes and labor services on the village communities, kings, churches, and other landlords could force the peasants to produce a surplus to feed the towns and the construction workers.

Western and Central Europe seem to have conformed to this general pattern. Their societies were stratified long before the period considered here, but before the end of the first millennium A.D. the facilities for transport of food were so poor that the European kings and other big landlords were forced to move from one of their estates to another in the course of the year.[14] They and their followers would remain for some time in a castle or manor, hunting the game and consuming the local wine, cereals, meat, fruits, and so forth. When the surplus was consumed, they moved on to another of their properties. Only after a road network was built in the following centuries could the royal courts stay permanently in capital towns. For many centuries more, however, road transport remained inefficient, and towns had to be either so small that transport distances could be small too, or supplied partly by water. Many European towns appeared on the banks of rivers or on the seashore.

It may be objected that if the towns made use of water transport, they could have appeared while population densities were low. But a minimum population density is needed in the area which exports the food to an urban center. As was mentioned earlier, Rome got its food supplies from Egypt and other areas with high or medium densities, not sparsely populated Western and Central Europe. Sparsely populated areas could export live cattle on foot if there were grazings along the route, but they could not export cereals. Therefore, European towns supplied by long-distance water transport could develop only when other parts of Europe had reached population densities and a stage of agricultural development that made organization of food transports possible.

Methods of Dealing with Labor Shortage
The period between the appearance of urbanization in Europe and the industrial revolution was one of fluctuations in population size, as mentioned already. When population declined, due to epidemics or wars,

the agricultural system adapted by a shift back to more extensive systems in the areas substantially affected. Fields were turned into permanent pastures or left to grow forest, and fallow periods were lengthened, until population increase once more made intensification necessary.[15] Thus, European agriculture adapted in a flexible way to population increase and fluctuations. In contrast, in ancient societies adaptation to declining population size was likely to lead to neglect of investments and breakdown of flow irrigation systems.

European agriculture could adapt flexibly to fluctuations of population size, because there were accompanying changes in labor force and in demand for food. But if the nonagricultural population increased while the agricultural labor force increased at a lower rate or declined, an increase of output per agricultural worker was needed. This was not easy to accomplish with preindustrial techniques. Ancient societies accordingly based expansion of urban activities on seasonal labor services by their own peasants, conquered peoples, or slaves. They carried off the populations of conquered towns or neighboring tribes to supplement their labor force.

The ruling elite in Europe was as keen on building palaces, churches, monasteries, and fortifications as the rulers of ancient societies, and its construction activities were just as labor intensive. The ruling classes in Europe, however, did not use the same means to deal with labor shortage as the ancient societies. In Western and Central Europe, labor services were sometimes important in agriculture but rarely in urban areas, and keeping Christian slaves of European origin was abandoned before the beginnings of the urban period.[16] Therefore, other means had to be used to make urban expansion possible. One of these was to draw labor out of agriculture and supply the town population with food imported long distance, by means of water, from other parts of Europe having less dynamic urban growth. Another was to use labor-saving methods and equipment in urban activities. A third was to draw labor out of agriculture and run the risk of insufficient food supply.

The first two of these measures became important during and after the industrial revolution; but in the preceding centuries of preindustrial urbanization, the chief means of dealing with labor shortage was to draw additional labor for the army, for construction activities, and for urban jobs from the agricultural labor force. There was usually keen competition for scarce labor, and most often agriculture lost in this competition. Nothing could be more inappropriate than to characterize the European economy in this period as a labor surplus economy. On the contrary, one of the most serious problems in the period of preindustrial urbanization in Western and Central Europe was insufficiency of food production, due not to shortage of land, but to shortage of labor.

In periods of stagnating population, increasing demand for manpower for the army and for nonagricultural occupations reduced the absolute size of the agricultural labor force. The remaining agricultural population had to reduce the area under cultivation, and the supply of food fell short of demand. In periods of increasing population, the share of the youth leaving the countryside for the army or the towns was so large as to cause food supply to fall short of demand. In both cases, more land would be kept as pasture or forest, or fallow would be left for more years, than would have been the case had the agricultural labor force been larger. Except for a few areas, which we shall discuss in the following chapters, Western and Central Europe had sufficient land for short-fallow cultivation until the next wave of sustained population growth in the eighteenth and nineteenth centuries.

In other words, the effective restraint on food production was not lack of potential for increase of output but lack of labor to utilize the existing potential. Therefore, in years of poor harvest, the output of food was insufficient to feed the whole population, and if stocks were low, the result would be soaring food prices and famine. Harvest fluctuations were larger in Europe than they seem to have been in ancient societies with flow irrigation. Substantial stocks of food were needed to secure the supplies in years of poor harvest. If the agricultural labor force was so small that it could cultivate only enough land to supply the population in years of normal harvest, but no surplus for stock building, a bad harvest or two would result in soaring grain prices. The poor would be squeezed out of the market and starve. Those peasants unable to retain sufficient stocks for themselves, perhaps because these were confiscated for use by the army and the urban population, also would starve.

Administrative technology, the art of organizing society, was at lower levels in Europe than in the ancient societies, including pre-Columbian America. In years of bad harvest, especially when they coincided with years of warfare, purchases or expropriations of food for the army and the towns drained the rural areas in Europe of food and left the local population, or part of it, to starve.[17] The worst period of famine in Western Europe seems to have occurred in the seventeenth century.[18] This was a period of very low—if any—population growth, in which the armaments race between European countries gained momentum and towns grew in size.[19] Under these conditions, agricultural labor shortages were unavoidable. Between 1500 and 1700 the population of London seems to have grown from around 50,000 to around 500,000, and in years of bad harvest, its needs were met by starving the peasants in the countryside.[20] In France the reason the famine of 1709–10 was so severe was that when a cold winter severely reduced the harvest the government gave priority to extraordinary supplies to the army fighting in Flanders, and to the towns.[21] The improvement of the transport network in the urban period reduced the risk of local famines in regions hit by a local harvest failure. But the risk of rural famines due to expropriations or sale of a large share of a small harvest to the towns and the army was increased. Regions usually having food surpluses were forced or tempted to sell too much in years in which the harvest was small; the remaining local supply was insufficient to feed the local population.

It was not always agriculture, however, which lost in the competition for scarce labor. In some cases, governments took steps to prevent too much labor from being drawn out of agriculture. This happened especially in periods of rapid urban expansion, when the towns attracted so much labor from the countryside that the army and agriculture were short-handed. Peasants and their sons were then forbidden to leave their villages and obliged to work for their landlord in the peak season.[22] Or weaving was prohibited in the month of peak demand for agricultural labor.[23]

Scarcity of labor was more pronounced in some periods than in others. The demand for soldiers and for labor for construction activities of different types, urban production, and services fluctuated. Moreover, the supply of labor changed abruptly during and after major wars and epidemics. After the Black Death, the reduction of the labor force caused acute labor shortages, and real wages were at high levels in the following period.[24] Usually, however, wage levels were regulated by custom, and legal prescriptions and guild rules prevented the change in wage rates and transfer of labor from one occupation to another that would have facilitated the adjustment between demand and supply. When enterprises in the towns were unable to attract labor from the countryside, they were motivated to apply labor-saving equipment.

It was mentioned earlier that before urbanization appeared in Western and Central Europe, this area was nearly a millennium behind China in technology. The late start was probably the main reason why a revolutionary technology could be produced in such a short time.[25] For millennia, low population densities prevented most of Europe from adopting many of the high-level technologies developed in the ancient urbanized societies. This handicap was removed when population density increased and urbanization spread.

Of course, low population density did not completely prevent technological progress in Western and Central Europe, since many technological inventions have very little relation to population density. Metals and water mills for crushing grains were found in the preurban period; in the eleventh century, England had more than five thousand water mills in operation.[26] But when the density needed for urbanization was reached and transport facilities improved, the way was opened for all the urban-linked, advanced technologies and intellectual achievements which had accumulated in other parts of the world. The initiative and creativeness which accompanied the concentration of the elite in urban centers in many ancient societies assumed revolutionary strength in Europe. Europe could import the inventions and scientific achievements which ancient societies had to think out.[27]

In the course of preindustrial urbanization in Europe, many labor-saving methods were taken over from technologically advanced areas in west and east Asia, and improvements on them were made. Mills powered by animals, water, and wind spread in many regions. Most were for grinding grain for bread and beer, and for pressing oil, but some were also used in the textile and metallurgical industries.[28] In the thirteenth century, looms of a type long in use in Syria and Egypt were introduced. When this caused a bottleneck at the spinning stage, the technology of spinning wheels was imported from China.[29] Thus, Europe benefited from the possibility of combining technologies of other regions. Later, this type of interlinked technological change became a characteristic feature of the industrial revolution. Meanwhile, the time lag between inventions made in Asian societies and their application in Europe was radically reduced as the urban period proceeded: for instance, the spinning wheel came into use in Europe only two centuries after its invention in China.[30] The examples of the spinning wheel, loom, and powered mills indicate that industries with mechanized equipment were by no means a European invention, but the labor shortage in Europe provided incentive to import such techniques and to experiment with further labor-saving methods and equipment.

9 RAW MATERIAL SUPPLY AND SPECIALIZATION OF LABOR

The increasing population density in Europe facilitated development of specialized crafts and manufactured goods. In areas of dense population, a large number of customers lived within a relatively small territory. Direct contact with customers was possible and transport costs for products could be kept at a minimum. A densely populated area, moreover, offered the advantages that levels of infrastructure investment were high according to the standards of the time, and that the market was large enough for specialization among the craftsmen, who were therefore more skilled than those in sparsely populated areas.

Manufacturing industries were even more dependent upon good infrastructure and a large market than were crafts. They required skilled workers and traders as well as the financial services and management and administrative skills which were concentrated in urbanized areas. Therefore, the areas in Europe which first developed manufacturing industries were those with the highest population densities—Tuscany, and the Low Countries—where there was already a tendency to concentrate production processes under one roof in the form of a manufactory in the Middle Ages. Such concentration occurred only later in France and England.[1] In addition to the high population density, Italy benefited from contacts with the technologically advanced Arab world, and the Low Countries profited from unusually good conditions for water transport.

If dense population had many advantages for manufacturing industry, it also had disadvantages, mainly related to supply of fuel and raw materials. As manufacturing developed in the most densely populated areas of Europe, the problem of raw material supply became more severe. It was approached by different means. One was density-related trade, that is, long-distance imports of raw materials from more sparsely populated areas. Another solution was to develop substitutes for scarce raw materials, and a third was to move the industries to areas with better supplies of raw materials. The attempts to solve the problem of raw materials had far-reaching effects. New industries appeared, transport technology was improved, and manufacturing spread to more and more areas. This process of change led to the industrial revolution, which accelerated it, and it seems still to be accelerating. This chapter deals only with its early stages.

DENSITY-RELATED TRADE WITHIN EUROPE AND WITH OTHER CONTINENTS

From ancient times, some long-distance trade in land-using products existed in Europe, carried by boats on rivers and along seashores. Small quantities of products obtained mainly by pastoralism and hunting and gathering, especially hides, furs, wax, and tar, were acquired by traders from more advanced parts of Europe. This density-related trade was similar to that which Arabs and Europeans developed much later with sparsely populated areas of Africa. When urbanization spread in the most advanced parts of Europe, traders already engaged in long-distance trade on a small scale had incentive to expand it to include more bulky goods. Improvements in transport and shipping were required, and seafaring nations in Europe competed in developing better methods of shipbuilding and navigation. All the seas of Europe became the scenes of this trade, which over the centuries grew in quantity and carried more and more bulky goods.

The first industries in Europe produced mainly textiles and metals. Some of the textile raw materials, like flax and silk, were labor intensive and suited for production in the densely settled areas in which the manufacturing took place. Wool, however, was a land-using product, which had to be imported as the industry grew larger. The metal industries became dependent upon imports of metal when the densely populated areas in which they began ran short of forests for charcoal production. The shipbuilding industry, which was a precondition for long-distance trade, also had to gather its timber supplies far away from the densely settled coastal towns in which it was located. Industrial centers as a whole were dependent upon long-distance food imports, when land or labor shortage developed in neighboring areas.

The early centers of manufacturing in Tuscany and the Low Countries, with their dense population, were the first in Europe to develop intensive systems of agriculture.[2] In the period in which other parts of Western and Central Europe shifted to short-fallow systems, these more densely populated areas began to abandon short fallow and introduce more intensive systems, including intensive animal husbandry and water control. In the eleventh century, draining, irrigation, and other investments needed for intensive agriculture were undertaken in northern Italy, and dikes and polders were built in the Netherlands as early as the tenth century.[3] In the fourteenth and fifteenth centuries, fallow in these densely populated areas was replaced by fodder crops for domestic animals and by industrial crops. In most other parts of Western and Central Europe, similar changes had to await the wave of population increase in the eighteenth and nineteenth centuries.

As early as the tenth century, towns in the Netherlands imported cereals from the shores of the northern seas, but only around 1500 did bulk shipments become feasible.[4] It became cheaper for German towns as well to get cereals by boat than overland from German villages. Spain began to import cereals from the Baltic in the fifteenth century, and England, in the sixteenth century.[5] At that time, the Low Countries were heavily dependent upon imports of cereals, and in the mid-sixteenth century, imports seem to have accounted for 12–15 per cent of their total grain consumption.[6] A very large share of urban consumption was dependent on imports. Imports allowed many towns to grow beyond the capacity set by local food production. They could use the land in the neighborhood for intensive cultivation of products which were difficult or impossible to transport over long distances, and reduce their production of cereals and other more easily transportable products. But a town could, of course, engage in this form of specialization of labor only if it had suitable export products or trading profits, with which to pay for the food imports and imports of land-using raw materials.

The areas which exported food and land-using raw materials to the growing industrial areas in Western and Central Europe included not only northern and eastern Europe, which were linked to the urbanized areas by water transport, but also England and Spain before these grew more densely populated and developed their own industries. In the course of time, the wool industry in the Low Countries became increasingly dependent upon wool imports. At the beginning of the urban period in Europe, England had lower population density than the neighboring areas on the Continent and was an economically backward area which relied on exports of cereals and wool to the more advanced continental areas. A triangular trade developed, in which the woolen industries in the Low Countries partly supplied their home market but partly exported cloth to Germany, thus providing themselves with the means to buy wool in England and cereals in Germany.[7]

However, with increasing population size and urbanization in England, the home market became large enough to support processing industries. England changed from a deliverer of wool to a large center of woolen industries, which produced both for the growing home market, including the army, and for exports to the Continent and to the colonies. In order to produce increasing quantities of wool in a country with increasing population density, England had to transform arable fields into pastures for sheep, and to shift from being an exporter of cereals to a net importer of cereals and other food. In other words, England used its labor for industry, its land for sheep, which required little labor, and its export earnings for food imports. This is a very peculiar pattern, since it implies that increasing population and a shift to a more extensive use of land go together. It is not, however, typical of the agricultural changes which accompany industrialization.

After the industrial revolution, density-related trade with overseas areas became much more important than inter-European trade in raw materials and food. But in the period of preindustrial urbanization, few of the imports to Europe from overseas areas were density related. The types of ships which could cross the oceans could carry little freight, and ocean transport was too costly to make bulk shipments of food and raw materials feasible. Therefore, imports from other continents were mainly of three types: high-value products like furs and precious metals; high-quality textiles and other high-value manufactured goods from the technologically advanced areas of Asia; and small amounts of products which for climatic reasons were unsuitable for production in Europe, such as cocoa, coffee, tea, spices, tobacco, and cotton. Among these products only furs, cotton, and manufactured goods from Asia could be considered density related. The Asian exports of manufactured goods reflected the higher technological level of the old, densely populated, urbanized economies of Asia, compared with newly urbanized Europe, which could manufacture only goods which were unattractive to the refined taste of the Asian upper classes.[8] Europe paid for manufactured goods and for other, climate-related imports from Asia mainly with precious metals, part of the spoils from the plunder of the American colonies. Silk, tobacco, and cotton were labor intensive rather than land using, but cotton was a good substitute for wool, and it therefore developed into one of the major European imports, providing the basis for one of the industries playing a central role in the industrial revolution.

After vast overseas territories had been conquered, long-distance trade provided a strong motivation to design ships which could carry heavy and bulky commodities across the ocean within a reasonable time.[9] However, it took more than three centuries before the efforts succeeded to the extent that large-scale bulk shipments became feasible. It was not until the mid-nineteenth century that iron became cheap and the invention of the steam engine and the screw made it possible to construct large, relatively fast moving, ocean-crossing steamships.[10] Only then did cereals, the major land-using product in inter-European trade, get competition from overseas. A few decades later, experiments with refrigeration techniques opened the way for overseas imports of meat and fruits.[11]

EFFECTS OF FOREST SHORTAGE

Hitherto, the most important density-related material, wood, has barely been mentioned. With increasing population density in Europe, shortage of wood became a major problem. Many of the technological innovations in the eighteenth century were the result of attempts to develop substitutes for wood as fuel and as raw material for industry and construction.

Timber for the shipbuilding industry became so scarce in Europe that in spite of its bulk, it very early got room on the oceangoing ships from North America. Wood for shipbuilding was floated down rivers to the ocean or the big lakes; in the winter the snow cover was used for transport to the river.[12] When transatlantic timber transports started, timber had long been an important item in inter-European trade. The limitation on ocean-crossing capacity protected sparsely populated timber-exporting regions in Europe from overseas competition. Some of these regions established sawmills driven by water power. Such industries were in use in Germany from the fourteenth century; in the sixteenth century, when timber shortages in Western and Central Europe became acute, they were introduced in Scandinavia and used for processing timber for export.[13]

The shortage of timber in the densely populated regions, which technologically were the most advanced, was only one aspect of the general dilemma of increasing scarcity of wood. Scarcity was the result partly of reduction of forest area to make room for additional fields, and partly of population increase which meant a lower supply of wood per head. Shortages affected the supplies of timber for shipbuilding and other construction, fuel wood for industries and households, and charcoal for the metal industries.

By contrast to many dry areas in other continents, in Europe the problem of fuel wood was mainly an urban one; most villages continued to have fuel wood for their own purposes. It was most serious for Italian industry, because the Mediterranean area had no coal as a substitute for fuel wood. By contrast, the densely populated Low Countries became pioneers in coal consumption in Europe, and in the thirteenth century seem to have been the largest coal consumers in the world, surpassing China.[14] Owing to their high population density, the Low Countries also pioneered the introduction of other technologies to alleviate the effects of population pressure on natural resources. Fuel shortages began much later in England, which was more sparsely populated. Owing to its rapid growth in the sixteenth century, however, the London region ran short of forest, and England replaced the Low Countries as the largest coal consumer.[15] Coal could be transported by boat directly from the mines to London.

The effect of the shortage of fuel in Western and Central Europe was technological change. Rising fuel prices in the fourteenth century led to experimentation with water-powered hammers, and in the following centuries, water power became an important substitute for fuel wood. The technical problems posed by coal, such as pumping water out of the mines and the problem of land transport, induced further technological innovations, including steam power and the invention of railways.[16]

In spite of the increasing use of substitutes for wood, the period before the industrial revolution continued to be a "wooden age." Timber and its by-products, especially potash and charcoal, played an indispensable role in practically every industry, and between 1500 and 1700 one region of Europe after another ran short of forest areas for woodcutting.[17] Although there was a gradual shift to stone and bricks for urban housing, timber remained the basic structural support, particularly for more modest residences, shops, and stalls.[18] Even the coal mines used increasing amounts of timber to support the shafts as mines became larger and deeper. With increasing population, reduction of the forest area, and increasing demand for fuel wood, more and more European industries shifted to coal or water power, or both. But the iron industry still used charcoal to smelt ore, and in one European country after another, increasing shortage of forest areas for charcoal production, sometimes accompanied by administrative restrictions on the use of forest for this purpose, curtailed the production of iron.[19] Only after the industrial revolution could iron become an important substitute for wood.

Small quantities of iron were produced in European forests since the first millennium B.C., but in the period of technological regression in the middle of the first millennium A.D., most of the centers of European production closed. With the appearance of urbanization, demand for iron rose steadily, and in the twelfth and thirteenth centuries intensive search for iron deposits went on all over Europe. Increasing production pushed up prices of fuel, inducing substitution of coal and experiments with water-powered forges. But iron production remained small. Estimates for around A.D. 1500 range 40–60 thousand tons,[20] which is more than one-half but less than one whole kilo per inhabitant in Europe. In 1750, on the eve of the industrial revolution, the output of iron was some three times larger, but since population had doubled, per capita output was still only some 1.2–1.3 kilos per inhabitant. Today only a few of the least developed countries have such a low per capita consumption of iron, and in the countries of Western and Central Europe, consumption is some 400–700 kilos per capita.[21]

During the whole of the period leading to the industrial revolution, the military sector took most of the supplies. Like other industries, manufacture of armaments began in the most densely populated and technologically advanced areas—the ones with the largest market. Northern Italy, the Low Countries, and southern Germany were important early producers of military equipment.[22] Lack of charcoal, however, became a threat to production. The first to suffer from lack of forest for charcoal production were Italy and other Mediterranean countries, in which not only population pressure, but also forest fires in the dry and hot summers reduced the forested area.

Many parts of the European continent became relatively advanced while still well supplied with forests, and iron and other metal production moved to these areas where wood was abundant.[23] However, the transport costs from forested areas to the centers of consumption kept prices high and limited consumption, especially for civil purposes. England had lower population density than continental Western and Central Europe and a more humid climate. Therefore, England had good possibilities as a producer of timber and metals, and moreover offered favorable conditions for water transport of heavy products. But when population increased and military demand rose sharply in the sixteenth century, wood for timber and charcoal became scarce. England then turned to Ireland as a major supplier of timber, and iron was produced in Irish forests until by the end of the century little forest was left.[24]

With increasing mechanization, the military sector demanded more and more metals. In the sixteenth century, large numbers of infantrymen were issued firearms, and large sailing ships bristled with cannons. In the following centuries, the armament race between European countries continued to exert pressure on metal supplies and forest areas. The European governments took more and more interest in promoting industries which produced armaments, uniforms, and other equipment for the armies, and especially in the manufacture of iron and bronze.[25] In the seventeenth century, arms manufacture was carefully supervised by governments or conducted in government establishments. Mass production methods first appeared in armaments factories and shipbuilding yards. Specialist corps of engineers and artillerymen were formed, and logistics played an important role in the preparation of military operations.[26]

Just as in many ancient urbanized societies, the preoccupation of the rulers with military matters acted as a stimulant to technological change. Boring machines, driven by water power, first came into use for making cannons, and blast furnaces were first developed for manufacture of cannonballs.[27] Many improvements in construction techniques, in transport, and in other infrastructure were directly or indirectly related to military needs. Later, when metals became less scarce, military innovations became useful for civilian purposes. Canal and railway transports benefited from innovations originating in armaments production.[28] The role of the military sector in promoting the industrial revolution should not be underestimated. Strong military demand prevented substitution of metals for wood for civilian purposes. Agricultural and other tools would at best have metal reinforcement on parts requiring great strength and durability; machinery too was of wood with metal reinforcements. As late as the seventeenth century, even scientific instruments were of wood with some parts in brass.[29]

DENSITY-RELATED CHANGES IN LOCATION OF INDUSTRY

Around 1700, England and the other major Western and Central European countries had population densities at group 7 level. In contrast, Scandinavian countries and European Russia still had group 3–4 densities, i.e., less than eight persons per square kilometer. So Western Europe gradually became dependent upon iron made in these countries. Transport to the West was by boat; transport within the exporting country was often by sledge in the winter season. In the beginning of the eighteenth century, imports from Sweden covered more than forty per cent of England's consumption of iron,[30] and by mid-century Russia had developed into the largest iron producer in the world.[31] The imports were due not to any shortage of ore in the densely populated countries— most of them had abundant ore—but to insufficiency of forest areas for production of charcoal to smelt the ore. The increasing dependence on imports for the most crucial raw material for military supplies acted as a very strong inducement for developing new technologies for metal production.

The introduction of iron production based on coal instead of charcoal is a classic example of a demand-induced innovation. It was promoted by population pressure on forested land in Western and Central Europe, leading to increasing shortage of wood. Coal was already used to forge iron in Germany in medieval times; around 1600, when the wood shortage became serious in England and the use of coal was spreading in other industries, the idea of using coal for iron production was discussed. A treatise appeared in 1613, but experiments were for a long time unsuccessful.[32] At the end of the eighteenth century, when experiments with substitution of coal for charcoal in iron production finally succeeded, the Western and Central European economies were released from the straitjacket of their dependence on the forest.[33] Production of iron miltiplied rapidly. The military sector could get much larger and cheaper supplies, and iron replaced wood in ways hitherto impossible because of restricted supply and high prices. Within a century from the introduction of the new technology, not only tools and machinery, but ships, wagons, bridges, roads, and buildings used iron, and the railway and steam engine appeared.

The introduction of the new technology resulted in an abrupt change in the sources of supply for iron. Sparsely populated countries lost their relative advantage. Russia lost its export markets, and Sweden could preserve a much reduced volume of exports only because of the exceptional quality of its ore. The new iron technology proved so efficient that it was even introduced in sparsely populated countries with abundance of forest, although the change from charcoal to coal took somewhat longer in France[34] and the United States,[35] with large forest resources, than in England, with its forest shortages and exceptionally favorable location of coal and iron ore. Before long, production of ordinary iron by means of charcoal ceased everywhere. Forested areas were no longer an attraction for the iron industry, which now located near deposits of coal and markets for metals.

It is interesting to note the difference between the new and efficient iron technology, which ousted the old technology everywhere, and the changes in agricultural technology discussed in earlier chapters. Agricultural technologies, such as water control, were less universally advantageous compared with old methods. They therefore were adopted only in areas in which population was too dense for continued application of the old methods. Thus, there continued to be differences between the agricultural technologies of areas with different population densities. There were, on the other hand, no differences between the methods used for iron production, after a relatively short transition period.

As a result of the new iron technology and the changes which went with it, a period began in which Western and Central Europe were technological leaders, owing to their large deposits of coal and ore in favorable locations. These deposits had the double advantage of attracting both raw-material-oriented and market-oriented industries. The result was a snowballing effect in England and the valleys of the Rhine and its confluents, where the rapid growth of industry attracted population from less favored areas. England prospered from depopulation of Scotland and Ireland,[36] and the Rhine valley absorbed the population surplus from eastern Germany.[37] This migratory movement made the industrial regions even more attractive for labor-oriented and market-oriented industries, and it became difficult for other areas to compete with them for new industries.

The shift of industry in Europe from south to north started long before the industrial revolution and proceeded gradually during the whole period of early industrialization.[38] With increasing population densities in northwestern Europe, the southern areas lost much of their advantage with respect to material and human infrastructure and also their attractiveness for market-oriented industries. Italian industries suffered from competition with industries north of the Alps, and Italian shipbuilding suffered earlier than others from forest shortage. The change to use of coal dealt the final blow to Italian industry. Lack of coalfields compelled Italian iron producers to continue with dispersed small-scale production based on charcoal, although charcoal had been scarce in Italy much longer than in other parts of Europe. Thus, possibilities for further industrialization were seriously restricted, and the whole period until new sources of energy began to replace coal was one of stagnation and decline for the Italian economy.[39]

The shift from south to north also proceeded north of the Alps.[40] Southern Germany, which had attracted industries based on water power, lost out to the northwestern region with its abundance of coal, ores, and navigable rivers. France, which was far ahead of England until the sixteenth century, fell behind in population growth and technological development in the following centuries. Even the old technological leader in the north, the Low Countries, lost out to England. The sparsely populated countries in north and east Europe had less to lose and more to gain by the industrialization in northwestern Europe, because they got larger markets for their exports of food and raw materials other than iron. Sweden had the double advantage of having a strong natural resource base, including water power and some coal, and being one of a small number of sparsely populated countries in a more and more densely populated, rapidly industrializing continent which could be reached by water transport on the northern seas. Moreover, snow and ice in the winter season made land transport feasible, even before railways. The Swedish economy was hit several times, when the foreign markets for its major export products became less absorptive: copper, iron, timber, and paper were all affected. But each time a new product took the place of the previous one. With the help of increasing population density, Sweden's originally export-based industrialization came to include market-oriented industries.[41] We shall return to this problem of export-based or market-oriented industrialization in sparsely populated areas in part 4, which deals with the diffusion of industrial technology to non-European areas.

10 AGRICULTURAL CHANGE IN THE PERIOD OF DEMOGRAPHIC TRANSITION

In addition to the industrial revolution, Europe has experienced large changes in demographic trends since the eighteenth century. Rates of population growth accelerated, and in the nineteenth century reached annual levels of around one per cent or more. In the twentieth century, population growth decelerated, and it is now close to replacement level in many countries. Furthermore, there were considerable variations in the extent, length, and timing of the nineteenth century demographic transition. As Kuznets points out, the demographic changes were by no means timed to the onset of industrialization.[1] In England, population growth seems to have accelerated simultaneously with the industrial breakthrough. In France, however, industrialization occurred without much change in rates of population growth; and in other cases, for instance in Scandinavia, there was a long time lag between the beginnings of the demographic transition and the industrial breakthrough.

In spite of these variations, it seems true for England and for Western and Central Europe as a whole that the rising rates of population growth helped to accelerate the economic growth. The industrial revolution was an acceleration of the long process of technological change which characterized the urban period in Europe. In the seventeenth century, further growth of the European economy was restricted by shortages of raw materials, especially forest products in densely populated areas, and by labor shortage, as armies, urban areas, and agriculture competed for a labor force which increased very little in that century. Technological changes in the eighteenth century removed one of these restrictions, because coal and ore could now replace wood. And at least in England, the acceleration of population growth helped to remove the other. The European economy entered a period of unprecedented growth of total production and per capita income.

This interpretation of the industrial revolution may seem unrealistic to those who accept the widespread belief that, the lower the rate of population growth within a given society, the better the possibilities for industrialization. Adherents of this theory have, in fact, suggested that the period of "lull" in population in the period before the industrial revolution helped to bring it about.[2] This theory of "lull" is based upon the assumption that increasing family size reduces savings, and that the disadvantage of a lower supply of capital more than outbalances the advantage of an increasing supply of labor, when the additional population reach working age. Labor is underestimated because the preindustrial period is wrongly assumed to have been characterized by "oversupply of labor."

The idea that savings would be reduced by accelerated rates of population growth at the time of the industrial revolution seems as unrealistic as the theory of oversupply of labor in the preceding centuries. The rate of saving depends on the distribution of income and the social structure, features which were left out of account in Keynesian theory. Income distribution in Europe seems to have been highly skewed both before and during the industrial revolution. Phyllis Deane suggests that there was a high rate of savings among the rich, and that the technological innovations provided them with incentive to use these savings for industrial investments yielding high profits.[3] Moreover, a large share of the families were small producers, who were more likely to reduce consumption than savings when they had to secure the future for more numerous offspring. In a later section of this chapter, we shall return to this problem of changes in the patterns of consumption and savings during the industrial revolution.

The interrelationship between the accelerated growth of population and the accelerated technological changes in industry in Europe has been widely discussed. In accordance with Malthusian tradition, many scholars have suggested that the clue to the problem is an "agricultural revolution," which preceded both the demographic and the industrial changes. This eighteenth-century agricultural revolution is supposed to have released the demographic change by improving nutrition, and the industrial change by permitting a large transfer of labor from agriculture to industry.[4] In other words, the sequence is assumed to be similar to the one suggested by Lynn White for the period of prolonged population growth between the ninth and fourteenth centuries, discussed in chapter 8. It is suggested that the agricultural change in the eighteenth century was a movement along the horizontal axis in table 5.3, and that this movement made it possible to produce more food with a constant labor force, thereby promoting an increase both of population and of the nonagricultural labor force.

However, it is by no means obvious that labor productivity in agriculture improved in the eighteenth century, and the agricultural labor force was not constant, but increasing. The agricultural changes which took place at that time seem to have been a downward movement on the vertical axis in table 5.3, in response to demographic change, rather than any major movement along the horizontal axis due to improvement of the quality of inputs.[5] The latter type of change first occurred much later when agriculture could draw benefits from the technological progress in industry and transport following the industrial revolution.

THE FIRST AND SECOND "AGRICULTURAL REVOLUTIONS"

According to the evidence concerning population changes in Western and Central Europe presented by Kuznets,[6] rates of growth accelerated from around one-half of one per cent annually in the mid-eighteenth century to around one per cent annually at the end (see table 10.1). Rates of population growth are assumed to have been even lower before mid-century. Rates of natural population growth of around one per cent or even higher seem to have been typical in the nineteenth century, and this had important effects on population density. It can be seen from table 5.2 that in the mid-eighteenth century, all European countries except Italy and the Low Countries had medium or sparse population density; at the end of the nineteenth century the whole of Western and Central Europe was densely populated, with the highest densities occurring in England, the Low Countries, and Germany. This large increase in population density, which corresponded roughly to a trebling of population—more in some countries—occurred in spite of continued net emigration, which became very large in the second half of the nineteenth century.[7]

The change from medium to high population density was accompanied by radical changes in the agricultural system. Annual cropping was introduced, replacing the existing system of short fallow with domestic animals grazing fallow and natural pastures. The latter system, discussed in chapter 8, was introduced during the long period of pop-

TABLE 10.1 DEMOGRAPHIC CHANGES IN EUROPE, 1750–1950

Century	Birth Rates				Mortality Rates				Rates of Natural Increase			
	Engl.	France	Scand.	Others	Engl.	France	Scand.	Others	Engl.	France	Scand.	Others
Mid-18th	3.7	4.0	3.5		3.2		2.9		0.5		0.6	
End 18th	3.7	3.3	3.4	3.8ᵃ	2.5		2.5		1.2		0.8	
Mid-19th	3.3	2.7	3.3	3.5	2.2	2.4	2.1	2.6ᵇ	1.1	0.3	1.1	0.8ᵇ
End 19th	3.0	2.2	3.0	3.2	1.8	2.1	1.7	2.0	1.2	0.1	1.2	1.2
Mid-20th	1.6	1.9	1.8	1.8	1.2	1.2	0.9	1.0	0.4	0.7	0.9	0.8

ᵃ Only Netherlands.   ᵇ Excluding Switzerland.
DATA SOURCE: Simon Kuznets, *Modern Economic Growth, Rate, Structure and Spread* (New Haven, 1966), pp. 42–44.
NOTE: Crude rates in long periods, per cent per annum. Averages for country groups are unweighted. Other countries are: Germany, Netherlands, Belgium, Switzerland, and Italy.

ulation increase between the ninth and the fourteenth centuries, when population density changed from low to medium. Now, as population density went from medium to high, it was abandoned in favor of the more intensive system of annual cropping.[8]

These successive changes of agricultural system in Western and Central Europe correspond remarkably well to the results obtained by the cross-country comparison of population density and agricultural system in chapter 3. There we saw that the short-fallow system is typical in low-technology countries with medium population density and the use of plow animals, while annual cropping is predominant in low-technology countries with group 8–9 densities. In Western and Central Europe, short fallow and annual cropping were, in fact, introduced when densities reached the levels we found in chapter 3. Moreover, the regional differences in densities and in the timing of change from one agricultural system to another also correspond to the results of chapter 3. Regions like Italy and the Low Countries, which reached medium and high densities earlier than other parts of Europe, also .got more intensive systems earlier; countries in north and east Europe with lower densities got them later.

It was underlined in chapter 8 that in the centuries preceding the industrial revolution, the bottleneck in European agricultural expansion was labor rather than land. Otherwise, it could have been overcome by transfer of the techniques of intensive agriculture, used in densely populated areas like Italy and the Low Countries, to the areas ravaged by periodic famines. But in typical cases, methods of intensive agriculture were unhelpful because they were even more demanding in labor input per unit of output than was the existing short-fallow system. Intensive methods did, however, become a suitable solution to the problems posed by the multiplication of population in the eighteenth and nineteenth centuries, when the area of land per head was reduced radically and the labor force increased. Communication between countries was so intensive in Europe in the urban period that the lack of large-scale transfer of methods of intensive agriculture before the eighteenth century indicates that motivation was lacking. If population growth had accelerated earlier, the spread of intensive methods would no doubt have taken place sooner too.

As usual when intensive methods are introduced, investments had to be made in land improvement, especially draining, which is the most important type of water control in the humid climate of Western and Central Europe. Investments were also made in fences to keep animals away from the crops, and in barns, stables, and other enclosures. These agricultural changes did not change the basic fact that European agriculture relied on human and animal muscle power, and that there was little use of purchased inputs except for wage labor. There were some improvements of crops, animals, and equipment, and in England some experiments were made with agricultural machinery.[9] But these were minor elements in raising output, compared with the large increase resulting from more labor. This seems to be true of England,[10] France,[11] and Germany.[12] Thus, there was a long period in the eighteenth and nineteenth centuries in which the agricultural labor force continued to increase and real wages in agriculture stagnated.[13] This period lasted until the continuing demand pressure on food production, caused by population growth and industrialization, induced more radical changes, this time improvements in the quality of inputs.

This second phase of agricultural development started in England in the mid-nineteenth century and spread to other countries of Western and Central Europe in the second half of the century. Population growth continued to be rapid, except in France, and there was continuing intensification of agriculture, but there was also increasing reliance upon agricultural imports. Industrial and scientific inputs were applied to raise output more rapidly[14] and to permit an increasing share of the growing rural population to transfer to urban employment.

There were several important features in this second phase. Owing to the improvements in ocean transport, food supplies could now be supplemented by large imports of food and fodder from overseas. The shortage of fertilizer for the more and more intensive agricultural system induced first import of guano fertilizer from Latin America and afterward production and use of increasing amounts of chemical fertilizer. Mechanization of agriculture, based first upon horse and steam power and later on tractors and electrification, gained ground. Scientifically based improvements were made in seeds and animals. This new phase of agricultural development in Europe, unlike the first one, was not a transmission of techniques long in use in the most densely populated parts. The new techniques were based upon the new developments in transport, manufacturing, and science which accompanied the process of industrialization.

The industrialization of Europe had to be well advanced before these new methods could be used. They could spread only after the iron and chemical industries were large and their products so cheap as to be economical in agriculture and transport. Commercial fertilizer on a large scale could not be introduced before a railway network was built;[15] large-scale imports of food and fodder had to await the steamship; imports of animal products required refrigeration techniques.[16] All these were demand-induced inventions, but it took time to invent and bring them into commercial use. This second agricultural revolution resulted in much more radical change within the agricultural sector of the European economy than the first phase. It has been suggested that the term "agricultural revolution" might more aptly be applied to this change than to the earlier, less radical one.[17]

CHANGES IN PATTERNS OF CONSUMPTION AND SAVINGS

Since changes in nutritional levels are a crucial element in the Malthusian theory of the eighteenth-century agricultural revolution, it is pertinent to ask what is known about dietary changes during the period. There is no doubt that per capita consumption of vegetables, fruit, and animal products increased when railways sharply reduced their prices in urban areas, but this was long after the eighteenth-century agricultural revolution.[18] It is also true that agricultural output increased rapidly in the eighteenth century. But so did population, and indications of rates of increase are too few and localized to allow any general conclusion concerning changes in average per capita supplies of food. The best estimates are for England, where both population and total output of food seem to have expanded around twenty per cent between 1740 and 1770.[19]

The proponents of the theory of major nutritional improvement in the first phase of agricultural change focus on two factors: increase of livestock due to fodder production, and introduction of the potato as food crop and pig fodder. But these changes were adaptations to increased population density. Fallow and natural pastures for livestock were turned into arable fields, and in England, into pastures for sheep as well. Because the increasing urban middle class provided a strong demand for livestock products, the result was not decline of per capita supplies, but rather an increase in prices, which encouraged fodder production and substitution of pork for beef. Between 1770 and 1850, prices of meat and butter doubled in England, while prices of wheat were the same at the beginning and at the end of this period.[20] This change of relative prices was necessary to cover the additional costs of fodder production, but it must have pushed the poor to cheaper types of food, leaving a larger share of livestock for consumption by the middle class.

It is natural that in this situation the potato would become acceptable as a cheap substitute for other food, and a means to avoid starvation in large, low-income families. Potatoes were raised and consumed in Europe in the sixteenth century, but until the eighteenth century on a limited basis only.[21] They were admirably suited for use when the area of land per inhabitant declined and the labor force increased, since they yield more calories per hectare than cereals and demand more labor.[22]

Potato cultivation became widespread when population increase raised total demand for food, and the poor became willing to try new types of food and work harder to get it. But the spread of the potato in the first phase of the agricultural and demographic change may not have improved nutrition since there is also the increasing family size to take into account.

The use of potatoes as pig fodder helped to provide cheaper meat to consumers willing to substitute pork for beef, since pigs utilize fodder more efficiently than cattle. The spread of high-yielding but labor-intensive root crops like potatoes, turnips, and sugar beets was a response to the increasing population pressure on land resources in Europe. Maize was also introduced as food and fodder in the eighteenth century.[23] But it is not easy to tell what effect this substitution of foodstuffs had on health. It is necessary to distinguish between social groups when we pose questions about the effect of population increase on nutritional levels and patterns of consumption and savings. At the time of the industrial revolution, wage earners' incomes were too low for substantial savings. When family size increased, they had no other choice than to increase the number of active family members, if that was possible, or reduce consumption, mainly by shifting to less expensive types of food. It is difficult to reconcile workdays of 12–16 hours for miserable wages in the new factories[24] with the theory that the main cause of declining mortality was better resistance to disease due to improved nutrition. Apart from famine years, the ancestors of these people probably had better nutrition in the Middle Ages, when mortality was high, than in the eighteenth century, when it began to decline.

Between the rich and the wage earners in European societies were a numerous group of peasants, craftsmen, and other small businessmen, who did save and invest in their businesses. Did these people reduce their savings when their families increased? Or did they do their utmost to save more, in order to provide all their children with the means to remain in the lower middle class? If they gave their children's future priority over their own desire for leisure and small luxuries, they could work longer hours and cut consumption more easily than the wage earners. It might be argued that even the rich were more likely to cut luxury consumptions than savings, if they had a large family to provide for.

Admittedly, the reasoning above is based upon speculation. But there are no facts which support the theory of decline of savings as a result of accelerated population growth either. Concerning the phase between the mid-nineteenth and the mid-twentieth centuries, Kuznets has pointed out that his comparison of long-term rates of population growth and growth of per capita incomes, which is reproduced in table 10.2, shows no clear association between them.[25] France had lower than average rates of population growth, but neither higher nor lower per capita growth of income. But if there is no clear correlation of population growth with per capita growth of incomes, there is bound to be correlation with growth of total national income. Mainly because of low rates of population growth, total national product of France increased by little more than two per cent annually in the period considered in the table.[26] The average increase of other European countries was nearly three per cent, that of North America over four per cent.

Because the differences in rates of population growth continued for such a long period, the effects on total output were enormous. If the average rates of population growth shown in table 10.2 had covered a full century in all cases, the national product of France would have multiplied seven times, that of other European countries thirteen times, and that of North America 30–35 times. The scope for military investment and investment in transport, higher education, and so on, would be much larger in the latter cases than in the first. It should be noted that the countries which were the pioneers in the European industrialization—Italy, the Netherlands, and England—had lower rates of per

TABLE 10.2 RATES OF INCREASE OF POPULATION AND NATIONAL PRODUCTS, MID-19TH TO MID-20TH CENTURY

| Country | Average Annual Percentage Increase | | | Period |
| | Population | National Product[a] | | |
		Per Capita	Total	
France	0.3	1.8	2.1	1841/50–1960/62
England	0.6	1.4	2.1	1855/58–1957/59
Sweden	0.7	2.8	3.7	1861/65–1960/62
Italy	0.7	1.3	2.0	1861/65–1960/62
Switzerland	0.8	1.6	2.6	1890/99–1957/59
Norway	0.8	1.9	2.9	1865/74–1960/62
Denmark	1.0	1.9	3.2	1870/74–1960/62
Russia/USSR	1.0	2.0	3.3	1860–1958
Germany/Fed. Germany	1.1	1.6	2.9	1851/55–1960/62
Netherlands	1.4	1.4	3.0	1900/04–1960/62
Average[b] of 10 countries	0.8	1.8	2.8	
Japan	1.2	2.6	4.2	1879/81–1959/61
Canada	1.9	1.8	4.1	1870/74–1960/62
U.S.A.	2.2	1.7	4.3	1839–1960/62
Australia	2.4	0.8	3.4	1861/65–1959/62

[a] In constant prices.   [b] Unweighted.
DATA SOURCE: Simon Kuznets, *Modern Economic Growth, Rate, Structure and Spread* (New Haven, 1966), pp. 64–65.

capita growth after the mid-nineteenth century than other countries covered by the table. Thus, there continued to be a tendency for late-comers to pick up.

EFFECTS OF INDUSTRIALIZATION ON AGRICULTURE

Population increase and industrialization induced changes in patterns not only of food consumption but also of rural employment. Before the industrial revolution, agriculture was a part-time occupation; members of European peasant families must have spent a considerable share of their working hours producing tools, clothing, and household equipment for their own use, gathering or producing materials for these activities, and gathering and producing fuel for the household. Building and repairing dwellings must also have taken much of their time, as Chaianov emphasizes.[27]

It is true that in the urban period in Europe, the towns were inhabited by craftsmen and merchants, but relatively few of the urban-produced goods seem to have found their way to the villages. Except among landlords living in the countryside and the small minority of rich peasants, there was little market for urban goods in rural areas.[28] Increasing population density allowed some rural specialization, and in some areas village smiths, potters, and weavers made household goods and clothing.[29] However, a large share of consumption of nonagricultural products in rural areas seems to have been covered by own-use production. Much of the rural-to-urban transport of produce was a one-way traffic of agricultural produce to the towns. Towns did not pay for all the agricultural products purchased by sale of urban products to the peasants. They obtained much of their food supply and raw materials of agricultural origin via feudal dues, taxes, and rents.

Production by urban craftsmen was labor intensive, and output per work hour was probably not much higher than own-use production among peasants. The main difference was in the much better quality of the urban products.[30] But ordinary peasants could not afford to pay for quality. Transport costs between towns and countryside were high, providing a strong motivation for self-supply in rural areas, where they had little left when feudal dues, taxes, and rents had taken their share. Besides, they could themselves produce nonagricultural products without forgoing other income, because the work could be done in the off-season with the help of family members of both sexes and all age groups, using materials from their own fields or the forests to which they had access.

The industrial revolution changed this pattern. The industrial product from the new factories cost a fraction of the price of similar products

made by urban craftsmen,[31] and improvement of transport further reduced the price at which urban-made products could be acquired in
rural areas. Thus, it became much more attractive for peasants to buy
industrial products and give up own-use production.[32] The increase of
population facilitated this change, because it raised the demand for food
and induced additional labor input in agriculture.

The peasants had two means to provide additional money income to
purchase industrial manufactures. They could intensify agriculture and
use the off-season of one labor-intensive crop to work on another, and
they could intensify the system of animal husbandry. Or some of the
family members could work in the new factories or on the farms with
"put-out" work from the new factories, while the remaining family
members did the agricultural work.

The rise in livestock prices and the decline in prices of manufactured
goods together provided a strong incentive for these changes and made
them acceptable even though labor productivity was very low in the
additional labor-intensive agricultural activities. The system of short
fallow, which was now abandoned in favor of annual cropping, had
operated with heavy labor peaks. The seasons of land preparation and
sowing had been busy seasons for the adult male labor force, and the
seasons of hay mowing and grain harvests had kept all members of the
peasant families, including housewives, children, and old persons, in
the fields from sunrise to sunset. But for the rest of the year, the labor
input in agriculture had been relatively small. The new system of annual
cropping demanded a still higher labor input in the peak seasons, in
order to plow, sow, plant, and harvest the areas which had been left
fallow under the old system or used as permanent pastures. Thus, a
large share of the increase of the rural labor force, due to accelerated
population growth, was employed in agriculture. And a part of the
additional demand for agricultural labor was a demand for labor in
periods which had until now required little agricultural work. All members of the family were required to increase their annual labor input in
agriculture when intensive agriculture replaced the short-fallow system.

Many of the new crops, for instance potatoes and turnips, yielded
much more per hectare than grains or hay, but they required much work
with planting, fertilization, hoeing, and harvesting. After the introduction of the new system, acute labor peaks appeared in seasons which
had been dead under the old system. Therefore, not only adult men,
but also housewives, children, and old people had to increase their labor
input in agriculture. Feeding animals in stables or enclosures, instead
of leaving them to graze fallow and pastures, and investments in drain-

ing and fencing, further changed the seasonal pattern of European agriculture.[33]

The alternative solution to the problem of providing money incomes for purchase of industrial manufactures—having some family members change to industrial work, either in factories or at home—also involved the work of women and children. Much of the own-use production of nonagricultural goods in peasant households had been by women and girls, and often these were the ones who now got employment in manufacturing industries, especially textile factories. Sometimes such industries provided dormitories for girls from peasant families.[34] Because many who got employment in factories or in put-out work had before been employed in own-use production, industrial and other nonagricultural employment could expand rapidly, although the annual output per worker in agriculture seems to have increased slowly, and output per work hour is likely to have declined in the first phase of agricultural change. In Denmark, annual agricultural output per male worker declined 0.1 per cent in the period 1818–36. In the whole period 1818–76, it increased only 0.2 per cent annually.[35] If account is taken of the increase in labor input per worker due to intensification of agriculture, there must have been substantial decline of output per work hour. But living standards increased due to an annual improvement of more than one per cent in sectoral terms of trade and terms of trade with foreign countries.

The increased money earnings in peasant families, due to more work in agriculture, more employment outside agriculture, and better prices for agricultural products in terms of nonagricultural products, helped to create a rapidly growing demand for industrial products. Moreover, both the population increase and the increase of nonagricultural production and incomes raised the demand for agricultural products. Thus, because increase of population and industrialization went together, industrialization induced intensification of agriculture, and intensification of agriculture induced further industrialization, thanks to the widening market for industrial products in rural areas.

The shifts from part-time work to full-time work, and from own-use production to monetized production, went unrecorded in the summary statistics of labor force for that period. Neither census returns, when they exist, nor records of industrial employment are reliable guides to changes in employment. Not only off-season work in peasant families but also the shifts to agricultural wage labor, when rural crafts were replaced by industrial production and intensification of agriculture, are bound to be overlooked.[36]

The choice for a peasant family between intensifying agriculture and having some family members shift into industrial employment was of course influenced by the possibilities for marketing products of intensive agriculture and for getting industrial work. Also the choice of new crops to occupy what previously had been fallow land and pastures differed according to market possibilities.[37] Industrial crops would be preferred in areas where local industries provided a market for them; fodder crops, in areas where neighboring towns or cities provided a market for products of intensive animal husbandry. These differences have contributed to an impression that the creation of some particular industry or the growth of a particular town caused the shift from short fallow to the new intensive systems. But the choice of one or another crop to replace fallow should not blur the picture of the general process of change.

Multiplication of the European population in the eighteenth and nineteenth centuries made it necessary to use the land more intensively and plant crops in land which had been used as fallow and pastures. In some areas, this led to planting industrial crops or fodder crops; in some areas, for instance in Eastern Europe, it led to planting cereals for exports; and in other areas, including some poor areas of subsistence agriculture, it led to introduction of potatoes.

THE DEMOGRAPHIC CHANGES

The influence of population changes on agriculture is much easier to detect than the influence of nutritional and other changes on population trends. Statistics concerning causes of death are a recent invention, but eighteenth-century literary sources point to a major decline in a wide range of contagious diseases as the crucial element at the early stages of declining mortality.[38] However, there are also other opinions. It has been suggested that falling mortality rates were due to improved resistance to disease, which was itself due to better nutrition.[39] It has also been suggested, however, that major killers, such as typhus, smallpox, and dysentery, operated independently of nutritional conditions.[40] The large reduction in mortality among the upper classes that cannot have suffered from insufficiency of food speaks for the latter view. The high mortality among the wealthy in the previous centuries and the later decline have been well established by studies of mortality in royal, noble, and rich bourgeois families.[41] Only in one case, that of smallpox, had medical science and its application reached a stage which might help to explain the eighteenth-century decline of mortality. In England, inoculation against smallpox started in 1721; from 1750, the service was available free of cost to the poor. This availability probably contribuuted to the early decline of mortality in England and some other countries.[42]

Apart from smallpox, the contagious diseases seem to have receded as causes of death long before modern science discovered efficient means to combat them, and also long before effective public health services were introduced. These services date in most countries from the second half of the nineteenth century or even later.[43] It seems that practical insight and experience led to improvements in health measures even before modern science created a deeper understanding of the nature of disease. We have here a parallel to how industrial technologies were able to improve before science reached a stage where it was applicable to industrial problems.

In the case of health technology, there were also many demand-induced improvements. In the sixteenth century, recurrent epidemics in France induced police measures, removal of waste, and quarantine within and between towns, all of which probably helped reduce epidemics. From around 1520, epidemics hit France only once every twenty years, against once every two years before that time.[44] In the seventeenth century, further efforts were made to reduce mortality. In wars, especially the Thirty Years' War, disease apparently took a much heavier toll in army camps and in towns crowded with refugees than direct slaughter. The great loss of human life, and especially of their own mercenaries, caused concern among the rulers.[45] Strategic measures designed to save lives were developed, and military doctors did much to develop preventive medicine and sound hygiene.[46] These efforts probably contributed to the later decline of mortality. In the eighteenth century, quarantine and other preventive methods became more effective owing to improvements in administration. Midwifery also improved,[47] reducing mortality of mothers and infants. European women in the Middle Ages lived a shorter time than men, owing to high mortality in the childbearing years.[48] But in the nineteenth century, women lived longer than men in all parts of Europe.[49]

Many features contributed to the decline of mortality. One was a decline in the incidence of malaria in the eighteenth century, after resurgence in the seventeenth. There are reports of spread of malaria due to neglect of water control in periods of population decline in the seventeenth century,[50] and draining marshes and reclamation of swamps following the increase of population in the eighteenth century may have reduced it again.[51] There was probably more understanding of the importance of cleanliness and avoidance of contamination, and there were better means to improve cleanliness. Soap production seems to have increased considerably in England, and the availability of cheap cotton goods brought more frequent change of clothing within the economic feasibility of ordinary people.[52] Better communication within and between European countries promoted dissemination of knowledge, including knowledge of disease and the ways to avoid it, and may help to explain the decline of mortality in areas which had neither an industrial nor an agricultural revolution at the time.[53]

Although decline of mortality was the major cause of the acceleration of population growth, increase of fertility may also have contributed. Causes of increased fertility may have been reduced mortality for women of childbearing age, and increasing opportunities for nonagricultural work for both adults and children, in cases where high marriage age or other fertility-restricting measures had been operating.[54] Studies of family histories, based on church records, may help to throw light on fertility changes in the eighteenth century. In a village in the Swiss Alps, Netting[55] found fertility increased due to reduced spacing of births. Potatoes had replaced cereals as basic food in that village, and Netting suggests that the availability of mashed potatoes may have reduced the period of breast-feeding, or that better nutrition of the mothers may have reduced the period of sterility after the preceding birth.

After a period of varying length in different parts of Europe, high and perhaps increasing birthrates began to decline. The increase of population decelerated. The result was new radical changes in European agriculture. In the period of rapid population growth and intensification of agriculture, many farms were subdivided among heirs, and new small farms of less than family size were created, as a means to retain a reserve of wage labor for use in larger farms in the peak season. As a result, most European farms covered less than ten hectares,[56] and their owners could make ends meet only by means of intensive cultivation.

Declining birthrates in the twentieth century reduced the rate of increase of demand for food in Europe. Larger farms responded to sluggish demand for food and rising agricultural wages by reducing or eliminating wage labor, and many owners of small farms shifted to nonagricultural employment, wholly or partly. The agricultural labor force declined rapidly after 1950, when mechanization of agriculture became widespread, but production continued to increase, owing to substitution of industrial and scientific inputs for direct labor input. As production overtook demand, there was a gradual reduction of net imports to Europe.[57] Full self-sufficiency was reached in one type of food after another, and Western and Central Europe, formerly the world's largest importer of agricultural products, became a large exporter of food. Large government subsidies supported exports, and high levies restricted food imports. The radical changes in the pattern of European trade in food had important consequences for many non-European countries, and in parts 4 and 5 we shall turn to these problems.

IV Diffusion of Industrial Technologies

11 TRANSPORT TECHNOLOGY AND MASS MIGRATION

We have seen in parts 2 and 3 that before the industrial revolution one densely populated area after another became the technological leader. During the whole of this part of human history, the main advantage of a dense population, i.e., the better possibilities to create infrastructure, seems to have outbalanced the disadvantage of a less favorable ratio between population and natural resources. Europe succeeded Asia as technological leader, but only after it arrived at relatively high population densities.

The worst handicap to techonological development for sparsely populated areas during this period was the low technological levels in the transport sector, especially land transport. Long-distance transport was feasible only by water, and the inhabitants of large, sparsely populated continents were doomed to be illiterate subsistence producers. Their rich natural resources were of little use to them. This situation changed when long-distance transport improved. In the wake of the breakthrough of the new coal-iron technologies came railways, iron steamships, and, later, motor vehicles and airplanes. Each of these innovations curtailed the costs of long-distance transport of persons or merchandise, sometimes of both.

With these new means of transport, as with the old ones, densely populated areas benefited most, because they could better utilize the infrastructure, i.e., rail networks, ocean harbors, roads, and airports. The new means of transport did, however, make it feasible for areas of relatively low population density to export their rich natural resources to areas with a larger market. Therefore, in the centuries after the industrial revolution, some areas with low population densities underwent rapid technological change, as well as population growth resulting from mass settlement of immigrants from more technologically advanced areas. Little more than a century after the industrial revolution, one of these areas, North America, successfully challenged the technological leadership of Europe. In this chapter, we shall focus on the mass immigration into North America and the accompanying rapid industrialization, but we shall begin with a more general analysis of the relationship between population density and the use of rail and road transport.

THE DENSITY OF TRANSPORT NETWORKS

The invention of the railway was promoted by the desire to transport coal from mines to consumers without heavy investment in canal building.[1] The railways became a practical proposition when the new iron technologies sharply reduced iron prices. They quickly developed into an instrument of long-distance transport of passengers and bulky products. Most of the western and Central European networks were built in the period 1830–70, and in 1850 England and Germany already had 25–30 meters of network per square kilometer.[2] The result of the railway building was urbanization on a scale never seen before.[3] Not only towns on rivers and seashores, but also inland towns could now outgrow the limit set by the capacity for production of food and other necessary materials in the neighborhood. Thanks to the railway and the ocean-crossing steamships, large towns in Western and Central Europe could now be supplied from all parts of Europe and also sparsely populated, resource-rich areas across the oceans. The railway is famous for its role in opening up the vast empty spaces of the western hemisphere for economic development. The large investments which went into railway building were feasible, however, only if they served a dense population, or particularly rich natural resources secured a large amount of traffic. Many railway lines in sparsely populated areas were uneconomic, but were built by miscalculation or for strategic reasons.

Since railways are economical only in densely populated areas, the density of railway networks themselves, measured in meters of railway line per square kilometer of territory, is low in sparsely populated countries, even those at relatively high technological levels (see the upper half of table 11.1). The large differences according to technological level reflect the fact that development of a railway network at an early date was a precondition for development of industrialization. Countries with extensive rail networks are at high technological levels today, while nearly all countries with small networks or none are at low or relatively low technological levels. In the densely populated European countries, railway densities are 75–100 meters per square kilometer. In the past, they were even higher in some places; many countries reduced their network after the development of road traffic made many lines uneconomic. The large investment in railways in Europe in the nineteenth century provided the basis for the high technological levels then achieved. The dense railway networks were a necessary condition for the national and international specialization of industrial and agricultural production, on which the European industrial system was—and is—based. Some European railways were built for strategic reasons, but

TABLE 11.1 LENGTH AND QUALITY OF TRANSPORT NETWORKS AROUND 1970

Density Group	Technological Level								
	Low	Medium	High	Low	Medium	High	Low	Medium	High
	Meters Rail per Km²			Meters Rail per 1000 Pop.					
1–3	0.3		3.3	0.3		1.4			
4–5	1.6	7.3	14.4	0.2	0.7	1.3			
6–7	2.8	8.4	30.9	0.1	0.3	1.5			
8–9	5.1	30.3	75.8	0.0	0.4	0.6			
≥10		29.7	90.0		0.1	0.3			
	Meters Roads per Km²			Meters Roads per 1000 Pop.			Hard Surface Roads as % of All Roads		
1–3	21	(5)	103	13	(2)	55	7	(70)	21
4–5	46	79	260	5	8	23	9	15	31
6–7	71	74	713	2	3	24	12	61	58
8–9	149	347	1060	1	3	9	30	66	75
≥10		775	2693		1	8		65	66

DATA SOURCE: International Union of Railways, *International Railway Statistics* (Paris, 1972); United Nations Industrial Development Organization (UNIDO), *Industrial Development Survey* (Vienna, 1974); International Road Federation, *World Road Statistics* (Geneva-Washington, 1973). NOTE: Number of countries included: for railways 71, including 12 without railways; for roads 92.

because they linked densely populated areas, they too induced development of industry and agriculture in the areas they served.

Although the differences in the size of the railway network between densely and sparsely populated countries are large, they are nevertheless smaller than the huge differences in population density. The length of the railway network per inhabitant is larger in sparsely populated countries, as shown on the right of table 11.1. Since the length of the network per inhabitant can be considered a crude measure of per capita costs of providing a country with railways, the implication is that sparsely populated countries had to pay more per inhabitant for a sparse network than densely populated countries for a dense network. In other words, the burden of railway building was relatively small in densely populated Western and Central Europe, which in the nineteenth century already had high levels of commercial production and enough traffic to allow a good capacity utilization of the network. Transport of bulky products became relatively cheap, and urban areas became less restricted by the capacity for food production in their surroundings. Moreover, coal and materials could now be transported cheaply to market-oriented industries located in large urban centers. The result was the trend toward development of large urban centers which characterized the nineteenth century.

For a region in which the potential volume of traffic was too small to warrant the large costs of installing and operating a railway line, invention of the railway brought no change. It was still a handicap to have a sparse population. Those sparsely populated areas which got an early start in industrialization and are at high technological levels today are areas which were able to pay the high per capita cost of extensive railway construction in the nineteenth century. They were areas with exceptionally good potential for exports of food and raw materials, and in which European or local investors accordingly found it profitable to finance railway building. Parts of North America belong to this category, and so do Russia and Sweden, which built railways with heavy reliance upon foreign financing.[4] Also, strategic considerations sometimes induced building of uneconomic railway lines.

The lower part of table 11.1 provides information for road networks in 1970. The importance of roads for sparsely populated countries can be measured by the much higher density of the road network, compared with the railway network. The road network of sparsely populated high-technology countries is denser than the railway network in densely populated high-technology countries. However, for roads as for railways, networks are much more dense in countries with high than in countries with low population density. Within high-technology countries, the range is from one hundred meters of road per square kilometer in countries with group 1–3 population density to nearly three thousand meters in countries with group 10 density, and the quality is better in the densely populated countries. Moreover, for roads as for railways, sparsely populated countries built longer networks per inhabitant, i.e., they had to invest more per capita to get their small networks.

REDISTRIBUTION OF WORLD POPULATION
The development of large urban centers, which became possible in the railway age, created a mass migration within Europe, as large numbers of rural people migrated to the growing industrial centers. Improvements in ocean transport created another mass movement of people and products which further reshaped the map of the world. It was mentioned in chapter 9 that in the nineteenth century, increasing iron production and declining prices of iron, together with the invention of the steam engine and the screw, revolutionized conditions for bulk shipments over the oceans. Iron ships equipped with steam engines and screws permitted an enormous expansion of cross-ocean transport of bulky materials and food, and at much cheaper prices than sailing ships. Therefore, the overseas colonies became much more useful supplements to the European economy. The result was more intensive development

of the existing colonies, and expansion of colonization to new areas. Europe (excluding European Russia) covers only three per cent of the world's land territory, but in the eighteenth century this small area housed some sixteen per cent of the world population. By contrast, North America and Oceania, which cover twenty per cent, seem to have had some four million inhabitants at that time, i.e., one-half of one per cent of the world population (see table 11.2). This tiny population included European immigrants and descendants of European immigrants who had arrived earlier.

When bulk transports became possible in the nineteenth century, Europe had a vital interest in large-scale imports of products of agriculture, pastoralism, and forestry, as well as mining products. But to obtain substantial supplies from near-empty lands, it was necessary to multiply the local labor force by mass immigration. Until 1800 immigration was on a small scale, but in the nineteenth century it accelerated.[5] Thanks to immigration and rapid natural population growth among the immigrants and their descendants, the population of North America and Oceania rose from the above-mentioned 4 million in the mid-eighteenth century to some 180 million two centuries later. Thus the population of North America and Oceania in 1950 was nearly half that of Europe, although it had been less than three per cent of Europe's two

TABLE 11.2 ESTIMATES OF WORLD POPULATION BY REGION, 1750–2000

Year	Europe	Russia[a]	N. America & Oceania	Total Cols. 1–3	Latin America	Asia	Africa	World
Population in Millions								
1750	125	42	4	171	16	498	106	791
1850	208	76	28	312	38	801	111	1262
1950	391	180	179	750	164	1372	219	2505
2000	540	321	330	1191	626	3757	834	6408
Density Group								
1750	6	2	1		1	6	3	4
1850	7	3	1		2	6	3	5
1950	8	4	4		4	7	4	6
2000	8	5	5		6	9	6	7
Percentage of World Population								
1750	16	5	1	22	2	63	13	100
1850	17	6	2	25	3	63	9	100
1950	16	7	7	30	7	55	9	100
2000	8	5	5	18	10	59	13	100

[a] Population and area of USSR today.
DATA SOURCE: United Nations, *Determinants of Population Trends* (New York, 1973), p. 21; United Nations, *The Population Debate, Dimensions and Perspectives* (New York, 1976), vol. 1, p. 36.

centuries earlier. The share of North America and Oceania in world population was seven per cent by 1950.

Mass immigration went from Europe and Africa to North America, Oceania, and Latin America, from European Russia to north and central Asia, and from Europe to North and South Africa. Kuznets suggests that between 1880 and 1910, twenty per cent of the population increase in Europe went overseas, and most remained to rear their children.[6] Because of the effects of the mass migration on both sides of the oceans, Europe's share of total world population did not change much in spite of accelerated rates of population growth. Total population in continents with predominately European population, however—i.e., Europe, America, and Oceania—went up from less than a fourth of world population in 1750 to more than a third in 1950. At the same time, the population of Asia seems to have declined from 63 to 55 per cent, and that of Africa from 13 to 9 per cent. After 1950, this trend was reversed, owing to the acceleration of population growth in low-technology areas.

The radical redistribution of world population in the nineteenth century went together with change in technological leadership, as already mentioned. Extremely rapid technological changes occurred in the areas with the most rapid growth of population. Population density in the United States went up from group 1 level in 1750 to group six level in 1950. During that same period, a territory used mainly for hunting and long-fallow agriculture by a sparse Indian population became the technologically most advanced country, after having deprived Europe of its newly acquired leadership. Other areas with mass immigration had rapid technological change, and they are all at either group 4 or group 5 technological levels today.

FOOD SUPPLY SYSTEMS IN "FRONTIER" COUNTRIES

The extremely rapid technological development in the areas of mass immigration from Europe had many causes. First, these areas had rich natural resources and a low man-land ratio. Second, the mass immigration of European labor meant that they had a flexible supply of labor, and that they benefited from skills and technological knowledge developed in Europe. The New World, especially the large cities in the U.S., provide us with a new example of the explosive technological and scientific advance which occurs when an elite from many different locations comes together under circumstances in which new demands call for new approaches and solutions to challenging problems. Third, the problem of infrastructure investment, which was the main handicap for sparsely populated areas, was less difficult to solve in the areas of mass immigration because they had a skewed distribution of population. A small transport network, although it gave access to only a small share of the natural resources, might be within reach of a large share of the population. Moreover, foreign capital was available for financing of infrastructure investment.

Let us begin with the man-land ratio and the skills. When the first settlers arrived in North America and Oceania, the scattered indigenous populations subsisted by means of extensive systems of food supply, either hunting and gathering or long-fallow agriculture. They lived in areas which had no infrastructure of the types to which the settlers were accustomed. These settlers came from areas with much higher population density, where they had used the land for short-fallow agriculture or—later—for annual cropping. All the settlers seem to have adapted to the lower man-land ratio in their new homelands by shifting to a more extensive system of food supply. Some made a very big leap backward, and adopted the extensive systems used by the indigenous population, which had been abandoned long before in the settlers' areas of origin. Some early settlers became hunters, or combined hunting with long-fallow agriculture in the huge forests at their disposal. But they of course used weapons and axes of European origin when they made the big leap back to hunting and gathering or forest fallow.

When cattle and sheep were brought to the new lands, many settlers became pastoralists, or, in the modernized version, ranchers. Ranching, like hunting, could be applied on the "frontier." The frontier was the area not yet in use for settled farming, and not supplied with the infrastructure necessary for commercial farming and deliveries to far-off customers. The ranchers either applied the ancient system of walking cattle herds, grazing them along the route and slaughtering them after arrival in areas of consumption, or else left most of the carcasses of slaughtered animals to rot in the pastures, selling only the hides or the wool. Some settlers continued to use plows and draft animals but shifted to a more extensive system. They abandoned labor-consuming practices like fertilization and protection against erosion. Instead, they shifted cultivation to new land when yields declined after a period of cultivation without protective methods.[7] In other words, they shifted backward from a European-type short fallow or annual cropping to a modernized long-fallow system, a sort of bush fallow using European-type equipment. The settlers have been blamed for the devastating methods they used, which exhausted and eroded the land, but their output per man hour was higher than in Europe where some labor went into soil protection.

By combining extensive systems of food supply with high-level technology (for the standards of that time), the settlers obtained higher output per man hour than any other food producers, in Europe or elsewhere. We can compare their situation with that of other food producers at that time by means of a table drawn up in the same way as table 5.3, which compared the situation of food producers in different parts of the ancient world. This is done in table 11.3. Like table 5.3, table 11.3 is based upon the assumption that output per man hour is declining within each vertical column, and increasing across the columns from left to right. This means that the North American Indians had far better output per man hour than the Indians in Mesoamerica, who used intensive agricultural systems with very primitive tools (chapter 5). But the North American Indians had lower output than the settlers who lived on the frontier and used the same extensive systems as the Indians, but better tools. The frontier settlers probably also had higher output per man hour in food production than those in the settlements to the east, who used more intensive systems with inputs of similar quality. However, part or all of this advantage was lost because they had to travel by foot or horseback over long distances to exchange their products for high-quality weapons and other equipment. All the settlers were clearly advantaged compared with the peasants in Europe because they combined more extensive systems with similar quality tools.

Table 11.3 not only illustrates that settlers had an advantage in moving farther and farther west in step with the continued westward movement of the frontier. It also suggests the trap in which the American Indians were caught when the frontier closed. They had been lured into moving westward by the relatively high output per man hour they could obtain farther west even without European-type equipment. But they lost this advantage when the frontier closed and they were confined to reservations on which they had too little land per head to subsist by extensive

TABLE 11.3 AMERICAN AND EUROPEAN FOOD SUPPLY SYSTEMS IN THE EARLY COLONIAL PERIOD

| Density Group | Quality of Inputs | | | |
| | Low | | High | |
	Area	System	Area	System
1–3	N. American Indians	HG + P + FF	Settlers on frontier	HG + P + FF
4–5			Settlers east of frontier	BF
6–7			Peasants in Europe	SF
8–9	Mesoamerican Indians	AC + MC		

systems of food supply. They were without the skills necessary for more intensive systems, because they had isolated themselves, or been isolated by the settlers, while all others advanced in skills. Early settlers also were faced with a dilemma. Because of large land resources and European skills and equipment, they could easily produce large surpluses of agricultural products. But by living scattered, they could not benefit from the types of infrastructure to which they were accustomed in Europe and only at very high costs could they exchange agricultural products for other items. They were faced with a new version of the old dilemma of having to choose between scattering widely with high output per man hour in food production, and concentrating population to benefit from infrastructure investment. Many early settlers renounced the standards of infrastructure to which they were accustomed in Europe, and settled in small, nearly self-sufficient communities.[8] Others made a compromise, and settled close to the frontier, where they could live more scattered than in Europe and have at least a rudimentary infrastructure.

The Movement of the Frontier

The first settlers arrived at a near-empty territory with a healthy climate and rich natural resources. They built one or a few small harbor towns, which they supplied with some infrastructure. Then they slowly penetrated the neighboring areas in step with the increase of population in the colony.[9] They first moved along the coast and adjacent rivers and later penetrated the interior. By this slow penetration, they could preserve an advantageous man-land ratio in the part they were occupying; that area could then be economically supplied with some infrastructure. The huge areas west of the frontier contributed little to the economy, but were no burden either. The settlers took no interest in the scattered indigenous and immigrant population in those areas until they had themselves become so numerous that they needed to settle them in order to continue extensive agriculture. The result was the skewed distribution of population within the areas of mass immigration, as mentioned above—group 4–5 densities or even higher in settled areas while most of the territory continued in group 1. With continuing immigration, the areas with higher density grew larger, the frontier moved, and new nuclei of settlement appeared in other parts of the territory. The indigenous population, if not killed off, continued with subsistence production in a more and more reduced area.[10] The distribution of population continued to be skewed, with the areas of highest densities becoming urbanized and so well supplied with infrastructure that they could become large-scale suppliers of raw materials and food to Europe.

These special features of skewed distribution of population and mass immigration facilitated railway building, because even a small network could be within reach of a large share of the population. Railways were built in areas with much higher than average population density and rich natural resources, or to serve future immigrants, who were brought in and settled in the areas served by the new railway. The cost of railway construction per kilometer of line was low in the large empty plains of the western hemisphere; railway building was further facilitated by large grants of land to the companies and, in many cases, by supply of capital, know-how, and equipment from Europe. Settlers were brought from Europe by the railway companies and sold land along the rail lines, to promote production and ensure utilization of the capacity of the line. Expectations of the companies were somtimes overoptimistic, however, and many railways never brought their owners anything but losses.

The improvements in ocean shipping, which made big grain exports to Europe profitable, provided incentive to push the frontier further inland by means of railway building. Without railways linked up with export harbors, the large exports of cereals would not have been possible. In spite of its huge areas suited for wheat production, Argentina was a wheat importer; districts used later for wheat growing were ranch land until railways linked them to the harbors on the coast.[11] Around 1880, the technical conditions for grain exports to Europe were fulfilled, as mentioned earlier. At that time, agriculture in the United States was more extensive than that of Europe, with higher output per worker. Table 11.4 indicates that in 1880, output per hectare of agricultural land measured in wheat equivalent was half as large in the U.S. as in Europe. An American male worker used 2–4 times more land than a European male worker, and his output was much larger. The only exception was England, which used a large share of the territory as pasture for sheep and cattle. The higher output per worker in the U.S. compensated for the high costs of transport from producer in America to consumer in Europe; American grain was so competitive in Europe that its arrival precipitated a serious depression in European agriculture.

During the following ninety years, the gap in intensity and output per worker between the U.S. and Europe widened further. In the U.S., agriculture was mechanized, small uneconomic farms in the East were abandoned, and large farms in the West became larger and used less hired labor. Agricultural area per male worker increased from 25 to 160 hectares, and output per male worker increased from 13 to 157 wheat units. By contrast, in Europe small farms intensified, as mentioned in chapter 10, and the decline in the number of agricultural workers was smaller than in the U.S. Thus, in 1970 the area per male worker in

TABLE 11.4 AGRICULTURAL AREA, OUTPUT IN WHEAT UNITS, AND MALE LABOR FORCE, 1880–1970

	USA	England	Denmark	France	Germany	Japan
1880						
Hectares per male worker	25	15	9	7	6	1
Output per hectare	0.5	1	1	1	1	3
Output per worker	13	16	11	7	8	2
1970						
Hectares per male worker	161	34	18	16	12	2
Output per hectare	1	3	5	4	5	10
Output per worker	157	88	94	60	65	16
Average annual percentage increase						
1880–1970						
Hectares per male worker	2.1	0.9	0.8	0.9	0.7	1.0
Output per hectare	0.7	1.0	1.7	1.4	1.6	1.4
Output per worker	2.8	1.9	2.5	2.4	2.4	2.4

DATA SOURCE: Hans P. Binswanger and Vernon W. Ruttan, *Induced Innovation, Technology, Institutions and Development* (Baltimore, 1978), pp. 48–49.

Europe was 10–20 per cent that in the U.S., and output per male worker was one-third to one-half that of the U.S. This widening gap helps to explain the increasing protectionism and subsidization of agriculture in Europe.

As we saw, the slow growth of demand for food in the twentieth century, as well as the protectionism, reduced the demand for agricultural imports in Europe, limiting export possibilities from the U.S. and other grain-producing countries of mass immigration. Because the rate of increase of home demand for food in the U.S. also slowed down, owing to lower birth rates, less immigration, and lower income elasticity, food production ran far ahead of amounts required. Government aid, in the form of price support and area restrictions, induced more intensive cultivation, with the result that output of food continued to increase. The U.S. has had to dispose of much larger agricultural surpluses than Europe, by means of subsidized exports and grants. We shall come back to this problem of surplus disposal in later chapters.

Industrialization in the United States
The low man-land ratio in the areas of mass immigration was an advantage not only for agriculture, but also for forestry. In a period when Western and Central Europe suffered from shortage of timber, fuel wood, and charcoal for iron production, North America benefited from an abundance of forest. As late as the mid-nineteenth century, the U.S. could still derive ninety per cent of its fuel from the forests.[12] Timber

was the first bulky product to compete successfully for the limited capacity on ocean-crossing sailing ships. Later, in the age of the steamship, the shortage of forest in Europe and its abundance in North America provided the most important inducement for development of Canada.

Before the huge increase of population in the nineteenth century, the population of the U.S. was largely rural and self-sufficient. The small demand for industrial manufactures and equipment was met by imports, largely from England, because the American market was too small for the establishment of manufacturing industries.[13] However, iron products were heavy, and the cost of transport from Europe was therefore high. Cost, together with the abundant supply of wood for charcoal, induced early establishment of an iron industry in the forested areas in the Northeast, which had rich iron ore. This early iron industry became an important element in the early industrialization of the United States. The American iron industry benefited from a natural protection of high transport costs from Europe and lower fuel costs than those of the European iron industry.

The U.S. had good-quality coal, and it was used for iron production before the railway age because coal deposits were located close to the system of interconnected rivers and lakes in the Northeast. Nevertheless, the abundance of charcoal delayed the change from charcoal to coal for iron production. Even after the Northeast changed to coal, other regions continued to use charcoal, until railway building lowered the transport costs for Northeastern coal-made iron so much that charcoal-based industries in other parts of the U.S. had to close.[14]

The rapid expansion of iron and iron-processing industries in the age of railway building made the Northeast the core area of industrialization. The location of the coal deposits and the most important iron industries in the Northeast contributed to concentration of both population and industries in that region. The skewed distribution of population and the large immigration together created sufficiently high population density to make market-oriented industries feasible at a time when the U.S. as a whole was still sparsely populated. Although movement from East to West in large numbers continued during the nineteenth century, there continued to be a strong concentration of population in the Northeast and the adjacent region of the Great Lakes. Because this region, with its deposits of coal and iron, so quickly got a large and relatively dense population, full-scale industrialization, including heavy industry and market-oriented consumer industries, could develop early in the United States. In 1950, forty-three per cent of the U.S. population lived in an area roughly bounded by Boston, Washington, and Chicago. This area accounts for less than eight per cent of the U.S. territory but housed sixty-eight per cent of the U.S. manufacturing industry.[15] Its population density, at group 8 level, was as high as the average for Europe, while the rest of the U.S. had group 5 density on average.

Industrialization in the United States was home-market-based rather than export-based. Both the consumer goods and the producer goods industries were designed to supply the rapidly expanding home market. It was the enormous growth of population, labor force, and market for industrial products which made the miracle of American nineteenth-century industrialization possible.[16] Only much later did the U.S. develop into a major exporter of manufactures. Another important reason for the rapid technological development in the U.S. was the skilled labor force. Immigrants came from that part of the world which was most advanced in technology at that time. They possessed the skills needed to accomplish a technical revolution. Even "unskilled" immigrants were familiar with life in a technologically advanced society, and those who had been forced from their villages by poverty were accustomed to hard labor. Many of the immigrants, however, were of another type. They were skilled farmers, craftsmen, and merchants, attracted by the opportunities of the New World, or highly trained professionals fleeing from racial and religious persecution. Because most immigrants were attracted by superior opportunities of the New World, America benefited from a flexible labor supply. When the demand for labor increased, more migrants were attracted,[17] and it was never necessary to starve agriculture of labor, or to wait for natural population increase.

Studies of the American and the European labor markets have shown that emigration from Europe was larger in good than in bad years, because good and bad years largely coincided on both sides of the Atlantic.[18] The response in the European labor markets to the pull of American demand was of course less in countries with strong internal demand for labor. Therefore, in the course of time, the share of migrants from the less industrialized countries of Southern and Eastern Europe increased. The flow of immigration to the U.S. never ceased for four centuries. During the first, rural period, the territory received mainly peasants endowed with the skills of European agriculture. Later, when urban centers grew up, they attracted immigrants with industrial or other urban skills. In contrast to the pattern of urbanization in countries without immigration, the early towns in America did not grow by attracting the populace of neighboring rural areas, ill adapted to the demands of an urban economy. A large share of the immigrants to expanding towns in the United States were people accustomed to urban life in Europe and skilled in urban occupations.

Even after the industrial revolution in the U.S., immigrants continued to account for a large share of the increase of population. Kuznets has shown that the net addition to the population due to intercontinental migration accounted for five per cent of the increase in the first two decades of the nineteenth century, but increased to thirty per cent in the last two decades of the century. If the age and sex distribution of the migrants are taken into account, they may have been a quarter of the addition to the labor force in the period after 1820, and one-half of the addition in the last two decades of the century.[19] Around that time, one-third of the labor force in the United States was foreign born.[20] Under these circumstances, transfer of technology from Europe to the United States was smooth and immediate. The continued flow of migrants automatically brought knowledge of the latest technological advance in Europe to the U.S. A large share of the American labor force entered the labor market equipped with new skills acquired in Europe and therefore able to apply European technology.

As the century advanced, the U.S. changed from a receiver of technological innovations from Europe to a center of development of new technology. America presents us with a new example of the revolutionary effects of the gathering of people under new circumstances and confronting new problems, in addition to the earlier examples from ancient societies and from Europe. To millions of immigrants, the change of scenery and the newness of the problems they faced presented a challenge; they reacted by developing initiative and a spirit of creativity which were unfettered by the guild restrictions and bureaucracies in their former homelands. Moreover, the steadily increasing demand for labor, and the floor to wages provided by the opportunities in agriculture, gave inducement to experiments with labor-saving equipment and methods, in both industry and agriculture.[21] The period after 1850 was one of massive westward shift of the agricultural frontier. In this period, railway construction, settlement, town building, and industrialization combined to push up the demand for labor, and American firms were experimenting with the use of machinery to replace labor.

Unlike in the Old World, in America workers had a positive attitude to mechanical improvements to relieve the drudgery of manual unskilled labor.[22] The U.S. benefited from a labor force which combined European skills with a positive attitude to labor-saving equipment. In the nineteenth century, the United States moved ahead of Europe in mechanization of both industry and agriculture. Because of the urgency of the transport problem in the vast continent, it also became the pioneer in mechanized road transport on a mass scale. The pioneering effort of the U.S. in developing the truck into a means of mass transport is an example of a demand-induced innovation in response to demographic conditions. In spite of the large investment in railways, most of the territory in the U.S. could not be reached economically from a line. The need for feeder transport to the railways more efficient than horse-drawn carts was much more acute than in Europe, with its dense railway networks. Together with the easy acess to mineral oil, this explains why the U.S. pioneered the automobile industry, which played the crucial role in raising American technological levels higher than Europe's.

Between 1840 and 1960, the national product increased 4.0–4.5 per cent annually, in contrast to less than three per cent for most Western and Central European countries (see table 10.2). There do not seem to have been significant differences in rates of growth of per capita national product in these two areas. It was the much more rapid growth of population in the U.S. which accounts for the spectacular growth of its economy. This growth of total income provided much more scope for improvement of military and civil infrastructure, including transport and communication, higher education, and research, as already mentioned.

Other areas of mass settlement by Europeans had advantages similar to those of the U.S., as concerns skilled labor and capital imports from Europe. But because their natural resources were less rich and diversified, and because immigration started later, the absolute size of immigration remained much smaller, and the development of a market sufficiently large for home-market-based industrialization was not so rapid. Transport costs were also a more serious problem, because the populations were relatively small and population densities low.[23] Therefore, these other areas industrialized later than the U.S., and some are still only semiindustrialized.

12 SPARSE POPULATION AS OBSTACLE TO INDUSTRIALIZATION

We have seen that after the industrial revolution, it became possible for a sparsely populated area by very rapid technological development to become the leading industrial nation in little more than a century. We have also seen that this technological development was based upon mass immigration from the most technologically advanced areas, and upon an automatic transfer of skills. The U.S. and the other areas of European mass immigration had a temperate climate, which was attractive for Europeans. In sparsely populated areas with hot climates, Europeans were uninclined to settle, especially if the climate was humid too. Most of Africa, excluding North and South Africa, and parts of Latin America and Southeast Asia belong to this category. These areas were potentially as important to the European economy as were the temperate areas. They were potential exporters of land-using products, for instance timber and minerals. Moreover, they were potential exporters of "climatic goods," especially tropical beverages, tobacco, cotton, rubber, and sugar cane, which could not be produced in Europe or in the overseas areas with temperate climates. With later development of refrigerated transport, fruits and vegetables were added to this list. There were two possible sources of supply of such products to Europe: densely populated areas, mainly in south Asia, or the sparsely populated areas mentioned above. It is the second of these alternatives which will be discussed in this chapter, together with the technological and demographic effects of export production in these areas.

Since mass immigration from Europe could not be counted on here, export production had to be by a small number of European managers and administrators using large numbers of non-European workers and mid-level personnel. But the local population was too small and scattered to supply manual labor for large-scale exports. Labor had to be brought in from other districts or continents. Especially important were migrations of Asians to Africa and of Africans to Latin America and southern North America.

USE OF STICK AND CARROT FOR RECRUITMENT OF LABOR

The demographic effects of export production for European markets varied widely. Some areas, for instance, Malaysia and the Caribbean Islands, got mass immigration of non-Europeans: Indians and Chinese in Malaysia, and African slaves in the Caribbean. The population therefore increased rapidly, as in the temperate areas, while exports of slaves led to decline of population in parts of West Africa. In other areas, mainly Africa, where the additional production was obtained by concentration of a larger part of the existing population in areas of colonial development, population trends could hardly avoid being affected, either because mortality went up or down or because sex-selective long-distance migration reduced fertility.

Thus, while the areas of mass immigration of Europeans became "frontier economies" with concentrated settlement of Europeans and scattering of the indigenous population, hot, humid areas with little immigration became "enclave economies." The local population and the immigrants concentrated in small enclaves, while the areas in between became nearly empty. Population trends and patterns of settlement in the hot areas were thus very different from those in areas of mass European settlement. There were important implications for infrastructure investment and for later industrialization; the large empty spaces between the enclaves and the much less favorable demographic trends were obstacles to transformation of the scattered enclaves into larger economies.

Most of the indigenous population in the sparsely populated, hot colonies were pastoralists and long-fallow producers, but many items of consumption, including export crops, were gathered rather than produced, especially in the early period after European arrival.[1] For instance, palm oil and rubber were gathered, and tropical wood is still gathered without replanting in most areas. Minerals were often obtained by small-scale production in open air deposits, and transported by human carrier to rivers and seashores. The system operated with very little infrastructure investment.

To obtain labor, the Europeans often used methods similar to those of the ancient empires. Labor services were imposed on the local food gatherers, pastoralists, and long-fallow cultivators, or they were enslaved by raids or collusion with indigenous chiefs. Long-term contracts were signed by chiefs or by the laborer himself. Indian contract labor for railway building in East Africa and Chinese contract labor for mines in Malaysia are well-known examples. In West Africa, slave raids to recruit labor for American plantations induced the local population to scatter even more and to settle in inaccessible regions. Many areas of West Africa became depopulated, partly because the population was carried away as slaves, and partly because those who escaped went elsewhere. According to one estimate, an area with an estimated population of twenty million may over a long time have exported 0.5 per cent of the population annually.[2] This was no doubt considerably more than the natural growth of population.

However, the Europeans used not only the stick, but also the carrot in their efforts to provide labor for export production. The literature from the colonial period reflects the disagreements between protagonists for the two methods. Boeke[3] was a well-known defender of compulsion as the most effective system, while Furnival[4] believed in the profit motive in dealing with the indigenous population. The carrot was purchase of crops and other products for export at favorable prices compared with those of European manufactured goods which could be acquired in exchange for them. The European manufactured goods partly satisfied new demands and partly replaced products made for own use. Before the arrival of the Europeans, there was very little specialization of labor in the sparsely populated areas. Parts of West Africa seem to be an exception, with considerable trade in agricultural and nonagricultural products before the arrival of European manufactured goods.[5] Population densities may have been relatively high, before the exports of slaves to America became of large dimensions. But for the most part, the settlements were too small and scattered to provide markets for specialized craftsmen, and each family produced not only its own food, but also other items needed or desired. By an additional input of labor, either in production of export crops or as wage laborers, the indigenous population could now abandon part of their nonfood production and replace it with manufactured goods from Europe.

These goods had the same effects on the subsistence producers in the sparsely populated hot colonies as on European peasants during and after the industrial revolution in Europe. Both groups increased their labor input in agriculture to purchase manufactured goods, instead of producing items which fulfilled similar wants. Total agricultural output as well as output per worker increased, and in both cases the increase was primarily due to an increase of labor input per family, and not to any significant increase in output per man hour in agriculture.

But there was an important difference between the increase in labor input during the industrial revolution in Europe and that which accompanied the introduction of export crops in the sparsely populated hot colonies. In Europe, the change was promoted by population increase and included a change of food supply system from short fallow to annual cropping. More food was produced with different methods, and the increasing total food surplus went to feed the increasing urban population which produced the manufactured goods and worked in related activities. In the colonies, there was no need to change the food supply system. Food continued to be produced for subsistence by means of long-fallow methods. At most, there was a shift from forest fallow or pastoralism to bush fallow in areas in which opportunities for cash crop production led to substantial immigration.

In areas of long-fallow agriculture, women usually perform a substantial part of the agricultural work, while men hunt or take part in wars and leisure activities. The European colonialists, taking advantage of this sexual division of work and leisure, induced or forced the underemployed men to become wage laborers on plantations or small-scale producers of export crops. The new cash crops became "men's crops," although women often helped to produce them. Nothing was done to encourage surplus production of food crops. These remained "women's crops," produced for family consumption as a part of women's traditional obligations.[6] Because the food crops were produced for family consumption and were part of women's traditional obligations, neither colonial administrators nor the leading male villagers took any interest in improving the crops or the methods of production. The sex division of labor in most areas of long-fallow agriculture helps to explain the continuing low technological levels in food production in the sparsely populated hot areas, and the huge widening gap in labor productivity between sparsely populated areas with and without mass immigration of Europeans.

The production of cash crops, in addition to the subsistence production of food, could be accomplished with a relatively light work burden for the family as a whole, because the favorable man-land ratio made long-fallow agriculture possible. Table 12.1, which includes the results of eighteen studies of labor input in different parts of Africa, reveals a relatively low labor input. Average weekly work hours in agriculture was fourteen hours for men and boys and fifteen hours for women and

TABLE 12.1 LABOR INPUT IN AFRICAN AGRICULTURE

Hours Worked per Week in agriculture	Number of Case Studies	
	Men and Boys	Women and Girls
1–5	1	2
5–9	2	1
10–14	5	5
15–19	7	4
20–24	2	5
⩾25	0	1
Total no. of case studies	17	18
Average weekly hours	14	15

DATA SOURCE: Ester Boserup, *Woman's Role in Economic Development* (New York, 1970), p. 21.
NOTE: Five of the studies exclude both boys and girls.

girls. All the studies relate to areas in which both subsistence food crops and export crops are produced. Some of the export crops, like cotton, were labor-intensive. The burden of agricultural work carried by all these families is lighter than that of peasant families in more densely populated areas with more intensive agricultural systems. The work burden carried by women, however, is large, since women also had to perform domestic duties. Since this double work burden is an obligation rooted in the traditional marriage system, which gives men command over female labor, it could perhaps be said that a large share of the added work input in agriculture was obtained by means of the stick, and not the carrot.

TRANSPORT INVESTMENT AND LABOR MIGRATION
Before the age of railways and trucks, human porterage was the only transport in most of Africa, and it is still used in some areas.[7] The organization of human porterage in Africa was primitive compared with that of pre-Columbian Mesoamerica. Cash cropping was limited by the price of porterage per kilometer, which was 3–6 times that of rail transport.[8] But railway building usually was uneconomic in sparsely populated areas (see chapter 11). The exceptions were areas of rich mineral deposits; two-thirds of the African railways built in the colonial period connected mines to a coastal harbor. The others, including the strategic line in East Africa, reportedly suffered losses.[9] But mineral resources so rich that a railway is built to make exploitation possible are few and far between. So the sparsely populated hot colonies got very few railways. Among the twenty African countries included in table 11.1 (all those for which information is available), only the Union of South Africa with mass immigration of Europeans had more than six meters of railways per square kilometer in 1970, and six countries had no railways at all.

Construction of railways led to an acceleration of labor migration, partly because labor had to be recruited over a wide area for the construction of the railway, and for employment in the mining center it should serve, and partly because there was an interest in providing it with traffic once built by encouraging cash cropping in adjacent areas.[10] Attempts were made (not always successfully) to get the local population to settle near the railway[11] and work in plantations managed by Europeans or produce cash crops in small holdings. In some areas, where railways linked up with water transport, as in the Lake Victoria region of East Africa[12] and the Upper Niger valley in West Africa,[13] major areas of cash cropping developed, with respectively cotton and groundnuts the major export crops. But this development was made possible only by mass migration from other districts.[14] Therefore, in most of the African continent, cultivatable land, forests, and mineral deposits were not utilized. The sparse population outside the small enclaves of colonial development had the choice of remaining subsistence producers or migrating, assuming that they were not removed by force or prevented from migration by police measures, as often happened.

Because of the lack of infrastructure and the small size of the labor force when measured against the natural resources of the huge African continent, there was no possibility for development of more than a limited number of relatively small enclaves. Densely populated colonies with a less favorable natural resource base had at least the advantage, compared with Africa, that their natural resources were more likely to be within reach of an existing transport network, and therefore more economical to exploit.

Most studies of colonial development focus upon the changes which took place within the enclaves, but pay little attention to the areas which took part in the development only as exporters of labor. It is crucially important for understanding the technological development in the sparsely populated hot areas to take account of the effects of labor migrations in the areas of out-migration. The exodus of labor to the enclaves produced a widening gap in population density and techno-logical levels similar to that in ancient times between the city-states and the surrounding tribal areas. While the enclaves got relatively rapid population increase, and more rapid increase of able-bodied young workers than of total population, the labor-exporting areas got decline of the able-bodied work force and little if any overall population increase. Thus, in the latter areas, the obstacles to development became reinforced by the migrations.

In some areas of East Africa, one-half the adult men left the villages;[15] in other areas, 60–75 per cent emigrated.[16] The role of the migrants in the local subsistence system was taken over by the women, who had to do still more than their traditional part of the work with food pro-duction and other economic activities, in addition to the domestic work. However, even with additional work by women, a deterioration of the subsistence economy was hard to avoid.[17] The women, children, and old men left in the villages survived because the extensive subsistence systems they used required a relatively small labor input per unit of output. Nevertheless, emigration of half, or more than half, the able-bodied male labor force put a large work burden on women, who also had to take care of the young and the aged. This exploitation of female labor in the labor-exporting areas meant that young adult males could be recruited for wages which covered little more than minimum sub-sistence costs for a single person. Moreover, single men could be housed in dormitories; thus social infrastructure costs to the mining and plantation companies were at a minimum. Therefore, wage costs could be competitive with those in densely populated colonies, although there was no shortage of land to exert a downward pressure on wages.[18]

With the appearance of the truck came improved possibilities for cash cropping in areas of relatively low population density. In Africa, the cost of transport from the producer to the railway was reduced to twice the rail cost per kilometer, and roads were cheaper to build than railways.[19] The high cost of porterage, compared with costs for transport by truck, provided incentive to build feeder roads to the railways in areas with cash cropping served by railway transport, i.e., within the existing enclaves of colonial development. There was little incentive to construct roads in areas without railways and cash cropping, however. Thus the areas of labor emigration were bypassed by road building, because their population was too small and sparse to make it worthwile to transform them into areas of cash cropping. The skewing of the transport system in favor of the enclaves continued to be an important feature in the sparsely populated hot colonies. The technological gap continued to widen, because the enclaves now also benefited from road motor transport.

In a sparsely populated area in which all families are producing the same products for family use, there is no market for local production of food or other items: commercial production must be based upon transport to distant markets. If the population is isolated from potential markets by large empty spaces without infrastructure for modern transport, the ratio at the village level between prices paid to the producers for a surplus and prices of products they can acquire will be unfavorable to them. They will prefer to keep a low labor input in agriculture and have a high degree of self-sufficiency of both agricultural and nonagricultural products.[20] In the areas of labor emigration, distances to potential markets are much longer and transport infrastructure much poorer than in Europe at the time of the industrial revolution, when favorable terms of trade between manufactured goods and local agricultural surpluses induced European peasants to become commercial producers on a large scale.[21] Owing to the unfavorable local terms of trade between industrial manufactured goods and local food surpluses in the labor exporting regions of the sparsely populated hot areas, the village populations and pastoralists still prefer to let their young men acquire money as migrant workers rather than become commercial producers. As a result, labor-exporting areas are caught in a vicious circle, or even a downward spiral. Because of the low population density and the high degree of subsistence protudion, it is uneconomic to supply these areas with a road network. On the other hand, without a road network, there are no possibilities for any major change from subsistence production and exodus of labor. The situation does not improve with improvement in the enclaves; it deteriorates, because the enclaves become even more attractive for youth in the labor-exporting areas.

The statistics for the density of road networks in table 11.1 reveals that a very large share of the territory in sparsely populated low-technology countries continues to be out of reach of facilities for modern transport. Road networks are only 20–50 meters per square kilometer, and only 7–9 per cent of these are hard surface roads. By comparison, road networks in most of Europe are over a thousand meters per square kilometer, and between two-thirds and three-fourths are hard surface roads. There are still large areas, for instance in the interior of Africa, which can sell nothing but cola nuts and live cattle. Cola nuts have low weight and volume relative to their value, and the cattle can be walked to the distant markets. They usually arrive in such poor condition, however, that the profit from raising and transporting them is extremely meager. Proponents of the theory of inevitable "labor surpluses" in rural areas of preindustrial societies consider labor migration the only means to reduce or avoid this underutilization of labor. It is true that without the exodus of young male workers from the sparsely populated areas with poor transport facilities and little or no cash cropping, the average labor input would be low. But this underutilization of labor disappears each time improvement of transport facilities makes cash cropping economical in a new area.

CHARACTERISTIC FEATURES OF COLONIAL URBANIZATION

The need to handle the transport and exports of mineral, forest, and agricultural products led to the emergence of some harbor towns and other urban centers in the enclaves. Here ancillary services for export activities and colonial administration were handled, as well as the import, transport, and distribution of European manufactured goods on which mining and plantation workers and cash croppers spent their money incomes. The indigenous population in the sparsely populated colonies were nearly all illiterate long-fallow cultivators and pastoralists, and they possessed none of the skills in demand in the colonial towns. Immigrants from Europe could be attracted to the hot regions only by incomes which were even higher than those offered persons with similar skills in areas with temperate climates and high income levels. So only a small number of European managers, businessmen, and administrators settled in these colonial towns; all other service occupations were filled by immigrants from non-European countries with preindustrial urbanization—mainly Asians from densely populated urbanized areas with low wage levels for urban skills. Southeast Asian colonial towns became populated with Chinese and Indians, East African towns with Indians, and West African towns with Lebanese.

By contrast to the indigenous population, these people had ancient traditions of bazaar trade and crafts. They were accustomed to urban life and money transactions. Some were recruited by the Europeans. Most, however, came on their own, attracted by the possibilities for earning money incomes, which were high by their standards although much too low to attract European immigrants. These immigrants filled all the jobs as clerks, supervisors of indigenous, unskilled labor, small tradesmen, and small craftsmenf—jobs which were indispensable for the functioning of urban economies and for handling transactions with mining and cash-cropping areas. Except for surplus food grown and sold by local market women in areas close to the town, virtually all trade in rural and urban areas was handled by these immigrant communities. Only a few manual services, if any, were performed by members of the indigenous population.[22] The existence of this immigrant middle class made it unnecessary for the managers of the urban economies to encourage literacy or other urban skills in the indigenous population. The little education for a small indigenous elite was provided voluntarily by missionaries.

When urbanization appears in a technologically backward region, an inflow to the new towns of foreigners from already urbanized regions is characteristic. These foreigners take over the skilled occupations which the indigenous population lack abilities to fill. When urbanization appeared in Europe north of the Alps, there was an inflow of Italians, Jews, and other peoples from the Near East. Later, when urbanization appeared in northern Europe, there was an inflow of German merchants; in Eastern Europe and Russia, Jews became an important element of the urban population. However, in the sparsely populated hot colonies, the technological and educational gap between the indigenous population and the immigrants was even wider, and the foreigners were never so dominant in European towns as they became in the colonial towns. They monopolized access to all jobs requiring any but the most primitive skills, thus barring the indigenous population from contact with modern technology.

Colonial towns differed sharply from other preindustrial towns, because they did not fulfill the usual function of producing nonagricultural products in exchange for food from the surrounding rural areas. In preindustrial Europe and other densely populated areas, agricultural production in the rural areas developed in step with nonagricultural production in the towns; the rural areas provided a market for the produce of the towns, and the towns provided a market for the products of the rural areas. However, in the sparsely populated hot colonies, this link between urban and rural development was broken. The surplus production from the rural areas was exported, and towns and rural areas were supplied by imports. The colonial towns were only intermediaries in this foreign trade, providing administrative services. The imports of European manufactured goods and of products from the lands of origin of the urban middle class acted as a formidable obstacle to development of urban crafts and industries. The failure to develop crafts and traditional industries later acted as a deterrent for industrialization, because no industrial skills were developed.

For a number of reasons, the colonial towns became dependent upon food imports. One reason was the foreign tastes of the inhabitants. Another was the lack of transport facilities in rural areas. Food was cheaper from other continents than from rural areas in the same colony. Even a town as far from the coast as Nairobi, on the East African railway, imported food by water and rail from other continents, because the surrounding road network was so poor.[23] Finally, there was the system of subsistence production by women. The women's obligation was to supply their families with food, and they rarely had energy left to produce more than that. Women who lived within walking distance of urban markets had very little to sell.[24]

The failure to produce food surpluses to supply the towns meant that when a rural area ceased to be a subsistence economy only, it became heavily dependent upon foreign trade. The foreign trade component of total national income is very large in this type of economy, on both the export and the import side, while the internal monetized sector is very small. The gap widens very rapidly as more areas of subsistence production change over to production for exports and old enclaves of mining and cash cropping attract an increasing share of the total population. There would seem to be large scope for import-replacement industrialization in such economies, but in reality the obstacles to industrialization are more serious than in other economies. The lack of industrial skills has already been mentioned. Such skills can be learned, however, while the obstacle provided by lack of sufficient markets for home-based industrialization is much more difficult, if not impossible, to overcome.

Here it is useful to look back at table 6.1. We see that a manufacturing industry located in the center of a 60-kilometer-radius area with a population density at group 3 level will have a population of only 30–40 thousand to draw on. But if population density is at group 9 level, two million persons will live in the area. Moreover, if population is two million, the transport network is likely to be so good that sales will be profitable over a radius of much more than 60 kilometers. Therefore, manufacturing industries may be profitable even in cases where the majority of the population are too poor to be customers, if the population density in the area is high enough.

In areas in which the local market for sale of manufactures is small, industries based on rich mineral deposits or other raw-material-oriented industries may nevertheless be set up. But if the area is sparsely populated, these industries are usually limited to crude processing and fail to attract market-oriented processing industries around them. It was mentioned in chapters 9 and 11 that the iron industries set up in Western Europe and the U.S. Northeast attracted processing industries, which again attracted immigrant labor, thus further raising population density and attractiveness for industry in the area. But this snowballing effect appeared because these industrial districts already had high population densities when the coal-iron technology had its breakthrough. By contrast, in the sparsely populated hot colonies, population density in the mining districts was much lower and the transport networks in the colonial mining areas much poorer, than those of Western Europe and the U.S. Northeast during the period of industrial breakthrough.

Therefore, neither mining nor administrative centers in the sparsely populated hot colonies grew into centers of manufacturing. Creation of a new mining or administrative center might precipitate a construction boom, which attracted labor from elsewhere. But since there was no follow-up with establishment of processing industries and other market-oriented industries, the labor force would be reduced when the construction phase was over, or at least the snowballing effect known from more densely populated areas would fail to appear. Thus, these colonies remained without manufacturing industries in the colonial period, and in most cases they continue to have a very low degree of industrialization.

REGIONAL CONTRASTS IN DEGREE OF INDUSTRIALIZATION
Table 12.2 shows the correlation between population density and degree of industrialization. Most sparsely populated countries were unindustrialized (less than 15 per cent of GDP from manufacturing) in 1970. Most densely populated countries were, if not highly, at least partly industrialized (15–24.9 per cent of GDP). The table covers only 120 countries, but the correlation would probably be even higher if more could be included, because most of those left out are either unindustrialized countries with low population densities, or densely populated East European and Asian countries with relatively high degrees of in-

TABLE 12.2 FREQUENCY AND PERCENT DISTRIBUTIONS OF COUNTRIES BY PERCENTAGE OF GROSS DOMESTIC PRODUCT DERIVED FROM MANUFACTURING AROUND 1970

Density Group	0–14.9%	15–24.9%	≥25%	Total	0–14.9%	15–24.9%	≥25%	Total
	Number of Countries				Percentages			
1–3	11	3	1	15	73	20	7	100
4–5	17	8	5	30	57	27	17	100
6–7	28	12	2	42	67	29	5	100
8–9	9	8	9	26	35	31	35	100
≥10	1	2	4	7	14	29	57	100
World	66	33	21	120	55	28	18	100
Region								
Europe	0	3	14	17	0	18	83	100
America & Oceania	8	15	5	28	29	54	18	100
Asia	11	5	2	18	61	28	11	100
Arab reg.	10	7	0	17	59	41	0	100
Africa	37	3	0	40	93	7	0	100
World	66	33	21	120	55	28	18	100

DATA SOURCE: Same as table 2.3.

dustrialization. Thus, industrialization, which started in Western and Central European countries with relatively high population densities, good transport networks, and preindustrial urbanization, spread fairly rapidly to other parts of Europe, helped by the same factors. In 1970, all the European countries included in table 12.2 were highly industrialized, except for Iceland, Ireland, and Greece.

It should be noted that the classification by degree of industrialization in table 12.2 and the classification by level of technology used in earlier tables are not identical. Portugal, with low technological levels in most of the agricultural sector, was at medium technological levels in 1970, but derived much more than 25 per cent of GDP from manufacturing. By contrast, Canada, with high technological levels in the agricultural sector and rich natural resources, had high technological levels but derived less than 25 per cent of GDP from manufacturing. Similarly, not all unindustrialized countries were low-technology countries. Most of the large oil producers in the Arab region were unindustrialized in 1970, but at medium technological levels, thanks to their oil revenues. It can be seen from table 12.3 that among the sixty-six unindustrialized countries in 1970, only forty-nine were at low technological levels. Two low-technology countries derived more than 15 per cent of GDP from manufacturing. These were Zaire and Yemen DR, with crude processing of copper and oil, respectively.

No less than thirty-six of the unindustrialized, low-technology countries were African countries. There were only four African countries

TABLE 12.3 DISTRIBUTION OF COUNTRIES ACCORDING TO DEGREE OF INDUSTRIALIZATION AND TECHNOLOGICAL LEVEL AROUND 1970

Density Group	(1) (N)	(2) below 15% of GDP from manufacturing	(3) below 15% of GDP from manufacturing and with low technological level	(3) as % of (1)
1–5	45	28	24	52
6–7	42	28	18	44
8–9	33	10	7	21
Total	120	66	49	41

DATA SOURCE: Table 12.2 and appendix.

which did not belong to this group. Two of these, South Africa and Zimbabwe, had mass settlement of Europeans in the colonial period.[25] Most of the unindustrialized African countries were sparsely populated in 1970, and among those with higher densities, a large share probably were sparsely populated in all or most of the colonial period. The whole group of unindustrialized low-technology countries included only seven densely populated countries, but twenty-four sparsely populated ones. Among all the countries which had sparse population in 1970, more than half were both unindustrialized and had low technology, while only one of every five densely populated countries had such low degrees of industrialization and such low technological levels around 1970. But this small group is important because it included India and probably China.[26] We shall focus on the problem of low levels of industrialization in densely populated countries in chapter 13.

It is not surprising that Africa was at lower degrees of industrialization and lower technological levels in 1970 than the Arab region or Asia. These regions had higher population densities than Africa, preindustrial urbanization, and much better preconditions for industrialization. But Latin America had population densities nearly as low as Africa: why was that region so much ahead of Africa in industrialization? Out of twenty-two Latin American countries included in table 12.2, only six were unindustrialized, and only two were at low technological levels in 1970. Important parts of the explanation are the quite different demographic trends in the nineteenth century and the very different patterns of settlement in these two continents. Nearly all Latin American countries had mass immigration of Europeans or of African slaves; total population therefore grew much more rapidly than in Africa, as can be seen from table 11.2. Because of mass immigration, settlement was less scattered, with many areas of Latin America developing in a frontier pattern. Coastal towns attracted large numbers of immigrants, and there was sufficient population density in the coastal area for establishment of manufacturing industries. In other words, Latin America developed a pattern intermediary between that of the U.S., which was highly favorable for industrialization, and that of Africa, which was highly unfavorable for industrialization.

In addition to the more favorable demographic conditions, the Latin American countries became independent much earlier than the African countries. They also had less racial separation, because sexual relations between different ethnic groups were more frequent. There was more incentive for the Indian population to migrate to urban areas in Latin America and fewer restrictions on migration than was the case for Africans in the colonial period. But owing to the sparsity of population and lack of rural infrastructure in the interior, urbanization in Latin America became highly concentrated in coastal towns. There was a sharp contrast in technological levels between these towns and the rural areas in the interior, which housed a large share of the Indian population.

When the African colonies became independent, the sparse population was split up among more than forty countries. Most had just a few million inhabitants, and only four had more than 16 million in 1970. These were much smaller populations than those in other parts of the world. Moreover, countries with small populations in other areas are mainly small islands or densely populated coastal areas, which benefit from water transport to the rest of the world. African countries have their small populations widely scattered over huge areas, which often are landlocked. Neither small populations nor landlocked situations are necessarily obstacles to industrialization. In the densely populated European continent, with its advanced level of infrastructure investment, a landlocked country with a few million inhabitants can be highly industrialized. Switzerland, for example, owes much of its top-ranking position in the world economy to its central location. It is the isolation of the population in the huge continent of Africa which is the obstacle to industrialization. European countries with small populations have large markets within easy reach of their borders and need only free trade to become highly industrialized. But the countries with small and low-income populations and poor infrastructure in Africa are in a very different position.

13 CONDITIONS FOR TRANSFER OF INDUSTRIAL TECHNOLOGIES TO ASIA

Most of Asia and the Arab region had much better preconditions for industrialization than the sparsely populated hot areas discussed in chapter 12. North Africa and western, southern, and eastern Asia were ancient centers of urbanization. Such areas had skilled craftsmen and traders, persons with administrative skills, and, usually, a literate elite; some of them had universities and other intellectual centers. The urban centers were linked up with surplus-producing rural areas, which supplied them with agricultural products, and to which they distributed products of local and foreign origin. Their transport networks were more dense than those of sparsely populated areas (see table 11.1). Because of this urbanization and the more dense population, the trading links to rural areas, and the better transport networks, the market for industrial manufactures was larger in these areas than in the sparsely populated ones. It was because all parts of Europe possessed this type of preindustrial urbanization that the industrial revolution spread more quickly from one part of Europe to another than to most overseas areas.

There were already some manufacturing industries, especially textile industries, within North Africa and western, southern, and eastern Asia in the nineteenth century. The industrial enclaves in India and China were large, even compared with industrialization in European countries. It is only when the numbers and capacity of industries are measured against the huge Indian and Chinese populations that they appear insignificant. But instead of looking at India and China as units, if we consider only the regions of Bombay, Bengal, and Shanghai, we see some important cases of early industrialization in densely populated areas. Until the end of the nineteenth century, the Indian manufacturing industry, located mainly in Bombay and Bengal, was larger than Japan's.[1] In India as in China, however, the vast majority of the population lived outside the orbit of the industrial sector, in an extremely poor, rural, near-subsistence economy.

Around 1970, about 40 per cent of the countries in the Asian and Arab regions derived more than 15 per cent of their GDP from manufacturing (see table 12.2). Moreover, nearly all the countries in the Arab region and in east Asia had reached medium technological levels by 1970. The Asian countries which were still unindustrialized and at low technological levels were in south Asia and Southeast Asia. Whether China belongs to that group cannot be decided for lack of statistics, but it seems likely. In chapter 7, we mentioned some sign of strain on the Chinese economy due to continuing high and increasing population density. India and the other densely populated Asian countries also faced increasing population pressure in the centuries before and after the industrial revolution in Europe. But population density in Asia varies. The relatively few countries with medium and low density were all unindustrialized and at low technological levels in 1970, while many at medium technological levels had extremely high population densities (see appendix). Japan had higher population density than nearly all the others, and the highest technological level.

Japan's early industrialization has been considered a mystery or a miracle because of its high population density and acute scarcity of agricultural land. In 1880, when Japan's industrial breakthrough began, agricultural area per male worker was one hectare in Japan compared with nearly twenty-five hectares in the United States (see table 11.4). Japan had few mineral resources; it did not benefit from transfer or advanced skills by mass immigration; nor did it receive large capital imports. In other words, all the features which made early industrialization possible in the U.S. were absent.

To understand the early industrialization of Japan, it is better to leave aside the U.S. experience and instead focus upon the European one.[2] Thanks to rapid growth of population in the first millennium A.D., urbanization appeared in Japan before Western and Central Europe. In the eighteenth century the city that is now Tokyo seems to have reached half a million inhabitants.[3] The urban sector was at high levels of preindustrial technology, and rural districts had artisans who could provide the nucleus of a skilled industrial labor force.

Japan has many features in common with England, the pioneer in European industrialization. Both are island countries, located close enough to the continent to make transport easy. Both are located far from those parts of the neighboring continents which first assumed technological leadership. While technological leadership in Europe moved from south to north between the time of the Roman Empire and the industrial revolution, a similar movement in Asia was from west to east, starting in Mesopotamia and passing through India and China. It was only after the industrial revolution that Japan bypassed China by adopting European technology more rapidly. For long periods, England and Japan had lower population densities than neighboring continental countries, from which they had to import technology. As mentioned in chapter 9, England was a producer of raw materials for industries on the continent before it built its own and bypassed the continental countries in industrial technology. Similarly, Japan developed by importing technology from China including written language and other urban technologies.

CONTRASTS BETWEEN JAPAN AND ITS CONTINENT

In the nineteenth century, population density in Japan was at group 8 level. The rate of population growth seems to have been 0.1–0.3 per cent annually in the period 1720–1870.[4] After 1870 it accelerated to more than one per cent. In other words, in the period of industrialization, Japan had a population growth rate as high as that of Europe. Population pressure on land was much more acute, however, because Japan is so mountainous that even today, when population density is at group 10 level, seventy per cent is covered by forest. This population pressure did not prevent rapid growth of the Japanese economy. From 1880 to 1960, the average annual increase of per capita product seems to have been around 2.6 per cent, i.e., considerably higher than that of Western Europe and the U.S. (around 1.7–1.8 per cent annually; see table 10.2).

Industrialization in Japan was facilitated by preindustrial urbanization and high population density. Indeed, Japan would seem a more likely candidate for early industrialization than the United States. But China and India also had these favorable features, and yet had very slow technological change. Why could Japan utilize the advantages of a high population density—such as the availability of urban skills, a large labor force for infrastructure investment, and a large market—better than China and India? How could Japan, in spite of the high population pressure on land, obtain a rapid increase of both total agricultural output and output per agricultural worker? Why did a similar development not take place in China and India, which had less acute population pressure on land and a less rapid growth of population in the period 1870–1950? Many experts have posed these questions and suggested answers; we shall look at some of their answers in the remaining parts of this chapter, focusing on those with some relation to demographic factors.

Two important features favored industrialization in Japan, compared with China and India: more favorable conditions for transport and more positive government attitudes to industrialization and other modernizations of the economy. Japan benefited from its island location that allowed water transport around and between the Japanese islands and between Japan and the continent. By contrast, most of the territories of China and India were beyond the reach of water transport. Industries set up in coastal areas of China and India in the nineteenth century remained isolated enclaves, rather than becoming pioneers of general industrialization like the British industries in the eighteenth century, and the Japanese industries in the nineteenth. Because the island location facilitated water transport, Tokyo, like London, could become a very large city long before the invention of railway transport. When Japan engaged in industrialization on a large scale, the easy access to water transport made up for the disadvantage of lack of raw materials, especially coal and iron. Navigable water and dense population combined to make transport in Japan efficient and cheap, and when railways were built, the dense population assured a volume of traffic sufficient to keep rates lower than elsewhere and nevertheless earn high profits.[5]

In China, the system of canal transport, built at enormous costs in previous centuries, seems to have acted as a deterrent to modernization. Railways and roads are costly to build when they have many waterways to cross, and the existence of these waterways made it less urgent to build railways. Even in 1970, railway density in China was less than three meters per square kilometer. In contrast, Japan, which in the nineteenth century developed an effective transport system with water traffic, railways, and roads linked together, had a railway density of fifty-seven meters per square kilometer. In China, many years were wasted with futile discussions about the value or inconveniences of railways,[6] and the resistance to railway building went so far that the first foreign-built railway was dismantled.

In India, the British started railway building before 1850, i.e., twenty years before Japan. Indian railways were built partly to transport coal and partly to encourage production of cash crops, especially cotton for the British cotton-manufacturing industry.[7] But the network was thin. In 1870, India had 2 meters of railway per square kilometer, as against 80 meters in England. A century later, the Indian network, at 18 meters per square kilometer, is still less dense than were the English and German networks before railway building started in India. Insufficient railway building provides an important part of the explanation of the delay in industrialization outside Europe, the U.S., and Japan. No other country, except for the Republic of Korea and Taiwan, has networks so dense as had England and Germany in 1850.[8]

Before the age of road traffic, very few Indian villages were within reach of the rail network for transport of bulky goods. As late as the First World War, feeder roads to the railways were nearly absent,[9] while the Japanese government had promoted building dirt roads for horse traffic in rural areas in the nineteenth century.[10] This no doubt helps to explain the slow expansion of industrialization in India, compared with Europe and Japan. Because of its much better transport system, Japan could develop not only urban but also rural industrialization at an early date, while industrialization in India and China was restricted to a few urban centers with adequate transport facilities.

Even after the development of road traffic, the Indian situation did not improve in relation to Japan.[11] China's system, uncovered by statistics, is probably even more sparse. It was underlined in earlier chapters that densely populated countries can better afford a dense transport network than sparsely populated ones with similar income levels. But some densely populated countries lost this opportunity for early industrialization, because they failed to devote sufficient resources to investment in railways, roads, and other rural infrastructure. Therefore, the degree of industrialization is low in a number of densely populated countries, including India and China.

It was not only in the field of transport that the Japanese government did more than the Chinese government and the British administration of India. The general attitude of the latter was that India ought to be developed as a supplier of raw materials to British industries and a market for British manufactures, while establishment of industrial enterprises which could become competitors with the British ones should be avoided.[12] In China, administration attitudes to modernization were ambivalent, as already mentioned. The Japanese government, however, wholeheartedly promoted imports of Western technology as a means to preserve Japanese national independence and avoid conquest by the U.S. or European powers.[13] It encouraged shipping services, railways and roads, and postal and telegraph services. It invested in arms factories, shipyards, mines, and cotton mills which employed Western techniques with the aid of Western experts. And it undertook sweeping reforms of legislation to facilitate the westernization of the Japanese economy.

As mentioned above, Japan had developed by importing technology from the more advanced countries of the Asian continent, especially China. As seems usual for newcomers, Japan was more open to imports of technology than were old technological leaders like China and India. Since Japan had for centuries borrowed and adapted Chinese technologies to fit its own conditions, it is not surprising that it was equally prepared to borrow and adapt European and American technologies, when these surpassed China's. And, like Europe at the early stage of its urbanization and the U.S. early in its industrialization, nineteenth-century Japan could move rapidly ahead because others had already made the inventions which it could take over and adapt to its needs.

In Japan as in Europe, desire for military strength promoted industrialization. This motive induced European governments to promote development of infrastructure and establishment of industrial enterprises which produced military supplies or more indirectly served to bolster national strength. Military considerations also induced the British administration of India to some development of infrastructure, military establishments, and heavy industries, and were the prime motive for imports of Western technologies in China. However, the general resistance to modernization in China weakened the efforts even within the military sector.[14]

All experts seem to agree on the importance of government attitudes and policies in explaining the different rates of industrialization of Japan, China, and India. There is, however, a limit to what government support can accomplish. The government succeeded in Japan, because the country was densely populated, favorably located, and had high levels of preindustrial technology. But even strong and well-designed government support would not have been able to promote successful industrialization in areas with the demographic conditions, location, and technological levels which characterized many sparsely populated areas in Africa and elsewhere in the nineteenth century. The Japanese success cannot be explained by government policy alone; the favorable demographic, natural, and historical preconditions also must be taken into account.

Changes in Methods of Food Supply in Japan

Let us now turn to the question of food supply in Japan. Here again, the island location was an advantage compared with China and India. It may seem surprising that Japan could produce food for its dense population when a large share of its territory was unsuitable for agriculture, but it must be taken into account that the Japanese population could obtain an important supplement to its protein supply from fish and other seafood. Japan could gather a large share of its nonvegetable supplies in the surrounding seas, while only a small share of the Chinese and Indian populations had access to seafood. It is true that China supplements its China Sea fisheries with fish hatching in artificial ponds and flooded paddy fields. Even so, fish consumption in the Chinese diet was of much less importance than in the Japanese one. In India, the protein supply from fish is negligible compared with that obtained from milk and milk products.

It was mentioned in chapter 3 that the loss of vegetable calories is large when a human population obtains parts of its calorie supply through animal products. Until recently, Japan had a small consumption of animal products. This and the large consumption of seafood help to explain why the Japanese population could subsist on a smaller area of agricultural land per inhabitant than the populations in continental countries in which the population derives a large share of its calories from animal products.

Agricultural output also increased rapidly in Japan during the period of increasing population and rapid industrialization, although in the first half-century of industrialization few industrial inputs were used. Chemical fertilizer began to be important only after 1905,[15] and change to mechanized equipment was on a small scale until recently. The statistics for the period 1885–1919 show constant labor input in agriculture, low input of capital, and a low capital/output ratio in agriculture.[16] Therefore, most commentators ascribe the rapid increase of output mainly to improvement of knowledge, and especially to "model farmers" who were advised by government experts how to select the best seeds.

However, Japanese statistics for this period are deceptive. Ohkawa has revealed how little is known about capital inputs.[17] Only equipment, livestock, and trees and scrub used mainly for silk and tea production were counted in the statistics. The estimates for investment include neither creation of arable fields, nor irrigation and draining undertaken by family labor. After the agricultural reforms in the 1870s, peasants used family labor and landlords used hired labor to expand small-scale irrigation and draining, but these investments are not recorded in the statistics for capital inputs. Moreover, investments in major irrigation schemes and in transport facilities, which were indispensable for expansion of agricultural output,[18] are counted as investments in infrastructure and not in agriculture. With a more complete count of investments, Japan would probably emerge as a country with high rather than low capital/output ratio in agriculture in that period, compared with countries with lower population density and less need to supplement scarce land resources with capital investment.

The statistics concerning labor input are no better than those for capital investment. Until 1920, only the number of agricultural families was recorded in the statistics, defined as families in which at least one member drew its support from agricultural work.[19] The statistics did not account for changes in the amount of agricultural work done by family members, or for changes in their nonagricultural work. During the industrial revolution in Europe, there were large changes of both types, as mentioned in chapter 10, and Japan seems to have had a similar experience, as we shall see below.

In Europe, the first phase of the demographic transition and the agricultural changes accompanying the industrial revolution led to increased labor inputs, as the short-fallow system was replaced by that of annual cropping. Fodder crops and industrial crops were planted in land which had previously been fallowed or used as pasture. In Japan, fallowing seems to have been abandoned early,[20] and the accelerated population growth of the 1870s, seems to have led to a further shift from annual cropping to the still more intensive system of multicropping. The statistical picture is not very clear, but the first traces of multicropping in Japan date from the thirteenth century, when this technology was imported from China, which had introduced it two centuries earlier by importing early-ripening types of rice from Southeast Asia.[21] With increasing population density in China and Japan, multicropping spread from south to north, seemingly facilitated by investments in irrigation, made before feudal labor services were abolished around 1870. It is usually assumed that multicropping increased much after the reforms,[22] so that toward the end of the 1880s, thirty per cent of the cropped area was multicropped, usually with a winter crop of barley or wheat following the summer crop of rice.[23] In 1950, over half of the much larger area under cultivation was multicropped, and three crops were frequent.

It was shown in table 5.1 that the more intensive the food supply system, the more operations are needed, and, therefore, the larger the labor input is likely to be. The increase in labor input is particularly large when a shift occurs from annual cropping to multicropping, since in that case there will be both a repetition of the usual operations for the second crop, and a larger labor input in each crop. In Japan, much labor was spent on careful preparation of seed beds, followed by transplanting with checkrow planting, and careful removal of parasites by hand from each infected rice plant.[24]

Much labor also was spent on gathering sufficient fertilizer to make multicropping possible. Chinese labor-intensive methods for composting were used; later this system was combined with the results of German soil chemistry to produce high yields.[25] In Japan, chemical fertilizer was not a substitute for composting, but an addition. From 1883 to 1937, the input of chemical fertilizer (in fertilizer content) increased from zero to 93 kilos per hectare of cultivated land, but in the same period, the input of other fertilizer, i.e., gathered matter, fish, and other purchased materials, increased from 108 kilos (in fertilizer content) to 159 kilos per hectare.[26] The eagerness of peasants to gather materials went so far that in 1890, the government took over the common land and prevented their access to it, in order to protect the forests.[27]

Improved seeds from research stations became important only after 1917, but practical experiments contributed to increase of yields long before results of modern science could be applied practically. However, seed selection was only one of the measures which were used to raise crop yields and facilitate multicropping in Japan. Increased planting of larger areas with labor-intensive, high-yielding industrial crops also raised labor input and agricultural output. Mulberry trees provided the

raw material for the highly labor intensive silk production, which supplied the main export item of Japan, and multicropping of mulberry
trees was introduced, allowing two rearing periods for worms each year.
In 1886, five per cent of the mulberry trees were cropped twice each
year; in 1905, the percentage had gone up to thirty-three,[28] and in 1920
to fifty.[29] Tea and cotton were other labor-intensive crops. As a result
of all these intensive methods, agricultural output in Japan rose from
three units per hectare in wheat equivalent in 1880 to 10 units in 1970
(see table 11.4). Output per hectare of agricultural land in Japan was
then 2–3 times that of Europe and ten times that of the U.S.

THE ROLE OF FEMALE LABOR IN THE INDUSTRIALIZATION OF JAPAN

If the increasing and extremely high agricultural output per hectare was
obtained mainly by means of labor-intensive methods and crops, and
not only by use of "miracle seeds," the implication is that the constant
number of peasant families must have increased both the activity rates
and annual work input per active family member. There are, in fact,
several reasons to believe that this was what happened.

One reason is the change in the seasonal work pattern, which goes
with shift from annual cropping to multicropping. When a first crop is
followed by a second and third in the same field, a large share of the
additional labor can be done by the same persons, if they are induced
or forced to increase their annual work input in agriculture. Another
reason for assuming increasing annual work input by members of the
peasant family is that many of the additional labor-intensive operations
needed for multicropping are to a large extent female and child labor
ones.[30] Women and children transplanted and weeded, gathered fertilizing matter, helped harvest paddy rice and pluck tea, and provided a
large share of the work in sericulture. The laborious work of removing
the eggs of the rice borer was done by small girls.[31]

Although quantitative information about work input in agriculture is
unavailable for the nineteenth century, more recent information reveals
an extremely high labor input per hectare. In the mid-twentieth century,
the number of eight-hour workdays per hectare was around 500, in spite
of the use of much industrial input.[32] Since the area cultivated per male
worker was 1.4 hectares, work input per male worker must have been
some 700 eight-hour workdays annually, which of course implies a very
active participation by women and children.

The industrialization of Japan, especially the growth of silk and cotton
industries for home consumption and exports, also relieved members
of peasant families of some of the work with home production of nonagricultural items, especially processing textile raw materials. It was

mentioned in chapter 10 that industrialization in Europe was accompanied by important changes in the use of female labor. During the early stages of industrialization and acceleration of population growth, the intensification of agriculture provided new work opportunities for women and girls, in agriculture and in industries. This process was facilitated by the abandonment of own-use production of textiles and other nonagricultural products. In Japan, a similar change seems to have taken place, and on an even larger scale.

Japanese women and girls entered industrial employment in large numbers. The densely populated rural areas of Japan had long been seats of specialized crafts, and when the government promoted dirt roads for horse traffic in rural areas and abandoned restrictions on movements of goods from one district to another, the foundation was laid for rural industries based upon local raw materials. The result was rapid growth of small-scale rural industrialization based upon water power. In 1884, no less than seventy-seven per cent of the factories in Japan were located in rural areas, and this was still the location for more than half in 1892.[33] Members of peasant families, in need of additional incomes, provided a labor force accustomed to hard work and long hours and willing to work for low wages.[34] Most of these small rural industries were silk, cotton, and other textile factories, and most of their labor force were women and girls from peasant families.

When large-scale urban industries appeared, they also relied heavily on female labor. Textile mills recruited young girls from peasant families as contract labor for a period of 3–4 years. The contract was made with the parents in the village, who received most of the wages.[35] The girls were housed in dormitories on the premises of the factory and received only pocket money. In the late nineteenth century, 70–80 per cent of the workers in the textile industry were women, and numerous other types of factories, mines, and fisheries employed women.[36]

Work hours were long in Japanese industry. In one industrial district for which a study has been made,[37] work hours increased from 11.5 per day in 1885–87 to 13.1 in 1908–11, apparently without any increase of real wages per work hour. Moreover, most Japanese industries closed only two days per month.[38] The long hours in industry were probably acceptable because work hours in agriculture also were long. In other words, the Japanese economic miracle of rapid industrialization under high and increasing population pressure was possible because activity rates and work hours increased compared with the preceding period of lower population pressure.

Owing to the low wages, especially for female and child labor, Japanese textiles and other manufactured goods could conquer foreign markets in spite of protective tariffs and other protectionist methods. Moreover, low wages in agriculture and industry and high rents for land combined to create an unequal income distribution. Therefore, the rate of savings was high, and until 1905, Japan financed its industrialization, including railway building, without capital imports.[39]

In Japan, as in Western Europe, industrialization went together with change of sectoral terms of trade in favor of agriculture.[40] The improving terms of trade for agricultural products encouraged continued intensification of agriculture. Landowning peasants intensified because prices of agricultural products were high at the village level compared with wages and other costs; tenants intensified in order to support their families and pay the high rents to the landlord.[41] The government organized courses on intensive methods for the peasants, and used both the carrot and the stick. Labor-intensive methods, like transplanting and pest control, were made obligatory, and when education and incentives were insufficient to call forth the desired input of labor, police control, punishment, and taxation were used as well.[42]

EFFECTS OF THE DEMOGRAPHIC TRANSITION ON JAPANESE FOOD SUPPLY

In Japan as in Europe, agricultural development proceeded by successive stages related to population changes. In the first phase of the demographic transition, marked by accelerating population growth, agriculture was intensified by labor-intensive means, with little if any industrial inputs. This phase lasted in Western and Central Europe from the mid-eighteenth to the mid-nineteenth century, and in Japan from around 1870 to the first decades of the twentieth century. In Europe and Japan, this first stage was followed by a second stage which had two characteristic features. One was increasing reliance upon imports of agricultural products, mainly from European and Japanese colonies or previous colonies, as a supplement to home production. Like other empires ancient and more recent, Japan tried to secure its long-distance supplies of raw materials by military domination, and to increase its supply of food from areas under its domination by using Japanese settlers and Japanese advisers to direct the indigenous population. This development started with imports of soybeans from Manchuria in the beginnings of the twentieth century,[43] and continued after the First World War with imports of rice from Korea and Taiwan.[44] The other feature common to Europe and Japan at the second stage of agricultural development was increasing use of industrial and scientific inputs. In both cases, chemical fertilizer was the most important component.

It was mentioned in chapter 10 that in Europe declining birthrates and declining income elasticity for food reduced the demand for food and imports of food and led to accumulation of food surpluses. Japanese agriculture also entered upon a new stage when rates of population growth were sharply reduced after the Second World War. But this time, development in Japan was different from that of Western and Central Europe. In Western and Central Europe, government policy restricted imports and encouraged continuing use of intensive systems of agriculture. Japan increased its reliance on imports and deintensified the agricultural system, by a near abandonment of multicropping, accompanied by a shift from home-produced fodder to fodder imports.

The reason for this deintensification was concern for the widening gap in labor productivity between the industrial and agricultural sectors.[45] Japanese industry, rebuilt after war damage, had high labor productivity, while labor-intensive agriculture continued to have low labor productivity. Reluctantly, policy on imports of food and fodder was liberalized, and subsidies were granted to turn armaments factories into factories producing agricultural machinery, including garden-size tractors.[46] The sweeping results of this change of policy can be seen from table 13.1. Use of multicropping not only declined in the 1960s; it gradually disappeared. By 1970, the winter crop of barley, mainly used for draft horses, had been given up in step with the replacement of horses by tractors. Instead, large amounts of fodder for meat animals and poultry were imported, mainly maize from Thailand. The only second crop left was green manure, which occupied around ten per cent of the arable land. Also the labor input per hectare sown with paddy declined, but there was little reduction of the arable area, probably because of a high property tax for land which was not in agricultural use.[47]

The change to less labor intensive production went together with an annual decline of around three per cent in the agricultural labor force, a change on many farms from full-time to part-time farming, and a change of the traditional Japanese diet to a mixed diet including livestock products, which also reflected diminished population pressure. It was

TABLE 13.1   INPUTS AND OUTPUTS OF JAPANESE AGRICULTURE, 1951–70

	1951	1956	1961	1966	1970
Eight-hour workdays per hectare	495	625	523	439[a]	387[a]
Multicropping index	139	131	133	124	109
Fixed capital, excluding land[b]	6.9	9.2	10.4		
Gross output[b]	4.9	5.8	6.1	6.4	6.6

[a] Calculated from change in labor force, assuming no change in hours worked per worker.   [b] Measured in paddy equivalent (one unit = one metric ton).
DATA SOURCE: Shigeru Ishikawa, *Economic Development in Asian Perspective* (Tokyo, 1967); Ministry of Agriculture, *Selected Economic Indicators Relating to Agriculture* (Tokyo, March 1971).

based on imported fodder, as already mentioned. In other words, there was a shift in production, from multicropping with very little animal husbandry to annual cropping with domestic animals, and a related change of diet.

Agricultural experts have praised the Japanese system of intensive agriculture, which was developed in the period of acute population pressure on land, as a result of good agricultural technology.[48] However, the abandonment of this system in favor of a less intensive one, when population pressure on land was reduced, reveals that the intensive system had been a necessary evil. The cost of obtaining high output by multicropping had been low labor productivity, which became unacceptable when Japan became a highly industrialized society after the Second World War.

The Japanese statistics for the period of industrialization give a false picture of the development of labor productivity in agriculture, because they reflect changes in numbers of adult male workers, instead of changes in the actual labor input by men, women, and children. According to table 11.4, gross output in wheat units per male agricultural worker increased by nearly two and a half per cent annually between 1880 and 1970, similar in percentage terms to the increase in Western European countries. However, in that period, neither work hours nor activity rates by family members seem to have increased in Western countries, and are more likely to have declined, while both were rising in Japan. Not only changes over time but also cross-country comparisons become seriously distorted when the size of the adult male labor force is used as indicator of labor input. There are large variations from country to country in women's work input in agriculture, and also in length of workday and annual number of workdays for the male labor force.[49] These variations are important for comparisons between Japanese and Indian agriculture, as we shall see below.

OBSTACLES TO AGRICULTURAL DEVELOPMENT IN CHINA AND INDIA
Earlier in this chapter, the question was posed why China and India had a much less favorable development of agriculture than Japan. Since these countries' agricultural difficulties are most often ascribed to shortage of cultivatable land, we shall begin to answer it by comparing agricultural area per inhabitant and agricultural system. This comparison is made in table 13.2, which is computed from international statistics of around 1965–70.

The table shows clearly that conditions for agricultural production were much less favorable in Japan than in China or India. Around 1970, the irrigated and multicropped area per inhabitant in China was as large

TABLE 13.2 AREA OF AGRICULTURAL LAND PER INHABITANT IN JAPAN, CHINA, AND INDIA (in hectares)

	Japan	China	India
Irrigated and multicropped (MC)[a]	0.01	0.06	0.04
Irrigated and cropped annually (AC)	0.02	0.04	0.01
Rain-fed and cropped annually (AC)	0.02	0.05	0.17
Rain-fed and used for short fallow (SF)	0.00	[b]	0.08[c]
Permanent pastureland (P)[d]	0.01	0.23	0.03
Total agricultural area	0.06	0.38	0.33

[a] Assuming that all multicropping is on irrigated land. [b] Included in AC. [c] Assuming that the area classified as fallow is used in one-year-crop/one-year-fallow rotations. [d] The difference between China and the other countries is probably overstated owing to difference in definition of pastureland.
DATA SOURCE: Same as for tables 3.1, 3.3, 3.6, 3.10, and 3.12.

as the whole agricultural area per inhabitant in Japan; in addition, China benefited from much more other arable land and from vast pastures, mainly in the north and west. The arable area per inhabitant in India was six times larger than that in Japan and twice that of China. It is true that India had only half as much irrigated land per inhabitant as China, but on the other hand, India had five times as much rain-fed land as China. The irrigated area per head in India was nearly twice that of Japan, and the unirrigated area was more than ten times larger. Japan's better access to fish and seafood can by no means counterbalance these differences. In other words, there seems to be no doubt that what distinguishes Japan is that Japan utilized poor resources efficiently and India and China utilized better resources poorly. The reasons for this are to a large extent the same as those behind Japan's advance in the industrial field: a more active government promotion of technological change and better transport facilities in rural areas and between rural and urban areas.

The more densely populated the country, the more important is the role of government in agricultural development: further intensification in densely populated areas is likely to require much more investment, especially in irrigation, than expansion of production in sparsely populated areas. Government participation is particularly important in regions in which investment in large-scale water control is needed for intensification, as is the case in many areas of China and India. Before 1880, the densely populated eastern regions of China were probably not behind Japan in agricultural output per head and per worker.[50] But then Japan entered a period of active government support for agriculture and industry, accompanied by military expansion on the Asian continent. China, together with Russia, was the main victim of the Japanese military policy. Defeat by Japan and the Western powers contributed to the disorganization and decay of the Chinese economic and administrative system. It is not difficult to understand why Chinese agriculture regressed in the long period of war and civil war that followed.

Large parts of the rural areas in India also were in decay in this period. The policy of the British administration was to supply the large Indian towns and the plantation districts with food produced in a few areas equipped with irrigation facilities and having good transport links to the consumer areas. Punjab in western India and lower Burma are important examples of this policy. Areas less well supplied with infrastructure grew food for the local poplation, but sale of surpluses was low. In some areas, a policy of rent control deprived the local landlords of motivation for expansion, repair, and maintenance of irrigation facilities and other rural investment, thus causing regression of production and increasing the severity of rural famines in years of bad monsoon.[51]

India had an unusually low output per hectare for a country with such a high population density, as can be seen from table 3.13 (in which the only country recorded in technology group II with group 8–9 density is India). There was little fallowing, owing to the high population density, and little use of fertilizing matter in spite of the high density. Manure was used as household fuel rather than as fertilizer. Labor input per hectare was much smaller than in China and Japan.[52] Many were prevented from taking part in agricultural work by caste rules, which had developed much earlier, when there was no need for intensive agriculture. In many areas, virtually no agricultural work was done in the long dry seasons. Owing to the low output per hectare, output per worker was also lower in India than in all other countries with similar densities included in table 3.13. The low output of agriculture provides an important part of the explanation of the low overall technological level of India, as well as the low degree of industrialization.

V Demographic Transition and Technological Change in the Third World

14 EFFECTS OF TECHNOLOGICAL CHANGE ON RATES OF POPULATION GROWTH

The discussion of the diffusion of industrial technologies in part 4 emphasized the differences between areas which were quick to import European technologies, and areas where this process proceeded very slowly. In some cases, slow progress in industrialization was due to sparse and stagnating population, in others to disturbances by wars and civil wars. In many areas lack of national or colonial government support for technological change played a major role. After the Second World War, the last obstacle was removed in many parts of the world, as colonial governments, which had been indifferent or hostile to industrialization, were replaced by national governments for whom rapid industrialization was a major goal. A similar change in government attitudes occurred in many of the countries which had traditions of independence. Spurred by these political changes, rates of growth in the industrial sector increased after 1950. World Bank statistics indicate that between 1960 and 1976, the industrial sector growth rate in non-industrialized and semiindustrialized countries together averaged some seven per cent yearly. This is a higher rate than that of the industrialized countries except Japan.

Rates of population growth also accelerated in this period. It can be seen from table 14.1 that, excluding high-technology countries and some countries in technology group 4, virtually all countries had population growth rates of at least two per cent annually, and many had much

TABLE 14.1 DISTRIBUTION OF COUNTRIES BY ANNUAL RATE OF POPULATION GROWTH, 1960–76

Rate of increase (%)	Technology Group					
	I	II	III	IV	V	Total
<0	0	0	0	0	1	1
0–0.9	0	1	0	5	15	21
1–1.9	2	0	1	3	9	15
2–2.9	21	17	13	11	0	62
3–3.9	1	4	10	5	0	20
⩾4	0	0	1	1	0	2
Total number of countries	24	22	25	25	25	121

DATA SOURCE: *World Bank Report 1978* (Washington, D.C., 1978), pp. 100–101.

higher rates. To some extent, the recent development of technology and population in low-technology and medium-technology countries resembles earlier development in the now highly industrialized countries: technological change and demographic change accelerated together. The magnitude of the changes, however, was different. When Europe and Japan industrialized, rates of population growth were at levels which implied a doubling of population in 70–100 years; in today's industrializing countries, the rates are at levels which imply a doubling of population in 25–30 years, or even less in some cases.

A doubling of population in less than thirty years had of course been seen before; the rapid growth of U.S. population helped to make its industrialization possible (see chapter 11). However, U.S. population growth took place in an empty area, which became populated by mass immigration from the technologically leading countries. The rapid population growth in low- and medium-technology countries today is by natural growth, although immigration from other low-technology countries helps to raise the rates even further in some of them. Moreover, the rapid doubling of population is occurring not only in areas with sparse population, but also in areas with an already dense population and considerable population pressure on resources.

In Europe, as noted in chapter 10, there was no close relationship between industrialization and acceleration of rates of population growth. The same has been true in recent decades.[1] Rates of growth of industry and the economy as a whole varied widely between countries, and variations were not correlated with the much smaller differences in rates of population growth. Some countries had high total growth rates because they combined very rapid growth rates of population with rapid technological changes; others had slow technological change and nearly constant or in some cases even declining per capita output. The last three chapters in this study are concerned with the differing experiences in low- and medium-technology countries in recent decades. The discussion will focus upon some of the major problems posed by rapid demographic and technological change. This chapter deals with the effect of the major technological changes on rates of population growth. We shall begin with changes in mortality, but devote most of the chapter to the more controversial issue of the effects on fertility.

CAUSES OF DECLINE OF MORTALITY
In most low- and medium-technology countries, the decline in mortality has been very rapid. In many cases, mortality rates have declined from a level of 2–3 per cent annually before the Second World War to around one per cent recently.[2] The main cause of these radical changes has been

the development of efficient health technologies followed by sustained efforts to transfer these techniques from high-technology countries to areas at lower technological levels. In the 1930s, a breakthrough took place in medical research. It became possible to treat a wide range of diseases, many of which had been major killers. The medical research was done in the industrialized countries, and its first effect was decline of their already low mortality rates. However, because their mortality rates were already low, and because their birthrates were also declining, the effects on their rates of population growth were modest. Long-term rates of population growth continue to decelerate in the industrialized countries.

In most medium- and low-technology countries and colonies, rates of mortality were so high before the Second World War that rates of natural population growth often seemed to be lower than those of the industrialized countries, despite high fertility. This picture was sharply reversed after the war. Military demands promoted health technologies and their transfer from one region to another. The industrialized countries were concerned about the health of their own soldiers, especially when they had to fight in tropical areas, and about the effects of local epidemics on military operations and the functioning of the economy. These considerations induced research into and innovations in tropical medicine. The fight against other intestinal and infectious diseases was also intensified.

Governments in low-technology countries ranked improvements in health high on their list of priorities. Lowering mortality was not only popular but also relatively cheap. Part or all of the expertise could be provided through international aid. During and after the war, many types of new health techniques were transferred to areas at low technological levels, in all parts of the world. New medicines and vaccines were imported or produced locally, and extensive spraying was undertaken with startling effects, especially in the case of malaria. Improvements of hygiene contributed to lower mortality, as they had earlier in the industrialized countries.[3] Some of the worst killers were nearly eradicated, and mortality due to many other diseases was radically reduced in virtually all parts of the world, including areas which had few other changes in technology. Water-borne diseases, spread as a result of agricultural development, developed resistances to spraying, and sometimes such setbacks slowed the reduction.[4] However, these setbacks acted as stimulants to further research and to attempts to change to new methods.[5] Vaccination replaced extensive spraying, and new types of irrigation were developed which do not invite proliferation of disease-carrying insects.

The rapid decline in mortality in countries with widely different rates of agricultural and other economic growth indicates that new health techniques and health facilities, rather than nutritional and other economic changes, are the main explanation. But nutritional deficiencies are no doubt responsible for a fair share of the remaining differences in mortality. These differences are very large. We have used life expectancy at birth as one of our indications of technological levels; we see from table 2.3 that it varied from 41 years in technology group I, which includes mainly African countries, to 66 years in group IV, to 72 years in group V, which includes the industrialized countries. In areas of Africa which had the highest mortality rates around 1970, there is evidence that half the children died before the age of five. Local studies have revealed that a peak of child mortality coincides with the customary age of weaning.[6] Apparently change from breast-feeding to contaminated food, which was often nutritionally deficient, produced the high mortality at these ages. Coming on top of high infant mortality, it resulted in low life expectancy at birth. Similarly, in areas of south Asia with high mortality rates, nutritional deficiencies and contaminated food due to poor hygiene combine to produce high mortality, especially in the young.

REGIONAL DIFFERENCES IN FERTILITY RATES
Fertility is influenced by a multitude of factors, the most important of which is technological level. The relationship between technological level and fertility is not close in all cases, however, and other factors should not be underestimated. Ansley Coale has pointed out that statistical comparisons of fertility and technological level in different countries are ambiguous, because there is a correlation between level of technology and culture area.[7] All high-technology countries except Japan have populations of European origin. Most countries at group IV technological level and with low fertility are inhabited by people of mainly European or Chinese origin, or have large Chinese minorities. Coale concludes that the regional or cultural factor is evident in the recent history of fertility decline: European and Chinese cultures seem to be more receptive to fertility control than others. Nadia Youssef[8] also has noted regional differences in fertility. She focuses on the Arab region, the cultural area with the highest fertility, and suggests that some features in Muslim culture may provide obstacles to fertility decline.

The regional differences in fertility observed by Coale and Youssef can be seen in table 14.2. It is obvious that fertility varies not only with technological level (as is generally agreed), but also between countries at similar technological levels. East and south Asia, Europe, and tem-

TABLE 14.2   TOTAL FERTILITY RATES, 1970-75

Region	Technology Group					
	I	II	III	IV	V	Total
Europe				3.0	2.3	2.4
East and south Asia	6.6	6.1	5.6	3.3	2.2	5.3
Oceania			(6.0)	(3.2)	2.9	3.7
Temperate America[a]				3.2	2.3	2.8
Other Latin America	(4.9)	(6.2)	6.5	5.0		5.6
Africa	6.0	6.0	6.5	(5.6)		6.1
Arab region	(7.2)	7.2	6.7	5.7		6.6
Total	6.2	6.2	6.4	4.2	2.4	5.0

[a] Canada, U.S.A., Chile, Uruguay, Argentina.
DATA SOURCE:United Nations. Here quoted from Tsui and Bogue, "Declining World Fertility: Trends, Causes, and Implications," in *Population Bulletin* 33, no. 4 (1978): 44–49.
NOTE: Total fertility rates indicate the average number of live births one woman would have, if throughout her childbearing years she experienced the age-specific fertility rates of all women in that population in a specified year. Unlike crude birthrates, total fertility rates are not affected by distortions in the age composition of a population.

perate America have virtually the same fertility rates in those technology groups for which comparison is possible, i.e., groups IV and V. Group IV, in which all the regions are represented, has fertility rates of 3.0–3.3 levels in the regions inhabited by peoples of European and Asian origin, but rates at 5.6–5.7 levels in regions inhabited by Africans and peoples of Arab culture. Tropical America, with a mixed population of American Indians, Africans, and Europeans, has a rate of 5.0, medium compared with other regions. Asia is also lower in group III, with a fertility rate of 5.6 against 6.5–6.7 in the other regions. At group II level, the Arab region has higher fertility than others, and at group I level, Asian fertility is higher than African. There are two reasons for the different pattern in the lowest technology groups: the Asian region includes three Muslim countries which seclude women and have very high fertility (Pakistan, Bangladesh, and Afghanistan); fertility is low in many low-technology countries of Africa. We shall come back to the relatively low fertility in Africa later.

Since European and Asian countries have similar fertility patterns, is there a common feature which may help to explain the similarity? Europe and Asia are the two densely populated continents. There are some reasons to believe that the differences between the food supply systems of densely and sparsely populated areas may promote different attitudes in rural areas to family size and fertility control.

EFFECT OF LAND TENURE ON RURAL FERTILITY
The culture groups which seem to have most fertility control, i.e., European and Chinese cultures, belong to areas which have long had

settled agriculture and high or relatively high population densities. The system of land tenure in such areas may create a conflict between the desire for large families and considerations of status and living standards. There is no such conflict in sparsely populated areas with long-fallow systems and tribal tenure, or in pastoral societies. We shall first look at the incentives to have large families in areas with long-fallow and tribal tenure, and afterward turn to Europe and Asia.

Under the system of tribal tenure, which still predominates in large parts of Africa, all members of the local tribe have access to clear land for long-fallow cultivation.[9] If such land is controlled by the local chief, he traditionally assigns more to large families. A man with two wives will get two plots, while a man with one wife will get one. Thus, as long as this system persists, a man obtains more land by marrying more wives and getting more children. The system still contributes to polygamy and the desire for large families.[10] It was mentioned in chapter 12 that in most of Africa, a large share of the agricultural work was and is done by women, and that children, even very young ones, perform numerous tasks in rural areas. A man with many children can have his land cleared for long-fallow cultivation by young sons, and all, or nearly all, other agricultural work done by women and smaller children. He need not pay for hired labor or fear for lack of support in old age. A large family is an economic advantage—a provider of social security, and of prestige in the local community. Therefore, the large family is the universally agreed on ideal in most African communities.

Rural women in Africa need many children to help them in their double role as agricultural workers and housewives under primitive conditions. Moreover, if they fail to produce any children, or stop childbearing at a young age, they risk being divorced and therefore having no support in old age. Women therefore are also strongly motivated to have as many children as possible. A survey of Yoruba women in Nigeria revealed that eighty per cent thought that children were wealth or were better than wealth. They did not think that on balance they consumed wealth.[11] However, despite the universal desire for many children, few African women succeeded in having large numbers of surviving children before the recent decline of mortality took place, and men succeeded only if they could afford many wives. Even today, African parents' desire for many children continues to be frustrated by low fertility and high infant and child mortality. Owing to venereal disease and malaria, rates of sterility are very high in some parts of Africa, as already mentioned.[12] Moreover, rates of involuntary abortion seem to be high owing partly to disease and partly to excessive burdens of hard work during pregnancy. And so in a continent in which children are considered as "wealth" rather than costs, most rural people are still unable to have the number of children they would like.

Let us now turn from Africa to European peasant communities in the period before the industrial revolution. This was many centuries after long-fallow systems and tribal tenure ceased to be typical of Europe. The predominant food supply system was short-fallow agriculture in permanent fields, as discussed in earlier chapters. The peasant families had holdings that were of different size but not proportionate to the number of family members. When the village population increased, hamlets might be created on the outskirts of the village territory. When the population density became so high that there was no room for additional hamlets, a family with more than one son had either to sub-divide the holding (if that was allowed) or to accept a decline of social status as some members became tenants or wageworkers for families with fewer offspring or more land. In that situation, second and third sons are not "wealth" for the family. A large family could no longer be a universal ideal. A rich man would obtain prestige if he combined much land with many sons, but poor families would not be respected for having more children than their holding could support. They were considered improvident breeders, who sacrificed the welfare of the family to satisfy their sexual desires. A new ideal appeared, that of "responsible parenthood." This ideal is not an urban invention, but an old peasant standard of decent behavior. Easterlin[13] suggests that this motive may account for the early fertility decline among American farmers as well.

A family with many children could hope to avoid subdivision of land or loss of status by arranging favorable marriages for their children, and prolonged negotiations about marriage arrangements for children of both sexes were a main preoccupation in peasant families. When a favorable marriage could not be negotiated, marriage might be delayed in the hope of better luck later. The end result might be celibacy. Marriage age in Europe seems to have been low in the Middle Ages and high later. Coale has labeled this change, which cannot be precisely dated,[14] the "Malthusian transition," because Malthus recommended delayed marriage and celibacy to reduce fertility. In Eastern Europe and Russia, delayed marriage appeared later than in more densely populated Western and Central Europe. It is tempting to suggest that the new pattern may have been promoted by the increasing difficulties with arranging favorable marriages, as population density increased. Habakkuk[15] has suggested that the delay of the Malthusian transition in Russia was due to the survival into the twentieth century of the customary redistributions of land in response to different rates of population growth in peasant families.

Celibacy and delay of marriage were the only methods of reducing fertility not banned by the Church. The effect of delayed marriage on fertility is often assumed to be unintentional. Many peasants probably did take into account, however, that if their children married young, the family might increase more than was desirable from the viewpoint of welfare and status. It should be added that not only land tenure but also other differences between the African and European agricultural systems motivated smaller family size in Europe. Child labor was much less important in Europe, since many operations performed by children in Africa were unneeded. Moreover, landowning peasants could live by hiring labor or leasing land, if they had no children to support them in old age. Only landless laborers depended upon their children in old age.

Much of this description of Europe could also be applied to China.[16] Despite the larger demand for child labor in the labor-intensive Chinese agricultural system, the small holdings provided strong motivation, for all but the rich, for not having too many children. In any case, Chinese peasants did restrict family size, by female infanticide and sale of female children to more wealthy families in need of servants. The custom of female infanticide was not limited to China. It was widespread in peasant families in Japan and northern India as well, where it lingers on in the form of fatal neglect of female children.[17] Many Asian peasants followed the advice of the ancient Greek author quoted in chapter 7, to have many sons and few daughters.[18]

EFFECTS OF INDUSTRIALIZATION ON FERTILITY

If concern about the size of the family farm provides motivation for fertility control, a decline of mortality will strengthen this motivation; increasing opportunities for nonagricultural employment due to industrialization will, on the other hand, weaken it. In Europe and Japan, and more recently in the Third World, acceleration of rates of population growth and industrialization have gone together. Thus there is pressure both to control and to relax control. This conflict is probably one of the reasons for the intriguing differences in time lag between decline of mortality and decline of fertility in different countries.

One spectacular difference is that between France, in which mortality and fertility declined nearly simultaneously, and England, in which a century separated the onsets of the two. There is some reason to assume that French peasants may have been more motivated to control fertility than peasants in most other parts of Europe. France seems to have been already ahead of most other parts of Western and Central Europe in population density before the Black Death in the fourteenth century (see table 5.2). In the eighteenth century, a large share of the French population were peasants with family holdings, and when mortality declined the combination of the two factors may have influenced peasant behavior more than increasing opportunities for nonagricultural employment.

The situation in England was quite different. After the seventeenth-century Revolution, land tenure developed differently than in France and most other parts of Western and Central Europe.[19] In the eighteenth century, when mortality decline strengthened the French peasant's motivation to limit family size, English peasants accounted for a small part of the agricultural population. This consisted mainly of hired labor and tenants,[20] who did not have the same motivation for fertility control as peasants with family holdings. Moreover, the great opportunities in England for nonagricultural employment for both adults and children did not invite to fertility control. A strong motivation was needed for such control, because religious and civil authorities in all Europe were strongly opposed to it, and only inefficient or dangerous and illegal methods were available. Before and after the fertility decline set in, European parents got large numbers of unwanted children.

The English model can perhaps be used to explain a more recent case of delayed fertility decline, that of Mexico. Mexico has long had very rapid rates of population growth and rapid urbanization and industrialization. In 1970–75, Mexico was at group IV technological levels, but total fertility was still at 6.5. In comparison, the average was 3.2 for countries in group IV levels in temperate Latin America, and 5.0 in tropical Latin America (see table 14.2). The only countries at similar technological and fertility levels were the Arab countries of Lebanon and Kuwait. It seems likely that the rapid development of nonagricultural activities in Mexico and the (illegal) possibilities for employment in the U.S. contributed to delay decline of Mexican fertility. The Indian population's preference for large families also may have played a role. However, the fertility decline seems now to have begun. According to one estimate, fertility should have declined from around 6.8 to 5.7 between 1968 and 1975.[21]

Another case in which good employment opportunities during the early stage of industrialization delayed fertility control is that of Japan. Before the industrial revolution in Japan, most of the population were peasant families with very small holdings, who practiced delayed marriage, female infanticide, induced abortion, and other folk methods of fertility control.[22] Toward the end of the eighteenth century, an unsuccessful attempt was made to increase fertility by subsidies. A century later, when industrialization began, increasing employment opportunities for women and girls removed the economic motivation for female infanticide. Small girls were used in the labor-intensive production of silk, tea, and cotton; they also worked at pest control by ridding, as mentioned earlier. Large numbers of young girls from peasant families got employment in rural and urban industries, earning money for their own dowries. When girls became a valuable asset for the family instead of a net expense on account of the dowry, female infanticide disappeared. The frequency seems to have declined in the 1870s, and it is assumed to have disappeared in the 1890s.[23]

Fertility declined in Japan after the Second World War, when large numbers of Japanese returned from former colonies, thereby increasing the pressure on land and employment opportunities and providing motivation for family restriction.[24] The number of illegal abortions rose steeply, and when abortion was legalized, birth rates descended to a low level. The decline may have been so rapid because fertility control was an old custom, and simply spread in response to new motivation. Japan was the first country with a background of earlier family limitation to get both motivation for and access to modern means of fertility control.

A Technological Revolution in Methods of Fertility Control

Rates of population growth were never high in Europe and Japan compared with those in low-technology countries today. Technological means for controlling fertility, however, are much better today than when Europe and Japan industrialized. This improved technology is largely a result of the population explosion, which raised fears and therefore stimulated research. When accelerated rates of population growth in low-technology countries began to cause concern in some of those countries, especially India,[25] and among Western experts and governments, the Western countries were at a general level of technology where virtually the whole population was motivated for fertility control. If large numbers of unwanted children were nonetheless born, it was because many methods were forbidden and others were unreliable. At first it was assumed that this situation was also typical for countries at lower technological levels. The emphasis was put on research to develop more efficient techniques and on making these available for Third World populations.

Grants were given for research, and expertise and financial aid were offered to establish family planning services to diffuse the new technologies. Donor countries put pressure on aid-receiving governments to accept the aid and take a positive attitude to fertility control. It may seem illogical that governments which restricted the access to birth control at home should exert pressure on other governments to accept services for its diffusion. But the Western governments simply transferred the principle of responsible parenthood to the field of international relations. A rich man (or government) recommends that a poor one stop having children, but does not take his own advice because he can afford them.

The liberal research grants to fertility research, together with the commercial demand in the West for better birth control, resulted in a number of new technologies, ranging from pills and loops to improved methods of abortion and sterilization. The first effect was in the industrialized countries where most of the research was carried out. Previously, parents were frustrated by the inefficiency and inconveniences of available methods of control. The combination of better techniques, a more open discussion of the subject due to the population explosion in the Third World, and expanded access to previously illegal methods under public pressure produced a major reduction of fertility in the industrialized countries, where total fertility rates often descended below replacement level.[26]

The diffusion of the new techniques in the Third World was rapid in some countries, but slow in many others. Estimates of the percentges in relevant age groups using contraceptives vary from 3 per cent in West Africa to 64 per cent in Hong Kong.[27] The wide differences reflected partly family attitudes and partly government attitudes. Table 14.3 is a regrouping, by technological level, density, and region, of data provided in a 1972 study of government efforts at fertility control. Scores ranged from zero to two, and positive scores were given for fifteen features (for instance, permitting use and imports of various technologies, establishment of services, supportive statements by political leaders, and so on). The table shows that the efforts were positively correlated with level of technology and population density. Parents are more motivated in countries at higher technological levels, and usually this motivation is reflected in more positive government attitudes.

The correlation with density reflects a natural concern by governments in already densely populated countries about the additional strain on resources caused by rapid population growth. Governments in sparsely populated countries are much less afraid of rapid population growth, and sometimes consider it an advantage. The influence of population density on government attitudes to fertility control appeared clearly at the World Population Conference in Bucharest in 1974.[28] The statements and votes of the delegates varied roughly in accordance with the difference in degree of population pressure on resources in the countries

TABLE 14.3 FERTILITY CONTROL EFFORTS, 1972

Density Group	Technology Group				
	I	II	III	IV	Total
	Average Effort Score				
1–3	0	0	0		0
4–5	1	1	1	7	2
6–7	1	3	7	14	6
8–9	2	16	13	13	11
≥10	(3)			24	20
Total	1	4	6	15	6
Region					
Africa	0.5	1			1
Arab region	(0)	(0)	4	0	3
Latin America	(3)	(0)	6	13	9
Oceania			(0)	(22)	11
East and south Asia	3	10	14	24	13
Total	1	4	6	15	6

	Distribution of Countries by Effort Score				
	Effort Scores				
	0	1–3	4–20	>20	Total
Africa	22	7	1	0	30
Arab region	9	1	5	0	15
Latin America	4	2	13	2	21
Oceania	1	0	0	1	2
East and south Asia	6	2	9	5	22
Total number of countries	42	12	28	8	90

DATA SOURCE: W. Parker Mauldin and Bernard Berelson, "Conditions of Fertility Decline in Developing Countries 1965–75," *Studies of Family Planning* 9, no. 5 (1978): 103.

they represented. Government representatives for many densely populated countries, in Asia and elsewhere, spoke and voted for fertility control. Hostility was voiced in speeches and votes by delegates of many sparsely populated countries, especially those in which efforts at industrialization and rural development are frustrated because of low population density. Differences in attitudes to fertility control reflect differences in resource endowment today; but they also are influenced by tenure systems and other effects of varying population densities in the past.

Twenty-two of the thirty African countries included in table 14.3 have a score of zero for government efforts for fertility control (lower part of table). Not only are there no family planning services, but efficient means of birth control are illegal and imports are prohibited. The hostile attitude of most African governments is not difficult to explain. Large families are the general ideal, because until recently there was little conflict between having many children and economic interests. Many parents even today would like to have more children than they have. Moreover, the low densities and the small size of population are obstacles to development in many areas. Tribal rivalry further acts to encourage fertility. Finally, in a continent in which women and children in rural areas bear a large share of the work burden of the family, many men fear that fertility control will undermine the traditional system of family labor, a step toward equality between the sexes. Fear that birth control may raise the traditional low status of women plays a major role in other parts of the world as well, especially in the Arab region. Most Arab countries have a score of zero and a total fertility rate of around 7. Governments are less hostile, and some are even positive, in Latin America, mainly because they are under pressure from parents who want access to better means than illegal abortions.

The situation is very different in Asia. Here, a number of governments in recent years have proceeded from propaganda and encouragement for fertility control to penalties to parents with many children. These include loss of various forms of favors, such as cheap housing and government employment. Following the lead of China, some Asian governments are even applying the method of neighborhood pressure.[29] These harsh methods have succeeded in reducing fertility spectacularly in three countries with authoritarian governments: China, Indonesia, and South Korea. But reactions to the Indian government's attempts demonstrate how much the public resents harsh methods in this field. It is an open question whether the tension resulting from such attempts is not worse than allowing rapid population growth to continue until parents become more motivated.

Meanwhile, voluntary means are underutilized in all parts of the Third World. There are only three medium- and low-technology countries in which all citizens have unencumbered access to all the modern methods. These three, China, South Korea, and Singapore,[30] are also among the countries putting pressure on parents. There is not a single country in the Third World in which the whole population has access to all the best modern means of control but is not pressured to use them. But in spite of the limited access to modern means of fertility control, the 1970s were a turning point in demographic development. In many countries, and in the world as a whole, birthrates were declining.[31] Rates of population growth will continue to be high in coming decades, owing to the youthful age distribution in most countries. But the first stage of the demographic transition, that of accelerating rates of world population growth, seems to be over. It is unlikely that decline of mortality will be so rapid as to cause further acceleration of population growth on a world scale.

15 INTERNATIONAL ADAPTATION TO DEMOGRAPHIC AND TECHNOLOGICAL CHANGE

During most of the twentieth century, birthrates have been declining in the countries at the highest technological levels, while rates of population growth have accelerated in countries at lower levels. Because there are close economic links between countries at different technological levels, the contrasting demographic trends have induced radical changes in international trade and factor movements. These changes in turn have affected the type of technological changes occurring within the national economies of both high-technology and lower technology countries. In this chapter, we shall look at the most important of these changes.

INTERNATIONAL TRADE IN RAW MATERIALS

For many centuries, a network of trade and factor movements linked the technologically leading areas with areas at lower technological levels, as we have seen. After the industrial revolution, these links became more close. In the period when Western and Central Europe was technologically more advanced than any other region, the European colonies and other non-European areas delivered large amounts of food, tropical products, and raw materials to Europe and received industrial consumer goods, equipment, capital transfers, and in some cases labor in return. These trade and factor movements were to a large extent adaptations to the differences in population density between Europe and other parts of the world. Because the imports of labor came from the areas leading in technology, immigration was a transfer of skills. Partly for that reason, the areas with mass immigration from Europe had very rapid technological change, while change was slow in areas depending on indigenous labor and techniques which were most often at preindustrial levels.

Many attempts have been made over the years to reduce the dependency of European industries on imported materials by developing substitutes. However, many substitutes were themselves produced from products which required supplies from outside, especially mineral oils. Self-sufficient in energy in the coal age—and with a small export surplus—Europe later became a heavy importer of mineral oil and other raw materials for energy production. Virtually all these imports come from medium- and low-technology countries.

Japan after its industrialization became even more dependent upon such imports than Europe. Countries of earlier mass immigration from Europe also became large net importers as they industrialized. Thus, today as in the past, there is a vast flow of raw materials and tropical crops from countries at lower technological levels to high-technology countries. To this has been added a large flow of energy in the same direction.

As suppliers of raw materials, tropical crops, and energy, most lower technology countries benefited from the rapid growth in high-technology countries following the Second World War. Because many of the raw materials and all the tropical crops were (and are) produced with preindustrial techniques, much of the production for export was labor intensive. When export demand and the rate of growth of the labor force increased, production expanded rapidly. It is true that in some densely populated countries, production of cash crops for export declined because more land was needed to produce food for the increasing populations. But in sparsely populated countries, where the limit to export production had been labor supply or lack of infrastructure or markets, production expanded all the more rapidly to fill the vacuum. Thus, in large numbers of developing countries, a large share of the increasing labor force was absorbed in expansion of production of cash crops and minerals for export, and the increasing export earnings helped to finance investments in urbanization, industry, and related infrastructure.

The increasing trade in raw materials, energy, and tropical crops between high-technology and lower technology countries creates a mutual dependency which is feared and resented by both partners. But there are other trade and factor movements linking the economies of countries at different technological levels. Table 15.1 provides a simplified overview of these relationships, and the important changes they have undergone since the end of the colonial period. The table shows the direction of major flows in the two periods.

The table indicates that the flow of raw materials and tropical beverages has been the most stable element in the pattern of international economic relations. There were major changes in the direction of flow of all other trade and factor movements. For food and labor, the net flows reversed direction. For industrial consumer goods and equipment and capital transfers, there have been important movements in the direction opposite that of the colonial period, although the net flows continue to be in the same direction.

The changes have been first of all related to the differences in demographic trends and the increasing industrialization in most parts of

TABLE 15.1 INTERNATIONAL TRADE AND FACTOR MOVEMENTS BETWEEN DIFFERENT TECHNOLOGY GROUPS, COLONIAL AND POSTCOLONIAL PERIODS

	Colonial Period		Postcolonial Period	
	Low and Medium Technology	High Technology[a]	Low and Medium Technology	High Technology[b]
Trade				
Raw Materials	→		→	
Energy	←		→	
Tropical beverages	→		→	
Food	→		←	
Industrial consumer goods	←		← →	
Equipment	←		← →	
Factor movements				
Capital	←		← →	
Labor	←		→	
Skills	←			

[a] Western and Central European countries.   [b] Countries listed in technology group V in appendix.

the world. While many flows in the colonial period were adaptations to differences in population density, as discussed in earlier chapters, many flows in the postcolonial period were adaptations to differences in population trends, i.e., low rates of population growth in high-technology countries and rapid rates in lower technology countries. Thus, food moved in large quantities from densely and sparsely populated countries with slowly increasing populations and high technological levels, to densely and sparsely populated countries at lower technological levels with rapidly rising populations. Similarly, labor, which in the nineteenth century moved from densely to sparsely populated countries, now moved in large quantities from countries with rapidly rising populations to countries with slow increase of population.[1] Finally, labor-intensive manufactured goods moved in increasing quantities from countries at lower technological levels with rapidly rising population to countries at high technological levels with slow population growth. We shall look at these changes in the following sections of this chapter.

REVERSAL OF THE TRADE IN FOOD

In the nineteenth century, England and other Western and Central European countries added to their home supplies by imports of food from other parts of Europe and overseas. In some countries, a large capacity for food exports catering to European markets was built up by expansion of transport networks and movement of the agricultural frontier. The development of food exports for markets in the industrializing countries of Western and Central Europe with increasing populations brought rapid technological change in the areas supplying the food. In many European countries and in non-European countries settled by immigration from Europe, the food exports helped to accelerate the change from subsistence production to commercial production with modernization of agriculture. Export earnings from food production were often the most important means to finance industrialization.

Today this way to industrialization is nearly closed, and the flow of food is from high-technology countries to countries at lower technological levels. As rates of population growth decelerated in Europe, the demand for food imports was reduced, as already mentioned. Moreover, government subsidization of European agriculture induced the small family farms to intensify production, with the result that many European countries turned from net importers to net exporters of food. This development was accelerated by the establishment of the Common Market for agricultural products, with its heavy levies on imports and subsidies to exports. There continued to be some imports of food and fodder from the traditional exporters, but most of these were now highly industrialized countries.

The sparsely populated countries in North America and Oceania built up an export capacity to supply Europe, as already mentioned. When European import demand was reduced, the demand from their own home markets also decelerated, owing to slowdown of immigration and decline of birthrates. However, food production continued to increase rapidly, helped by government support policies similar to those in Europe. For outlets for excess production and substitutes for sluggish markets, the large food exporters turned to the low- and medium-technology countries, as did European countries with export surpluses. The large exports of food from high-technology countries in North America, Oceania, and Europe in recent years are usually viewed as "gap fillers"; that is, rising exports from these countries are considered a response to the inability of lower technology countries to respond fully to acceleration of rates of population growth. This explanation, however, overlooks the crucial role played by the farm support policy in the exporting countries.

The exporting countries did not support their farmers in order for them to respond to a rising demand for food imports in lower technology countries.[2] They provided farm support and helped to dispose of the resulting food surpluses to prevent an increase in the gap between agricultural and nonagricultural incomes in their own countries. The subsidies and the grants of food were adjusted until the sum of commercial and subsidized exports reached a level corresponding to the needs of the national farm support policy. In this way, North America and Europe competed to get rid of food surpluses, even at great loss, and countries which ordinarily could not have afforded to do so became large food importers. In large numbers of medium- and low-technology countries, the favorable terms on which food imports were available induced governments to rely on food imports and neglect investments in agriculture and rural infrastructure.[3]

Because the food imports helped to keep food prices low in importing countries, production of non-food crops for export became more profitable than food production, and land or labor or both were shifted to non-food export crops, thus exerting a downward pressure on their world market prices.[4] The subsidized exports of food from the industrialized countries also provided a strong disincentive to established and potential food exporters in low- and medium-technology countries. Thus, in spite of large unutilized possibilities for expansion of food production, many sparsely populated Latin American countries had low or medium rates of increase of food production, and many potential food exporters among the lower technology countries were discouraged from making investments in food production and rural infrastructure which might have turned subsistence producers into commercial food producers. In countries in which food is produced for subsistence in rural areas and the urban sector is small, there is limited scope for commercial food production unless food surpluses can find markets outside the country. Increases in agricultural incomes become dependent upon exports of non-food crops; the choice then may be between continued subsistence production and heavy reliance on one or a few non-food export crops.

In east Asia, conditions for food exports were better than elsewhere because of Japan's increasing imports of food and fodder. Some east Asian and Southeast Asian countries made large investments to modernize agriculture and to develop roads and other rural infrastructure. Therefore, a number of Asian countries had very large increases of food production, which contributed to high growth rates of per capita incomes and promoted industrialization. If the food policy in other industrialized countries had encouraged food imports instead of subsidizing food exports, many lower and medium-technology countries would no doubt have invested more in food production, for home use and exports; more land and labor would have been used for food crops rather than non-food crops. But in many countries, industrialization benefited from the relatively low urban wage costs due to imports of cheap food. Thus, the food policy of the industrialized countries influenced not only the distribution of investment resources between food crops and non-food crops in lower technology countries, but also the distribution of resources between agriculture and manufacturing industry.

Population Density and Export of Manufactured Goods

The rapid increase of industrial production in many medium-technology and some lower technology countries had important implications for international trade. At the same time as lower technology countries developed a new dependence upon food imports from high-technology countries, many of them became less dependent upon imports of manufactured goods. The pattern of industrialization in most lower technology countries followed a common pattern.[5] The first stage was establishment of industries to manufacture consumer goods, especially textiles and footwear. This stage began in the late nineteenth century in India and China and in some of the countries which are now at medium technological levels. By 1970, large numbers of lower technology countries were far advanced in replacing imports of this type by home-produced goods. Many countries with reasonably large home markets also began to replace previously imported equipment and other capital goods with ones of their own.[6]

In some countries, the stage of import replacement was followed by a second stage, in which the country became an exporter of industrial products. These were mainly consumer goods, but in some cases included transport equipment, machinery, and other capital goods.[7] The countries which had reached this stage in 1970 were mainly densely populated countries.[8] It can be seen from table 15.2 that the share of exports consisting of industrial manufactured goods is linked both to overall levels of technology and to population density. Apart from countries at technology level V, only groups of densely populated countries derived more than fifteen per cent of export income from manufactured goods.

TABLE 15.2 EXPORTS OF INDUSTRIAL MANUFACTURES AS PERCENTAGE OF TOTAL EXPORTS

| Density Group | Technology Group | | | | | |
	I	II	III	IV	V	Total
1–3	2.4	13.1			23.7	12.0
4–5	5.6	5.4	11.1	9.8	43.1	12.9
6–7	7.9	4.6	13.9	14.1	59.6	15.1
8–9	11.3	36.4	13.1	33.2	67.9	42.1
≥10	(57.0)			68.2	73.4	68.8
Total	9.0	11.6	13.0	27.3	58.7	25.4

DATA SOURCE: Same as table 2.3.

There are several reasons for this. Many densely populated countries had ancient urbanization, an urban partly literate population, and skilled craftsmen and traders. Numerous of these had some manufacturing industries several decades before the period with which we are concerned in this chapter. They were, therefore, much better equipped for an advance in export markets than was the sparsely populated country with very little urbanization, in which the small market for nonagricultural products had been satisfied by imports from industrialized countries. Second, the densely populated countries had intensive systems of agriculture, and the rural population was accustomed to long hours of toil for low incomes. The rural-to-urban migrants in densely populated countries adapted more easily to the role of docile, low-paid worker in export industries than did rural-to-urban migrants who had produced subsistence and export crops in sparsely populated areas and were accustomed to shorter and less regular work schedules. Third, densely populated countries had more inducement to attempt a breakthrough in export markets for industrial products, because they had fewer possibilities for expanding exports of agricultural raw materials, tropical beverages, and food than had most sparsely populated countries. It usually was easy to expand the area given over to export crops in countries with low population density when accelerated population growth provided the additional labor. By contrast, as we have seen, in densely populated countries, with competition between use of land for food crops for the home market and use for export crops, possibilities for expansion of exports were limited unless exports of manufactured goods were increased.

In other words, many countries in the sparsely populated continents had rapidly increasing exports of agricultural products, which replaced earlier exports from Asia and other densely populated countries. These countries on their side replaced exports of agricultural products with exports of industrial products. India, Pakistan, and Bangladesh, with high population densities but low technological levels, derive 50–60 per cent of their export earnings from industrial products, though the income from them amounts to only $3–$6 per inhabitant per year. Such a concentration of exports on manufactured goods is not a sign of strength or of an advanced stage of development. Because of their unfavorable man-to-resource ratio, these countries are as vulnerable to conditions in markets for industrial products as are many sparsely populated countries to changes in markets for cash crops and minerals.

Exports of manufactured goods are even more closely linked to high population densities than is industrial production. It is possible to establish manufacturing industries catering to the home market even in small sparsely populated countries with scattered population, if the government is willing to protect high-cost industries. But export industries rarely are established if they need heavy subsidization. Thanks to the rapid and sustained population growth in the Third World, more and more countries have home markets which can sustain manufacturing industries. In 1950, the total number of sparsely populated countries was probably 66, and the number of densely populated ones, probably 29. According to estimates made by the ILO, the number of sparsely populated countries may decline to 35 by the end of the century and that of the densely populated may increase to 69.[9]

RATES OF GROWTH AND CAPITAL TRANSFERS

Owing to the rising demand for imports of manufactured goods and raw materials in high-technology countries, large numbers of countries at lower technological levels were able to have high rates of export-led economic growth as their rates of population growth accelerated. Some, especially small countries in east Asia, obtained this by means of exported manufactured goods; others, especially sparsely populated countries, by means of raw materials or tropical beverages. Table 15.3 shows annual rates of growth of per capita national product in the period

TABLE 15.3 DISTRIBUTION OF COUNTRIES BY INCREASE OF PER CAPITA NATIONAL PRODUCT, 1960–76

Annual Percentage Increase	Income Group[a]					
	1	2	3	4	5	Total
<0	4	2	2	2	1	11
0–1.9	12	8	3	5	1	29
2–3.9	5	11	13	7	17	53
4–5.9	3	2	3	4	4	16
⩾6	0	1	3	6	1	11
Total number of countries	24	24	24	24	24	120
Average Percentage Increase	1.5	2.2	3.2	3.6	3.3	2.9
Dollars per Capita Increase[b]	2	7	21	68	143	48

	Africa	Asia E+S	Arab group	America & Oceania	Europe	Total
<0	6	2	2	1	0	11
0–1.9	13	6	3	7	0	29
2–3.9	12	6	3	19	13	53
4–5.9	3	1	3	1	8	16
⩾6	0	5	3	0	3	11
Total number of countries	34	20	14	28	24	120

[a] Income groups have been calculated by ranging the countries according to size of per capita national product in 1960.   [b] In 1976 prices.
DATA SOURCE: *World Bank Report 1978* (Washington, D.C., 1978), pp. 76–77.

1960–76, the longest period for which reasonably reliable estimates are available for a large number of countries. A large majority of countries in Latin America, the Arab group, and Asia had more than two per cent per capita growth of output in this period of rapid population growth. Only Africa had a majority of countries with low or negative per capita growth rates.

The typical per capita growth rates were 2–4 per cent, much higher than in the preceding century in the countries which are now highly industrialized. We saw in table 10.2 that the typical per capita growth rate in Western and Central Europe between the mid-nineteenth and the mid-twentieth centuries was 1.5–2.0 per cent annually. And since rates of population growth were much lower than those of Third World countries today, the corresponding difference in growth rates for total national income would be very large.

Nearly all the countries with decline of per capita output, and two-thirds of those with growth rates below two per cent, were low-income countries in Africa and south Asia. We have already discussed the handicaps of these two regions in earlier chapters. Their effects continue to be felt. The situation for the countries in the lowest income groups is serious, not only because their rates of growth are lower than those of other groups, but because their income increases are so small in absolute amounts. Average annual increase of per capita income was only two dollars in the group with the lowest incomes, while countries in income groups 3 and 4 had increases of over $20 and nearly $70, respectively (see table 15.3).

It is apparent that countries at a certain income level and provided with some skills and infrastructure could usually obtain rapid increase of per capita incomes in the period of accelerating population growth, but that only very few of the poorest countries could do so. These differences in performance seem to be related to differences in capacity for exports. Most of the low-income countries with low or negative growth rates had few exports; their low export capacity prevented them from drawing benefit from the rising import demand in the high-technology countries. Twenty-one countries had less than $10 per capita exports in 1960,[10] and most of these had either less than one per cent or negative per capita growth of output between 1960 and 1976. It might have been expected that these countries would be the first to benefit from international development aid, but this was far from the case.

International development aid went to a large extent to political affiliates of the donor countries, and private capital investment went primarily to countries which were already at relatively high technological levels and therefore had the infrastructure and skills needed to secure an efficient utilization of capital imports.[11] It can be seen from table 15.4 that in addition to having extremely low per capita exports, the countries in the lowest income groups had virtually no long-term private capital imports and received extremely small per capita amounts of official loans and grants, compared with countries at higher income levels. These countries had no possibilities for financing rapid technological change. The handful of countries with low per capita exports in 1960 which arrived at medium technological levels in 1970 did so because they had become oil exporters or because they had strong political affiliation to a major donor country, which financed their development.

In the medium-technology countries, not only much larger capital imports, but also large domestic savings helped to finance industrialization and other technological advance. Similar to European experience, the industrial revolution in lower technology countries in recent decades resulted in large profits and savings out of profit. The high savings rates in most medium-technology countries are shown in table 15.5. In reality, savings are higher than shown in the table, because national accounts understate or leave out nonmonetized investment in agriculture. However, a share of these savings, particularly those of the large oil exporters, were invested in high-technology countries, thus producing a capital flow from lower technology to high-technology countries.

MIGRATION OF LABOR AND CAPITAL BETWEEN HIGH-TECHNOLOGY AND LOWER TECHNOLOGY COUNTRIES

It was mentioned earlier and indicated in table 15.1 that the recent pattern of labor migration is the reverse of that of the colonial period.

TABLE 15.4 NET INTERNATIONAL FLOWS OF DEVELOPMENT FINANCE PER ANNUM, 1969–73

	Average national income (dollars per capita)					
	0–100	100–199	200–399	400–799	≥800	Total
	Dollars per capita					
Long-term private capital	0.1	1.2	4.3	9.0	9.8	2.4
Long-term official capital	1.2	1.8	4.0	5.0	13.9	2.6
Official donations	0.4	0.8	3.8	0.4	2.3	1.0
Total development finance	1.6	3.8	12.1	14.4	26.0	6.0
Export value	6.0	17.0	67.0	72.0	216.0	
Total development finance (dollars per capita)	Number of Countries					
≤2	3	2	2	1	0	8
3–9	3	14	8	0	2	27
10–24	2	0	10	8	2	22
≥25	0	0	1	2	3	6
Total	8	16	21	11	7	63

DATA SOURCE: United Nations, *External Finance for Development: Recent Experience and Its Implications for Policies* E/AC. 54/L.82 (New York, 1975), tables 1, 8, 11.

TABLE 15.5 DISTRIBUTION OF COUNTRIES BY GROSS DOMESTIC SAVINGS AS PERCENTAGE OF GROSS DOMESTIC PRODUCT, 1976

Per Cent	Technology Group					
	I	II	III	IV	V	(N)
<0	3	1	1	2	0	7
0–9	10	7	1	1	0	19
10–19	6	7	8	4	3	28
20–29	0	4	8	10	13	35
≥30	1	1	5	3	2	12
Total number of countries	20	20	23	20	18	101

Per Cent	Africa	E + S Asia	Latin America	Arab Region	Europe N. Am. & Ocean.	(N)
<0	2	1	0	3	1	7
0–9	12	4	2	1	0	19
10–19	10	2	8	3	5	28
20–29	4	6	8	2	15	35
≥30	2	2	0	6	2	12
Total number of countries	30	15	18	15	23	101

DATA SOURCE: World Bank, *World Development Report 1978* (Washington, D.C., 1978), pp. 84–85.

In the nineteenth century, there were large flows of labor from densely populated high-technology countries to sparsely populated colonies and former colonies; there was no flow worth mentioning in the opposite direction, except for return migration. However, in the postcolonial period, rapid economic expansion and low rates of growth of the labor force in high-technology countries created a demand for immigrant labor. Many members of the rapidly increasing labor force in countries at lower technological levels seized this opportunity for earning higher incomes. The flow of labor changed direction. It is true that there continued to be some migration from Europe to the old areas of mass immigration, but this flow was now within the group of high-technology countries.[12]

Like the earlier migrants from Europe, many of the new migrants from lower technology to high-technology countries were skilled or highly educated people, but the skills they possessed were not new to the high-technology countries to which they migrated. The traditional way of transferring skills by migration of labor from high- to low-technology countries was practiced only to the extent that small numbers of managers and some technical experts from high-technology countries stayed for a few years in low-technology countries. Transfer of skills by means of migration from medium- to low-technology countries, however, seems to have been increasing.

The adjustment to differential demographic trends by movement of labor and labor-intensive manufactured goods from lower technology to high-technology countries was resented by organized labor and other interest groups in the high-technology countries, especially during the period of relatively high unemployment in the 1970s. There was some retrenchment from the liberal policies of the preceding decades. However, when legal and administrative measures limited flows of labor and products, capital movements from high- to low-wage countries become an alternative means of adjustment. Both national and (even more important) multinational corporations moved production from high-cost, high-technology countries to lower technology countries.[13] These became more and more attractive locations for industry, as infrastructure improved and the labor force became better skilled while continuing to work for comparatively low wages.

Because multinational corporations were large enough to finance large investments in research, many were technological leaders within their special field. Their bargaining position was very strong in relation to governments in both lower technology and high-technology countries. Therefore, they could obtain access to markets in high-technology countries for manufactured goods (and food) produced in lower technology countries better than could national industries in these countries. A large share of the exports of manufactured goods from lower technology to high-technology countries accordingly is handled by multinational corporations.

High-technology countries met with increasing competition from lower technology countries, not only in their home markets, but also in export markets. Again they used subsidies as a means to defend their export markets, and tried to tie international loans and grants to supplies of equipment and other trade. Nevertheless, trade within the group of low-technology countries began to rise more rapidly than trade between low- and high-technology countries. Trade among the Latin American countries and among countries in the Arab group and Asian countries rose especially rapidly.[14] This increase in trade helped these countries to reduce the negative effects which the economic recession in industrialized countries would otherwise have had on their development.

16 POPULATION GROWTH AND RURAL CHANGE

The acceleration of population growth in the Third World revived old Malthusian fears. We have seen, however, that in many earlier periods, the response to population growth was intensification of land use, and this experience was repeated in recent decades. In step with the increase of world population, intensive systems of agriculture replaced extensive systems in larger and larger parts of the world. Not only population, but also rates of growth of food production have accelerated.

In the period 1880–1960, when population in Europe and Japan increased around one per cent annually, total agricultural output and food production rose by around one and a half per cent per year.[1] After 1950, the average rate of increase of food production in Third World countries was roughly double that rate, though there were very large variations between countries.[2] Between 1952 and 1972, the typical rate of increase of food production was 2–3 per cent per annum, as can be seen from table 16.1. Fifty of the 111 countries for which information is available

TABLE 16.1 DISTRIBUTION OF COUNTRIES BY INCREASE OF FOOD PRODUCTION, 1952–72

	Annual Percentage Increase							
	<0	0–0.9	1–1.9	2–2.9	3–3.9	4–4.9	⩾5	(N)
Total Food Production								
Africa	0	3	6	12	6	6	1	34
South Asia	0	1	2	1	2	0	0	6
E & SE Asia	0	0	0	2	2	2	2	8
Arab region	1	1	2	3	3	0	2	12
Tropical America	0	0	4	3	2	5	5	19
Temp. Amer. & Ocean.	0	1	1	4	1	0	0	7
Europe	0	1	7	6	8	3	0	25
Total number of countries	1	7	22	31	24	16	10	111
Per Capita Food Production								
Africa	11	9	10	3	1	0	0	34
South Asia	4	1	1	0	0	0	0	6
E & SE Asia	1	2	1	3	1	0	0	8
Arab region	6	4	1	0	0	1	0	12
Tropical America	6	4	6	3	0	0	0	19
Temp. Amer. & Ocean.	2	4	1	0	0	0	0	7
Europe	0	6	8	8	3	0	0	25
Total Number of Countries	30	30	28	17	5	1	0	111

DATA SOURCE: FAO, "Population, Food Supply and Agricultural Development," in United Nations, ed., *The population debate* (New York, 1975), vol. 1, pp. 494–97.

had above three per cent annual growth of food production. A large majority of these were Third World countries.

If we compare the increase of food production in the countries with rapid population growth, i.e., those of Africa, Asia, the Arab region, and tropical America, with that in countries with low rates of population growth—in Europe and temperate America and Oceania—it is apparent that it was considerably higher in the first group (table 16.2). In some Third World countries, rapid rates of growth of food production were obtained by introduction of the technology of the so-called "Green Revolution," but the number of countries which made extensive use of these technologies was relatively small in the period covered by tables 16.1 and 16.2. Most of the expansion of food production was obtained by traditional methods, based upon use of human and animal muscle power with little industrial and scientific inputs (see table 3.8).

The increase of food production was impressive, measured by the standards of earlier periods, but it was much less impressive when measured against the growth of population. More than one-third of the countries with rapid population growth had decline of per capita food production, and another fourth had less than one per cent increase. Many of these imported food from the industrialized countries whose rates of increase of food production were high thanks to farm support policies. Four of the six countries in south Asia had lower rates of food production than of population. Other countries with decline of per capita food production had rich natural resources and preferred to import food and use their own resources, be it labor, capital, or land, for other purposes. It is significant that the Arab region, with large oil incomes and labor shortages, had the largest share of countries with declines in per capita food production. Half had lower rates of growth of food

TABLE 16.2 INCREASE OF FOOD PRODUCTION, 1952–72: PERCENT DISTRIBUTION

	Total Food Production		Per Capita Food Production	
Annual Percentage Increase	Africa, Asia, Arab region, Tropical America	Europe, Temperate America, Oceania	Africa, Asia, Arab region, Tropical America	Europe, Temperate America, Oceania
<0	1%		35%	6%
0–0.9	6	6%	25	31
1–1.9	19	25	24	28
2–2.9	27	31	11	25
3–3.9	19	28	3	9
4–4.9	16	9	1	
≥5	13			
Total	100%	100%	100%	100%

SOURCE: Table 16.1.

production than of population. In some countries with low or negative growth rates, civil wars or ill-conceived land reforms retarded agricultural growth. Others were traditional food exporters that suffered by competition from the subsidized exports of the high-technology countries.[3]

For lower technology countries, which were actual or potential exporters of food, the surplus of the high-technology countries provided a serious handicap to development of both agriculture and industry. To governments in food-importing countries, however, it seemed to offer many advantages. (1) Food prices in urban areas could be kept lower, thus keeping wage costs lower and reducing risk of inflation (or so it seemed until world market prices of cereals soared in the early 1970s). (2) With urban areas supplied by imported food, there would be less need to devote resources to rural investments, and therefore more resources would be available for industrial and urban development. (3) By yielding to donor pressure to accept food supplies, importers could hope to get a more willing ear to demands for other types of aid. (4) Counterpart funds for food imports provided the government in the food-importing country with financial means for investment or other expenditure, thus making it possible either to expand activities or to keep taxes low. (5) In many cases, governments could obtain more revenue if food imports caused a shift of resources from food production to production of export crops; this was because many governments derived a large share of total revenue from taxes on export crops or from large price differentials between government purchases of such crops and export receipts. All these advantages could be obtained immediately, while the disadvantageous effects of food imports—lack of rural development, large migration from rural to urban areas, increasing dependency upon the unpredictable policies of a few large food exporters—appeared more slowly.

DEMOGRAPHIC CONDITIONS FOR USE OF MODERN TECHNOLOGY
To economize on rural investments by supplying the towns with imported food was a dangerous choice because it prevented intensification of food production by means of modern inputs. Lower technology countries have much better means to accelerate food production than those available in the nineteenth century. New types of inputs have become available and many older ones are now of better quality. In practice, however, nearly all these inputs are unavailable to most producers in lower technology countries. In most of the areas that supply towns and export markets with agricultural products, no purchased inputs are used except hired labor. Use of most types of industrial and scientific inputs

is feasible only in rural areas which are well supplied with infrastructure. Purchased inputs, including chemical fertilizer, are often bulky and must be transported, traded, and stocked. Therefore, good roads to the village or the isolated farms are necessary, and so are local warehouses. For mechanical equipment, fueling and repair services must be available locally. An extension network may also be a precondition for the introduction of modern methods, especially if the agricultural structure is one of many small producers. Sometimes large-scale controlled irrigation must be provided or service facilities created for tube wells or other types of modern small-scale irrigation.

When Western Europe and Japan began to make use of industrial inputs in food production, their rural areas were already well supplied with necessary types of infrastructure. It is worth remembering that in the nineteenth century, when Western European agriculture reached a stage in which labor inputs were supplemented by industrial inputs, railway density in England and Germany was some 25–30 meters per square kilometer. Even today, railway density in India is only 18 meters per square kilometer, and much less in most other low-technology countries.[4] Moreover, India has less than 0.3 kilometers of roads per square kilometer, as against 1.0 kilometer of much better quality roads in high-technology countries with similar densities, and nearly 3.0 kilometers in Japan.[5] Such limited transportation facilities help to explain why, in 1970, agricultural modernization was still only beginning in India and other low-technology countries. In that year, India used 13 kilos of chemical fertilizer per hectare of arable land, as against 386 kilos in Japan.[6]

The Indian experience shows that rural infrastructure is a precondition for the use of industrial and scientific inputs in agriculture. It was mentioned in chapter 13 that the British colonial administration supplied Punjab and some other areas with good infrastructure, including transport facilities, perennial irrigation, and some extension services, so that these regions could be used to supply the large Indian cities with food. After independence, these areas, especially Punjab, spearheaded modernization and expansion of food production in India. During the 1960s, Punjab had an average increase of some seven per cent annually in agricultural output and attracted a large immigration from other Indian states.[7]

This agricultural development compares well with the high agricultural growth rates in Taiwan and South Korea, which were obtained by very large grants of foreign aid to areas which had been well supplied with infrastructure during the period of Japanese occupation. The experience of Punjab, however, is far from being typical of India, where most areas are severely handicapped by poor transport conditions and lack of other infrastructure.[8] As a result, the average increase of per capita food production in India in 1952–72 was less than one-half of one per cent annually, and food imports were large.

India is a densely populated country. The lack of rural infrastructure is an even more serious obstacle to agricultural modernization in sparsely populated countries. We have seen that the transport network in sparsely populated low-technology countries is so small that it can serve only a very small area; in addition, the lower the population density, the poorer the quality of the road network. It is interesting to compare table 3.8, which shows chemical fertilizer per hectare, with table 11.1, which shows the density of rail and road networks. We see a similar picture of large differences in favor of densely populated and high-technology countries, and the explanation is simple. A country is unable to use substantial amounts of chemical fertilizer, or other means to modernize agriculture, if most rural districts are out of reach of transport facilities because of sparse population or low overall technological levels, or both.

Modern transport facilities are not the only type of rural infrastructure which is uneconomic and therefore nonexistent or poor in quality in sparsely populated areas. Others are marketing facilities, repair shops, postal and telephone services, electricity, and social services such as educational and health facilities. Moreover, an important element in modernized farming, extension services to the individual producers, is uneconomic or of poor quality. It has been suggested[9] that to have a reasonably efficient extension system, the extension center should be located in a town of at least two thousand and should serve an agricultural population of at least five thousand, which should be within a seven-kilometer distance from the center if rural roads are poor and foot and bicycle transport the main means to reach the producers. If we accept these figures, at least seven thousand should live less than seven kilometers from the center. The population density would be at group 7 level, as can be seen from table 6.1. This density is 3–4 times the average for Africa and Latin America in 1970. Thus, except for areas with much more than average density, establishment of efficient extension networks would require large and probably uneconomic investments in rural roads.

TECHNOLOGICAL CHANGE AND LABOR MIGRATION
Because the infrastructure needed for use of modern inputs was lacking, most of the expansion of food production, especially in sparsely populated areas, was accomplished by traditional means. Many areas were

settled by squatters willing to accept rude conditions in areas with vacant land but without infrastructure. Food production was based on muscle power and fallowing. In many already-settled areas, land use was intensified by traditional means.

Large areas used for hunting and herding before population growth accelerated came to be used for crop production. Forests were cut down and wasteland was improved. In areas previously used as fallow, additional food and fodder crops were planted. Fallow declined in most low- and medium-technology countries for which information is available.[10] Multicropping spread,[11] but this change was usually associated with introduction of better seeds and chemical inputs in areas well supplied with infrastructure.

Settlement in areas without infrastructure or intensification of production by labor-intensive means made it possible for increasing numbers of rural population to subsist at traditional standards, but could not raise incomes above the customary level. In countries with increasing opportunities in other areas, rural youth was not ready to accept a traditional life without access to modern goods and services. The development of new means of communication and their diffusion to rural areas increased this disinclination. The migration from sparsely populated areas with poor infrastructure accordingly accelerated, and possibilities for expansion of food production were underutilized.

This acceleration of rural-urban migration is not a result of population growth, but a response to increasing rural-urban differentials in incomes, opportunities, and facilities. Because of expanding opportunities for industrial, administrative, and other service employment, the pull of the urban areas became much stronger, especially in newly independent and in oil-exporting countries. Areas of prosperous cash cropping for exports also became poles of attraction for labor from less prosperous regions. For instance, in Ghana a prolonged boom in cocoa production attracted a large inflow of migrant labor, mainly from areas with poor infrastructure in the interior of Africa. China and other communist countries reduced the amount of such migrations by administrative controls, as had many European governments in earlier centuries, and as did many colonial governments. But noncommunist countries usually allowed free movements, at least within the country, and often also emigration from the country.

In some countries rural-urban migrations became very large, especially when the pull of the towns went together with extensification of agriculture due to large-scale imports of food. In four countries in the Andean region, a large share of the land which had borne wheat in the 1950s was turned into pastures.[12] Consumers shifted consumption from other cereals to wheat, and eighty per cent of a much-expanded per capita consumption of wheat was covered by imports. Parts of Europe had also turned wheatfields into pasture when improvements of transport technology made large-scale imports of cereals feasible; in Europe, however, the excess agricultural labor which resulted from this shift to a more extensive agricultural system was absorbed in other activities. It was not always so easily absorbed in Latin American countries, which extensified agriculture in a period of accelerating population growth. In Africa, too, with its tradition of labor migration and rapid expansion of urbanization, rural-urban migration was large. Its sparse and scattered population and lack of rural infrastructure are still formidable obstacles to change. It is finding it difficult to switch from subsistence agriculture to commercial production of food to feed the rapidly growing towns.

But lack of infrastructure was not the only obstacle. Even areas close to towns often failed to produce surpluses of food, because of the traditional African system of food production (see chapter 12). Even when modern inputs are available, African women who raise the food have neither means nor credit to purchase them.[13] Therefore, the colonial system with imports of food to the towns continues to predominate. With rapid growth of towns, food imports have become very large,[14] although Africa could easily meet much more than its own demands, if more areas were supplied with the necessary infrastructure and male or female farmers were encouraged to engage in commercial food production.

In Africa and other areas in which agriculture relied mainly upon human labor inputs, out-migration was accompanied by a corresponding decline of output (or a slower increase, if only part of the population increase migrated). Production became insufficient to feed the increasing share of the population who lived in urban areas, and food imports or additional food imports to the towns became necessary. In other words, food imports promoted rural-urban migration, and rural-urban migration promoted food imports, in a vicious circle. Out-migration was largest from areas with the least possibility for use of industrial and scientific inputs in agriculture, because the producers had little incentive to use labor-intensive methods. By contrast, in areas with modern inputs, producers could obtain sufficient increases of output to be willing to put in more labor, raising their total output and income considerably by the combined effect of higher output per work hour and more work hours per worker. Thus, densely populated areas of Asia with modernized agriculture, like Punjab and Taiwan,[15] were able to retain a large share of the rural population increase in the rural areas. Punjab even attracted labor from other Indian states, as mentioned above.

However, not all types of rural modernization acted as restraints upon migration. Establishment of schools and increasing literacy in rural areas usually promoted migration. Parents often were motivated to send their children to school by the desire to give them opportunities to earn good incomes in urban areas. Although cash crops sometimes yielded good income, the crops might fail or export markets might collapse. A family of cash croppers with one or more members in urban employment had a kind of insurance against bad times. Popular pressure for establishment of schools in rural areas was strong, especially in Africa, where it quickly led to increased emigration.

There are no doles for immigrant labor in urban areas of the Third World. Rural youth from poor families must return to their villages when they fail to obtain wage employment or other income in the town. Their return serves as a deterrent for other potential migrants. Such a process of adaptation of the rate of migration to employment opportunities in urban areas operates less smoothly if the migrants belong to relatively well-off families. Such families are likely to finance long periods of unemployment rather than abandon the hope of getting returns for their investment. Urban unemployment thus may be large among educated youth, but small among illiterate youth, who are looking for unskilled, manual jobs. A labor force survey made in Nigeria toward the end of the 1960s[16] showed twenty per cent unemployment among persons with six or more years schooling, but without a school certificate; four per cent among those with less than four years schooling; and only one per cent among those aged more than twenty-nine years.

Divergent Trends in Technology

By contrast to high-technology countries, in most of which the agricultural labor force is declining by some three per cent per year, in lower technology ones the labor force is increasing by natural growth, which exceeds emigration. According to U.N. estimates, in only fourteen countries (excluding high technology ones) did the agricultural labor force decline between 1960 and 1970.[17] Ten of these belonged to technology group IV in 1970 and already had large urban sectors and relatively low rates of population growth. In countries at group I–III technological levels the average increase of the agricultural labor force was estimated to have been 1.0–1.5 per cent annually, but it should be taken into account that for most countries, these estimates are informed guesses.

Countries with rapid growth of total agricultural output needed an increasing labor force in agriculture since little modern input was used (see tables 3.8 and 3.11). The size of the rural-urban migration and its effects varied with the pattern of development in the country. To simplify, we may distinguish between four main patterns. First, in countries with rapid overall growth and rapid growth of agriculture, agricultural output often grew more rapidly than home demand for agricultural products. In such countries, either self-sufficiency for food increased or agricultural exports grew rapidly. They had labor shortages with increasing real wages in urban and rural areas. This pattern occurred in east Asia, Southeast Asia, and other regions. A few regions in India belonged to this pattern; they delivered a large share of their home-grown food supplies to the urban areas because agriculture grew slowly in other parts of India.

A second category includes countries with rapid overall growth, but slow growth of agriculture. The towns, and sometimes also rural areas, were supplied by food imports. Such countries had a widening gap between urban and rural incomes and very large pull-push rural-urban migration. This pattern was unstable if any recession reduced the capacity for labor absorption in the urban sector. Many Arab and Latin American countries, and some in Africa, belonged to this group.

Countries in the third group have low or medium population density and slow growth, both overall and of agriculture. These countries had expansion of the traditional types of production, more or less in step with population growth, unless they were food importing. Since there was little if any increase of real incomes, the most enterprising youths migrated to other countries. Many African countries and some in other parts of the world belonged to this pattern.

Finally, countries with dense population, slow growth (both overall and of agriculture), and no permission to emigrate had stagnation or decline of rural wages. Migration to urban areas usually resulted in return migration[18] but exerted a downward pressure on urban wages, which helped to make the country an efficient exporter of manufactured goods unless quota arrangements prevented its access to export markets. India is the outstanding example of this pattern.

In other words, the period of rapid population growth in lower technology countries had widely different effects in different parts of the world. A few countries accomplished both an industrial and an agricultural revolution. Many more made rapid strides in the industrial sector, but technological change in rural areas was modest, for reasons already discussed. Some countries failed to change substantially in the urban or the rural sectors. In countries at low technological levels, in which most of the population were occupied in agriculture, slow growth in the rural sector is very serious because the absolute level of production per worker is so low. There are no possibilities for improving the income of the majority of the population so long as the large share occupied in agriculture produce so little.

The First and Second Stages of the Demographic Transition

In countries in which population growth was rapid and economic growth slow, serious social problems emerged, but many families in countries with rapid economic growth and population increase also experienced deteriorating standards of living. The problems caused by high rates of population growth are somewhat different at early and later stages of the demographic transition, because of the changes in the age distribution of the population.

When declining mortality, especially among young children, causes an acceleration of rates of population growth, the size of nuclear families becomes larger than before. Except in countries in which children perform substantial amounts of productive work from a very young age, the burden on the adult family members becomes heavier. Unless the adults succeed in raising their incomes, the standard of living of the family will decline. At a later stage of the demographic transition, the size of nuclear families ceases to increase because fertility begins to decline. From this stage onward, the family problem is no longer to raise incomes in order to support an increasing number of children below working age, but perhaps to support adult but unemployed offspring.

Many parents succeeded in supporting increasing numbers of surviving children because they lived in countries with rapid technological change and increasing real incomes, or because they managed to raise family incomes in money or kind by an additional work input per adult. But many others, especially in countries with slow growth, had to reduce per capita consumption. Such a reduction did not necessarily imply any deterioration in nutrition, which would raise mortality rates. Most families, even very poor ones, can shift to cheaper forms of food. Cassava plays the same role as the potato played during the demographic transition in Europe.[19]

In Asia, such shifts seem to be an extremely important factor. In east and south Asia (excluding Japan and China) per capita production of cereals rose by about one-half of one per cent per year during the 1960s and consumption rose a little more, thanks to increasing imports. But per capita production of starchy roots increased by nearly three per cent per year[20] and it may have increased even more, since production of root crops for subsistence is difficult to estimate and is sometimes undervalued. This was for instance the case in Kerala, and this omission explains the surprisingly low figure for this Indian state in official statistics.[21] Livestock products, however, declined by around one-half of one per cent.[22] The rapid increase in production of starchy roots, and the decline in livestock products, indicate that many families were replacing some livestock products with vegetable food, and that poorer families were replacing part of their consumption of cereals with starchy roots. None of these shifts in consumption is damaging to health, if the crucial proteins are obtained from pulses or cererals, but this is not always the case (see chapter 14).

The problem of large family size was solved for many families when children married and set up households with incomes of their own. Other families solved the problem by means of emigration of one or more children, often the oldest son.[23] Emigration was most likely to happen in areas in which lack of rural infrastructure investment and other rural development, or rapid mechanization of agriculture, restricted local employment opportunities.[24] In such cases, the second stage of the demographic transition did not result in an increasing number of rural nuclear families, but in accumulation of young adults in urban areas.

Except for countries with very fast urban growth, unemployment among the youth in urban areas created political tension. If the urban unemployment resulted in return migration and discouraged further emigration of rural youth, the political tension spread to the countryside. Demands for redistribution of land emerged, and if large landowners introduced tractors to avoid labor troubles and demands for land reforms, the social and political problems were enhanced. Thus, at the second stage of the demographic transition, when the number of children per family is no longer increasing but the number of young adults in the country continues to increase rapidly, the most crucial factor is likely to be the ability of national governments to improve the utilization of the resources of labor, land, and capital by means of suitable economic policies.

In other words, the fate of a country at the second stage of the demographic transition is likely to depend on the ability of the ruling elite to organize society; that is, it depends on the level of "administrative technology." We have seen that some societies, for instance the pre-Columbian societies in the western hemisphere, and later Japan, were able to compensate for poor material technology or poor natural resources by organizational skills. But the leading elites in those societies had more time to adapt to population changes, because such changes were much less rapid than those in the Third World today. Moreover, in most of the countries which recently became independent, the ruling class is handicapped by insufficient experience; all or nearly all its members were denied responsible jobs and high-level education in the colonial period. Under these circumstances, they could hardly be expected to be able to solve the problems of rapid population growth and avoid economic and political difficulties.

Appendix

Countries Grouped by Density and Technological Level, around 1970

Density Group	Technology Group					
	I	II	III	IV	V	Unclassified
1						Falkland I French Guyana Greenland Mongolia Namibia Spanish Sahara Svalbard
2	Mauritania	Botswana Gabon	Libya		Australia Iceland	United Arab Emirates
3	C. Afr. R Chad Niger	Congo Oman Yemen DR	Saudi Arab.	Guyana	Canada	Afar-Isas Qatar Surinam
4	Mali Somalia Zaire	Angola Bolivia Sudan Zambia	Algeria Paraguay		NZ	Br. Honduras N. Caledonia N. Hebrides Solomon I
5	Cameroon Guinea Guinea Bis. Laos	Eq. Guinea Ivory C Liberia Madagascar Mozambique Tanzania	Nicaragua Papua NG Peru **Zimbabwe**	Argentina Brazil Chile Venezuela	Finland Norway USSR	
6	Afghanistan Benin DR Ethiopia Senegal Upper Volta Yemen AR	Kenya	Ecuador Honduras Iran Iraq Jordan Malaysia Swaziland Tunisia	Colombia Fiji Mexico Panama S. Africa Uruguay	Sweden USA	Bhutan

7	Gambia Malawi Nigeria Togo	Burma Cambodia Ghana Indonesia Lesotho Sierra Leone Uganda	Egypt Guatemala Morocco Syria Turkey	Costa Rica Kuwait	Ireland	Timor
8	Burundi Nepal	Pakistan S. Vietnam	Domin. R Philippines Thailand	Albania Cuba Greece Portugal Romania Yugoslavia	Austria Bulgaria Czechoslov. Denmark France Hungary Poland Spain Germany DR Germany FR Italy Switzerland UK	China N. Korea N. Vietnam
9	Haiti Rwanda	India	El Salv. Sri Lanka	Israel Jamaica Lebanon Trinidad		
10	Bangladesh			S. Korea	Belgium Japan Netherlands	Puerto Rico Taiwan
13				Hongkong Singapore		

Notes

CHAPTER ONE

1. Cyril Stanley Smith and R. J. Forbes, "Metallurgy and Assaying," in Charles Singer, et al., eds., *A History of Technology* (Oxford: Clarendon, 1957), vol. 3, p. 68.

2. Robert Redfield, *The Primitive World and Its Transformation* (Harmondsworth: Penguin, 1968; orig. pub. 1953), pp. 18–19.

CHAPTER TWO

1. J. Desmond Clark, "Early Human Occupation of Savanna Environments in Africa," in David R. Harris, ed., *Human Ecology in Savanna Environments* (London: Academic, 1980).

2. David R. Harris, "Alternative Pathways toward Agriculture," in Charles A. Reid, ed., *Origins of Agriculture* (The Hague: Mouton, 1977).

3. Joseph Needham, *Science and Civilization in China* (Cambridge: University Press, 1961—).

4. John D. Durand, "Historical Estimates of World Population," *Population and Development Review* 3, no. 3 (1977).

5. Colin Clark, *Population Growth and Land Use* (London: Macmillan, 1968).

6. Ajit Das Gupta, "Study of the Historical Demography of India," in D. V. Glass and Roger Revelle, eds., *Population and Social Change* (London: Edward Arnold, 1972).

7. Marcel R. Reinhard, André Armengaud, and Jacques Dupaquier, *Histoire Générale de la Population Mondiale* (Paris: Montchrestien, 1968).

8. William T. Sanders, "Population, Agricultural History and Societal Evolution in Mesoamerica," in Brian Spooner, ed., *Population Growth: Anthropological Implications* (Cambridge, Mass.: M.I.T., 1972).

9. Robert L. Carneiro, "The Measurement of Cultural Development in the Ancient Near-East and in Anglo Saxon England," *Transactions of the New York Academy of Sciences* 31, no. 8 (1969).

10. United Nations, *Developing Countries and Level of Development*, E/AC 54/L 81 Annex II (New York, 1975).

11. Pakistan and Bangladesh are shown separately in all tables, although the separation occurred after 1970. Indicators were available for 130 countries. Ministates are excluded (territory less than 10,000 square kilometers, and population less than one million). Taiwan and Puerto Rico do not appear in U.N. statistics, and China, North Korea, and North Vietnam were excluded due to lack of information. Seventeen other countries could not be included, mainly sparsely populated countries and dependent territories with small populations (see appendix).

12. It is obvious from the list of unclassified, sparsely populated countries in the appendix that none of these belonged to technology group V.

CHAPTER THREE

1. Ester Boserup, *The Conditions of Agricultural Growth* (London: Allen and Unwin, 1965).

2. T. W. Schultz, *Transforming Traditional Agriculture* (New Haven: Yale University Press, 1964).

3. Ester Bosrup, "Food Supply and Population in Developing Countries," in Nurul Islam, ed., *Agricultural Policy in Developing Countries* (London: Macmillan, 1974).

4. Joginder Kumar, *Population and Land in World Agriculture*, Population Monograph Series no. 12 (Berkeley: University of California, 1973).

5. Food and Agriculture Organization, *Production Yearbook* (Rome: FAO, 1972), table 1.

6. Boserup, *Conditions*.

7. Kumar, *Population*.

8. B. L. Turner, Robert Hanham, and Anthony V. Portararo, "Population Pressure and Agricultural Intensity," *Annals of the Association of American Geographers*, 1977.

9. Dana G. Dalrymple, *Survey of Multiple Cropping in Less Developed Nations* (Washington, D.C.: U.S. Department of Agriculture, 1971).

10. Richard B. Lee and Irven de Vore, eds., *Man the Hunter* (Chicago: Aldine, 1968). Colin Clark and Margaret Haswell, *The Economics of Subsistence Agriculture* (London: Macmillan, 4th ed. rev., 1970).

11. Ester Boserup, "Present and Potential Food Production in Developing Countries," in Wilbur Zelinzky, Leszek A. Kosinski, and R. Mansell Prothero, eds., *Geography and a Crowding World* (New York: Oxford University Press, 1970), p. 102.

12. Yujiro Hayami and Vernon W. Ruttan, *Agricultural Development: An International Perspective* (Baltimore: The Johns Hopkins University Press, 1971).

13. Ester Boserup, *Woman's Role in Economic Development* (New York: St. Martin's, 1970).

CHAPTER FOUR

1. V. Gordon Childe, *New Light on the Most Ancient East* (London: Routledge & Kegan Paul, 1952).

2. Robert McC. Adams, *Land behind Baghdad* (Chicago: University of Chicago Press, 1965).

3. Philip E. L. Smith, *The Consequences of Food Production* (Reading, Mass.: Addison-Wesley, 1972).

4. Lee and de Vore, eds., *Man the Hunter*. Sally R. Binford and Lewis R. Binford, eds., *New Perspectives in Archeology* (Chicago: Aldine, 1963). Kent V. Flannery, "Origin and Ecological Effects of Early Domestication," in Peter J. Ucko and G. W. Dimbleby, eds., *The Domestication and Exploitation of Plants and Animals* (London: Duckworth, 1969). Philip E. L. Smith, "Changes in Population Pressure in Archeological Explanation," *World Archeology* 4, no. 1 (1972). Mark N. Cohen, *The Food Crisis in Prehistory* (New Haven: Yale University Press, 1977). Robert McC. Netting, *Cultural Ecology* (Menlo Park, Calif.: Cummings, 1977).

5. Lee and de Vore, eds., *Man the Hunter*.

6. Cohen, *Food Crisis in Prehistory*.

7. Lee and de Vore, eds., *Man the Hunter*.

8. Carlo Cipolla, *The Economic History of World Population* (Harmondsworth: Penguin, 1962), p. 37.

9. Richard B. Lee, "Population Growth and the Beginnings of Sedentary Life among the Kung Bushmen," in Spooner, ed., *Population Growth*.

10. Smith, *Consequences of Food Production*. Rhys Jones, "Hunters in the Australian Tropical Savanna," in Harris, ed., *Human Ecology in Savanna Environments*.

11. Don E. Dumond, "Population Growth and Political Centralization," in Spooner, ed., *Population Growth*.

12. Cohen, *Food Crisis in Prehistory*.

13. Lee, "Population Growth."

14. Jacques Houdaille, "Les méchanismes régulateurs de la fécondité dans les sociétés traditionelles," in *International Population Conference: Mexico*, vol. 3 (Dolhain: IUUSP, 1977).

15. E. A. Wrigley, *Population and History* (London: Weidenfeld & Nicolson, 1969).

16. Harris, "Alternative Pathways toward Agriculture."

17. Stuart Piggott, *Ancient Europe* (Edinburgh: Edinburgh University Press, 1965), pp. 39–40.

18. Flannery, "Origin and Ecological Effects of Early Domestication."

19. Boserup, *Woman's Role*.

20. Fekri Hassan, "Determination of the Size, Density and Growth Rate of Hunting Gathering Populations," in Steven Polger, ed., *Population, Ecology and Social Evolution* (The Hague: Mouton, 1975).

21. Mark N. Cohen, "Population Pressure and the Origin of Agriculture," in Polger, ed., *Population, Ecology and Social Evolution*.

22. United Nations, *The Determinants and Consequences of Population Trends* (New York: United Nations, 1973).

23. Smith, *Consequences of Food Production*.

24. Lawrence J. Angel, "Paleoecology, Paleodemography and Health," in Polger, ed., *Population, Ecology and Social Evolution*, table 1, pp. 182–83.

25. A. Romaniuk, "Infertility in Tropical Africa," in John C. Caldwell and Chukuka Okonjo, eds., *Population in Tropical Africa* (New York: Columbia University Press, 1968).

26. Robert E. Ekvall, "Demographic Aspects of Tibetan Nomadic Pastoralism," in Spooner, ed., *Population Growth*.

27. Don E. Dumond, "The Limitation of Human Population," *Science* 187 (1975).

28. Lee, "Population Growth."

29. Hassan, "Determination of Size," table 1, p. 43.

30. Cohen, *Food Crisis in Prehistory*.

31. Smith, "Changes in Population Pressure."

32. Flannery, "Origin and Ecological Effects of Early Domestication."

33. Binford and Binford, eds., *New Perspectives in Archeology*.

34. Lee and de Vore, eds., *Man the Hunter*.

CHAPTER FIVE

1. George L. Cowgill, "On Causes and Consequences of Ancient and Modern Population Changes," *American Anthropologist* 77, no. 3 (1975).

2. In my earlier *The Conditions of Agricultural Growth* this distinction among inputs of different quality was referred to as a difference in the "make of tool" (pp. 26–27). The more general term is used in this study to underline that there were and are qualitative differences in inputs other than tools.

3. Sanders, "Population, Agricultural History and Societal Evolution." Michael D. Coe and Kent V. Flannery, *Early Cultures and Human Ecology in South Coastal Guatemala* (Washington, D.C.: Smithsonian Institution Press, 1967), p. 103.

4. Childe, *New Light on the Most Ancient East.*

5. Karl A. Wittfogel, *Oriental Despotism* (New Haven: Yale University Press, 1957).

6. Adams, *Land behind Baghdad.*

7. Sanders, "Population, Agricultural History and Societal Evolution," Philip E. L. Smith and T. Cuyler Young, "The Evolution of Early Agriculture and Culture in Greater Mesopotamia," in Spooner, ed., *Population Growth.* Robert McC. Adams and Hans J. Nissen, *The Uruk Countryside* (Chicago: University of Chicago Press, 1976). Karl W. Butzer, *Early Hydraulic Civilization in Egypt* (Chicago: University of Chicago Press, 1976).

8. Boserup, *Conditions.*

9. Wittfogel, *Oriental Despotism.*

10. Childe, *New Light on the Most Ancient East.*

11. Harris, ed., *Human Ecology in Savanna Environments.*

12. Boserup, *Conditions.*

13. B. Wailes, "Plow and Population in Temperate Europe," in Spooner, ed., *Population Growth.*

14. This is not meant to imply that a shift from bush-fallow without plow to short-fallow with plow would always be associated with group 6–7 densities.

15. Cipolla, *Economic History of World Population.*

16. Robert McC. Adams, *The Evolution of Urban Society: Early Mesopotamia and Pre-Hispanic Mexico* (London: Weidenfeld & Nicolson, 1966).

17. Smith and Young, "Evolution of Early Agriculture and Culture."

18. Dalrymple, *Survey of Multiple Cropping*, p. 10.

19. Needham, *Science and Civilization*, vol. 4, pt. 2 (1965), pp. 332 and 356–60.

20. Smith and Young, "Evolution of Early Agriculture and Culture."

21. Robert McC. Adams, "Early Civilization, Subsistence and Environment," in Carl H. Kraeling and Robert McC. Adams, eds., *City Invincible* (Chicago: University of Chicago Press, 1960).

22. Smith and Young, "Evolution of Early Agriculture and Culture."

23. Adams, *Land behind Baghdad.* Adams and Nissen, *Uruk Countryside.*

24. William T. Sanders and Barbara J. Price, *Mesoamerica: The Evolution of a Civilization* (New York: Random House, 1968), p. 78.

25. Adams and Nissen, *Uruk Countryside.*

26. Sanders and Price, *Mesoamerica*, p. 78.

27. Childe, *New Light on the Most Ancient East*, p. 114.

28. Adams, *Evolution of Urban Society*, p. 57.

29. Needham, *Science and Civilization*, vol. 4, pt. 2, pp. 356–60.

30. Adams, "Early Civilization, Subsistence and Environment."

31. Sanders, "Population, Agricultural History and Societal Evolution."

32. Adams, *Evolution of Urban Society.*

33. Cohen, *Food Crisis in Prehistory.*

34. Adams, *Evolution of Urban Society*, p. 39.

35. Sanders, "Population, Agricultural History and Societal Evolution."

36. Ibid.

37. Don S. Rice, "Population Growth and Subsistence Alternatives in a Tropical Lacustrian Environment," in Peter D. Harrison and B. L. Turner, eds., *Pre-*

Hispanic Maya Agriculture (Albuquerque: University of New Mexico Press, 1978), pp. 44–47.

38. Gerald W. Olson, "Some Pedological Observations of Soils in Maya Areas in Relation to Archeology," presentation statement at meeting of Society for American Archeology, Tucson, Arizona, 1978.

39. B. L. Turner II, "Ancient Agricultural Land Use in the Central Maya Lowlands," in Harrison and Turner, eds., *Pre-Hispanic Maya Agriculture*, pp. 163–83.

40. Gene C. Wilken, "Food Producing Systems Available to the Ancient Mayas," *American Antiquity* 36, no. 4 (1971).

41. Dennis E. Puleston, "Terracing, Raised Fields and Tree Cropping in the Maya Lowlands," in Harrison and Turner, eds., *Pre-Hispanic Maya Agriculture*, pp. 229–30.

42. Adams, "Early Civilization, Subsistence and Environment."

43. Eric R. Wolf and Angel Palerm, "Irrigation in the Old Acolhua Domain," *Southwestern Journal of Anthropology*, 11, no. 3 (1955).

44. Sanders, "Population, Agricultural History and Societal Evolution."

45. Ibid.

46. Piggott, *Ancient Europe*, pp. 43–52.

47. V. Gordon Childe, *The Prehistory of European Society* (London: Cassell, 1962).

48. Robert L. Carneiro, "Slash and Burn Cultivation among the Kuikuru," *Anthropologia* (Caracas, 1961).

49. Childe, *Prehistory.*

50. B. Wailes, "The Origins of Settled Farming in Temperate Europe," in George Cardona, Henry M. Hoeningswald, and Alfred Senn, eds., *Indo Europe and Indo Europeans* (Philadelphia: University of Pennsylvania Press, 1970).

51. Piggott, *Ancient Europe*, pp. 235 and 243–44.

52. Cipolla, *Economic History of World Population*, p. 41.

53. M. I. Finley, *The Ancient Economy* (London: Chatto & Windus, 1973), p. 123.

54. There was even some multicropping on irrigated land in the southern tip of the Italian peninsula in the Roman period. See Dalrymple, *Multiple Cropping.*

55. Reinhard, Armengaud, and Dupaquier, *Histoire Générale.*

56. It seems that plowing in classical Greece and Rome was with scratch plows without mulboards. See Wailes, "Plow and Population."

57. Adams and Nissen, *Uruk Countryside*, p. 83.

CHAPTER SIX

1. Lee and de Vore, *Man the Hunter.*

2. Majhamout Diop, *Histoire des Classes Sociales dans l'Afrique de l'Ouest* (Paris: F. Maspero, 1971), pp. 17–41.

3. Boserup, *Conditions.*

4. Adams, *Evolution of Urban Society.*

5. Robert L. Carneiro, "A Theory of the Origin of the State," *Science*, no. 169 (1970).

6. Smith, *Consequences of Food Production.*

7. Adams and Nissen, *Uruk Countryside*, pp. 21, 91.

8. Robert McC. Netting, "Sacred Power and Centralization," in Spooner, ed., *Population Growth.*

9. Sanders and Price, *Mesoamerica.*

10. Carneiro, "Slash and Burn Cultivation among the Kuikuru."

11. Wittfogel, *Oriental Despotism*. Sachindra Kumar Maity, *The Economic Life of Northern India in Gupta Period* (Calcutta: World, 1957).

12. Richard Duncan-Jones, *The Economy of the Roman Empire* (Cambridge: University Press, 1974).

13. Kingsley Davis, "The Origin and Growth of Urbanization in the World," *American Journal of Sociology* 60 (1955).

14. Smith, *Consequences of Food Production*.

15. Clark and Haswell, *Economics of Subsistence Agriculture*, pp. 196–97, 204.

16. Wittfogel, *Oriental Despotism*, p. 34.

17. Sanders and Price, *Mesoamerica*.

18. Finley, *The Ancient Economy*.

19. Clark and Haswell, *Economics of Subsistence Agriculture*, p. 192.

20. Sanders, "Population, Agricultural History and Societal Evolution." Adams and Nissen, *Uruk Countryside*, p. 17.

21. Turner, "Ancient Agricultural Land Use."

22. Sanders, "Population, Agricultural History and Societal Evolution."

23. William T. Sanders, "The Fon of Bahut and the Classical Maya," *Actes du XLII Congrès International des Américanistes* 8 (Paris: Société des Américanistes, 1976), pp. 396–98.

24. Wittfogel, *Oriental Despotism*, p. 55.

25. Adams, *Evolution of Urban Society*, pp. 115–16.

26. Sanders and Price, *Mesoamerica*.

27. Childe, *New Light on the Most Ancient East*, pp. 189–90, 203.

28. Sanders and Price, *Mesoamerica*.

29. Reinhard, Armengaud, and Dupaquier, *Histoire Générale*, pp. 39–46.

30. Finley, *The Ancient Economy*, pp. 107, 126.

31. Ibid.

32. Piggott, *Ancient Europe*, pp. 216–20, 236.

33. Finley, *The Ancient Economy*.

34. Wittfogel, *Oriental Despotism*.

35. Adams, "Early Civilization, Subsistence and Environment."

36. Robert McC. Netting, *Hill Farmers of Nigeria* (Seattle: University of Washington Press, 1969).

CHAPTER SEVEN

1. Childe, *Prehistory*, pp. 78–98.

2. Adams, *Evolution of Urban Society*, p. 126.

3. Childe, *New Light on the Most Ancient East*, p. 170.

4. Walter Minchinton, "Pattern and Structure of Demand, 1500–1750," in *Fontana Economic History of Europe* (Glasgow: Collins, 1972—), vol. 2 (1974), p. 140.

5. Adams, *Land behind Baghdad*. Adams and Nissen, *Uruk Countryside*.

6. E. A. Wrigley, *Industrial Growth and Population Change* (Cambridge: University Press, 1961), p. 13.

7. Childe, *New Light on the Most Ancient East*, p. 156.

8. Wittfogel, *Oriental Despotism*, p. 39.

9. Ibid., p. 25.

10. Adams, *Land behind Baghdad*, p. 105.

11. Duncan-Jones, *Economy of the Roman Empire*, p. 3.

12. Davis, "Origin and Growth of Urbanization," pp. 431–32.

13. Reinhard, Armengaud, and Dupaquier, *Histoire Générale*, p. 27.

14. Duncan-Jones, *Economy of the Roman Empire,* pp. 349–50, gives prices for slaves with different skills.

15. Sanders, "Population, Agricultural History and Societal Evolution." Adams, *Land behind Baghdad.* Adams and Nissen, *Uruk Countryside.*

16. Wittfogel, *Oriental Despotism,* p. 323.

17. P. A. Brunt, *Social Conflicts in the Roman Republic* (London: Chatto and Windus, 1971).

18. Duncan-Jones, *Economy of the Roman Empire.*

19. Adams, *Evolution of Urban Society,* pp. 59–63.

20. Anthony Preus, "Biomedical Techniques for Influencing Human Reproduction in the Fourth Century, b.c.," *Arethusa* 8 (1975).

21. Brunt, *Social Conflicts,* p. 136.

22. Quoted in Preus, "Biomedical Techniques," p. 256.

23. Duncan-Jones, *Economy of the Roman Empire,* pp. 294, 318.

24. William H. McNeill, *Plagues and Peoples* (Oxford: Blackwell, 1977).

25. Ibid., pp. 108–28.

26. Durand, "Historical Estimates of World Population," p. 272.

27. Angel, "Paleoecology, Paleodemography and Health," pp. 182–83.

28. Eric R. Wolf, *Sons of the Shaking Earth* (Chicago: University of Chicago Press, 1959).

29. Immanuel Wallerstein, *The Modern World-System* (New York: Academic Press, 1974), p. 112.

30. Wolf, *Sons of the Shaking Earth.*

31. Wolf and Palerm, "Irrigation in the Old Acolhua Domain."

32. Adams, *Land behind Baghdad.*

33. David S. Landes, *The Unbound Prometheus* (Cambridge: Cambridge University Press, 1969), pp. 29–30.

34. Wolf and Palerm, "Irrigation in the Old Acolhua Domain."

35. Needham, *Science and Civilization,* vol. 4 pt. 3 (1971), pp. 3 ff.

36. A. W. Skempton, "Canals and River Navigations before 1750," in Singer, et al., eds., *A History of Technology,* vol. 3, pp. 438–70.

37. Jacques Bernard, "Traders and Finance in the Middle Ages, 900–1500," in *Fontana Economic History of Europe,* vol. 1 (1972).

38. Maity, *Economic Life of Northern India,* p. 113.

39. Joseph Needham, *Clerks and Craftsmen in China and the West* (Cambridge: Cambridge University Press, 1970), pp. 340–46.

40. Needham, *Science and Civilization,* vol. 4, pt. 3, pp. 239–45.

41. Needham, *Clerks and Craftsmen,* pp. 28–30, 107–8.

42. Shigeru Ishikawa, *Factors Affecting China's Agriculture in the Coming Decade* (Tokyo: Institute for Asian Economic Affairs, 1967), p. 41.

43. John Lossing Buck, *Land Utilization in China* (Nanking: University of Nanking, 1931), vol. 1, pp. 15–16, and vol. 3, tables.

44. Needham, *Science and Civilization,* vol. 4, pt. 2, p. 558.

45. Lynn White, Jr., "The Expansion of Technology, 500–1500," in *Fontana Economic History of Europe,* vol. 1 (1972), p. 160.

46. Needham, *Science and Civilization,* vol. 1, pp. 240–43.

CHAPTER EIGHT

1. McNeill, *Plagues and Peoples.*

2. Emmanuel Le Roi Ladurie, "Zero Population Growth and Subsistence in 16th Century Rural France," *Peasant Studies Newsletter* 1, no. 2 (1972): 61.

3. Reinhard, Armengaud, and Dupaquier, *Histoire Générale*, p. 186.

4. J. C. Russel, "Population in Europe, 500–1500," in *Fontana Economic History of Europe*, vol. 1, p. 41.

5. United Nations, *Determinants and Consequences*, vol. 1, p. 18.

6. Ansley J. Coale, "The Demographic Transition," in United Nations, ed., *The Population Debate* (New York: United Nations, 1975), vol. 1.

7. Piggott, *Ancient Europe*, p. 52.

8. Inge Skovgaard-Petersen, "Oldtid og Vikingetid," in Inge Skovgaard-Petersen, Aksel E. Christensen, and H. Paludan, eds., *Danmarks Historie*, vol. 1 (Copenhagen: Gyldendal, 1977), pp. 63–64.

9. Richard C. Hoffman, "Medieval Origin of the Common Fields," in William N. Parker and Eric L. Jones, eds., *European Peasants and Their Markets* (Princeton: Princeton University Press, 1975).

10. White, "The Expansion of Technology," pp. 147–48.

11. Wailes, "Plow and Population," pp. 154–79.

12. Reinhard, Armengaud, and Dupaquier, *Histoire Générale*.

13. Boserup, *Conditions*.

14. Georges Duby, "Medieval Agriculture, 500–1500," in *Fontana Economic History of Europe*, vol. 1, p. 204.

15. B. H. Slicher van Bath, *The Agrarian History of Western Europe*, A.D 500–1500 (New York: St. Martin's Press, 1963).

16. Duby, "Medieval Agriculture."

17. Louise Tilly, "La Révolte Frumentaire: Forme de Conflit Politique en France," *Annales* 27, no. 3 (1972).

18. Reinhard, Armengaud, and Dupaquier, *Histoire Générale*, pp. 146–96.

19. Domenico Sella, "European Industries, 1500–1700," in *Fontana Economic History of Europe*, vol. 2, pp. 384–88.

20. J. D. Chambers and G. E. Mingay, *The Agricultural Revolution, 1750–1880* (London: Batsford, 1966), p. 10.

21. Tilly, "La Révolte Frumentaire," p. 753.

22. David S. Landes, "Japan and Europe," in William W. Lockwood, ed., *The State and Economic Enterprise in Japan* (Princeton: Princeton University Press, 1965), p. 125.

23. Sylvia Thrupp, "Medieval Industry, 1000–1500," in *Fontana Economic History of Europe*, vol. 1, p. 260.

24. Jean Fourastie, *L'Evaluation des Prix à Long Terme* (Paris: Presses Universitaires de France, 1969), pp. 147–70.

25. Landes, *Unbound Prometheus*, p. 27.

26. Thrupp, "Medieval Industry," p. 234.

27. A. R. Hall, "The Rise of the West," in Singer, et al., eds., *History of Technology*, vol. 3, pp. 716–17.

28. Richard Roehl, "Patterns and Structure of Demand, 1000–1500," in *Fontana Economic History of Europe*, vol. 1, p. 135.

29. White, "Expansion of Technology," pp. 160–61.

30. Needham, *Science and Civilization*, vol. 1, pp. 242–43.

CHAPTER NINE

1. Hermann Kellenbenz, "Technology in the Age of the Scientific Revolution," in *Fontana Economic History of Europe*, vol. 2, p. 245.

2. R. Zangheri, "The Historical Relationship between Agricultural and Economic Development in Italy," in E. L. Jones and S. J. Woolf, eds., *Agrarian Change and Economic Development* (London: Methuen, 1969). B. H. Slicher van Bath, "The Rise of Intensive Husbandry in the Low Countries," in Charles K. Warner, ed., *Agrarian Conditions in Modern European History* (London: Macmillan, 1966).

3. L. E. Harris, "Land Drainage and Reclamation," in Singer, et al., ed., *History of Technology*, vol. 3, pp. 300–315.

4. Wallerstein, *Modern World-System*, p. 96.

5. Herbert Moeller, "Population and Society during the Old Regime, 1640 to 1770," in Herbert Moeller, ed., *Population Movements in Modern European History* (London: Macmillan, 1964), pp. 35 ff.

6. Slicher van Bath, "The Rise of Intensive Husbandry," p. 39.

7. Jones and Woolf, eds., *Agrarian Change*, p. 6.

8. Hall, "Rise of the West," p. 710.

9. Kellenbenz, "Technology in the Age of the Scientific Revolution," p. 225.

10. W. Arthur Lewis, *Tropical Development, 1880–1913* (London: Allen and Unwin, 1970), p. 13.

11. A. J. Youngson, "The Opening up of New Territories," in *Cambridge Economic History of Europe*, (Cambridge: University Press, 1965), vol. 6, p. 172.

12. Ibid., pp. 158–59.

13. Kellenbenz, "Technology in the Age of the Scientific Revolution," p. 224.

14. J. U. Nef, "Coal Mining and Utilization," in Singer, et al., eds., *History of Technology*, vol. 3, p. 74.

15. David S. Landes, "Technological Change and Development in Western Europe 1750–1914," in *Cambridge Economic History*, vol. 6, pp. 325–26.

16. Nef, "Coal Mining," pp. 83–87.

17. Sella, "European Industries," pp. 392–93.

18. Roehl, "Patterns and Structure," p. 130.

19. Thrupp, "Medieval Industry," pp. 239–40.

20. Smith and Forbes, "Metallurgy and Assaying," p. 31. Rolf Sprandel, "La Production du Fer au Moyen Age," *Annales* 24 (1969): 312.

21. United Nations Research Institute for Social Development, *Data Bank of Development Indicators*, vol. 1 (Geneva: UNRISD, 1976), p. 59.

22. Sella, "European Industries," pp. 387–88.

23. Samuel Lilley, "Technological Progress and the Industrial Revolution," in *Fontana Economic History of Europe*, vol. 3, pp. 198–99.

24. Wallerstein, *Modern World-System*, p. 281.

25. Smith and Forbes, "Metallurgy and Assaying," p. 30.

26. A. R. Hall, "Military Technology," in Singer, et al., eds., *History of Technology*, vol. 3, pp. 347–48.

27. Kellenbenz, "Technology in the Age of the Scientific Revolution," p. 212.

28. Hall, "Military Technology," p. 373.

29. Derek J. Price, "The Manufacture of Scientific Instruments from c. 1500 to c. 1700," in Singer, et al., eds., *History of Technology*, vol. 3, p. 623.

30. Eli F. Heckscher, *Svensk Arbete och Liv* (Stockholm: Aldus Bonnier, 1969), p. 110.

31. E. Ames and N. Rosenberg, "Changing Technological Leadership and Industrial Growth," in Nathan Rosenberg, ed., *The Economics of Technological Change* (Harmondsworth: Penguin, 1971), p. 427.

32. Nef, "Coal Mining," p. 79.

33. E. A. Wrigley, "The Supply of Raw Materials in the Industrial Revolution," *Economic History Review*, 2d series, vol. 15, no. 1 (1962): 4, 16.

34. Claude Fohlen, "The Industrial Revolution in France, 1700–1914," in *Fontana Economic History of Europe*, vol. 4, pt. 1 (1973), p. 55.

35. Peter Temin, "A New Look at Hunter's Hypothesis about the Ante-Bellum Iron Industry," in Rosenberg, ed., *The Economics of Technological Change*.

36. Peter Mathias, *The First Industrial Nation* (New York: Scribner, 1969), p. 449.

37. Knut Borchardt, "The Industrial Revolution in Germany," in *Fontana Economic History of Europe*, vol. 4, p. 123.

38. Hall, "Rise of the West," p. 712.

39. Luciene Cafagna, "The Industrial Revolution in Italy, 1830–1914," in *Fontana Economic History of Europe*, vol. 4, pp. 286 ff.

40. Wallerstein, *Modern World-System*, pp. 226–27.

41. Heckscher, *Svensk Arbete och Liv*.

CHAPTER TEN

1. Simon Kuznets, "Population Trends and Modern Economic Growth," in United Nations, ed., *The Population Debate*, vol. 1, pp. 425–26.

2. Jones and Woolf, eds., *Agrarian Change*, pp. 5 ff.

3. Phyllis Deane, "The Industrial Revolution in Great Britain," in *Fontana Economic History of Europe*, vol. 4, pt. 1, pp. 201–2.

4. Paul Bairoch, *Révolution Industrielle et Sous-Développement* (Paris: SEDES, 1969), pp. 29 ff.

5. Boserup, *Conditions*, pp. 37–39; Chambers and Mingay, *Agricultural Revolution*.

6. Simon Kuznets, *Modern Economic Growth: Rates, Structure and Spread* (New Haven: Yale University Press, 1966), pp. 42–44.

7. Ibid., pp. 52–54.

8. Boserup, *Conditions*, pp. 36–37.

9. Folke Dovering, "The Transformation of European Agriculture," in *Cambridge Econmic History of Europe*, vol. 6, p. 643.

10. Deane, "Industrial Revolution," pp. 191–93.

11. Bairoch, *Révolution Industrielle*, p. 286.

12. Borchardt, "Industrial Revolution in Germany," pp. 91–92, 98–99.

13. Chambers and Mingay, *Agricultural Revolution*, pp. 136 ff.

14. Boserup, *Conditions*, pp. 112–15.

15. Jones and Woolf, eds., *Agrarian Change*, p. 11.

16. Michel Tracy, "Agriculture in Western Europe: The Great Depression, 1880–1900," in Warner, ed., *Agrarian Conditions*, p. 102.

17. Warner, ed., *Agrarian Conditions*, p. 7.

18. Deane, "Industrial Revolution," pp. 211–12.

19. Phyllis Deane and W. A. Cole, "British Growth, 1868–1959," in *Cambridge Economic History of Europe*, vol. 6, pp. 8–9.

20. *Chambers and Mingay, Agricultural Revolution*, p. 182.

21. Minchinton, "Pattern and Structure of Demand," pp. 125–26.

22. In the 1930s, labor input per hectare in potato production in Denmark was nearly four times as high as in grain production and ten times larger than in production of grass fodder, according to a large sample of farm accounts. These differences were larger than the differences in output per hectare measured in

calories. See Jens Warming, *Danmarks Erhvervs og Samfundsliv*, vol. 3 (Copenhagen: Gads Forlag, 1939), p. 319.

23. R. J. Forbes, "Food and Drink," in Singer, et al., eds., *History of Technology*, vol. 3, p. 13.

24. Deane, "Industrial Revolution," p. 221.

25. Kuznets, *Modern Economic Growth*, pp. 63–68.

26. Research and Planning Division, Economic Comission for Europe, "The French Economy: Basic Problems of Occupational Structure and Regional Balance," in *Economic Survey of Europe in 1954* (Geneva: United Nations, 1955), chap. 7.

27. A. V. Chaianov, *The Theory of Peasant Economy* (Homewood, Ill.: R. D. Irwin, 1966), pp. 174 ff.

28. Landes, "Japan and Europe."

29. Thrupp, "Medieval Industry," p. 231.

30. Ibid., p. 240.

31. Bairoch, *Révolution Industrielle*, p. 108.

32. Jan de Vries, "Labor/Leisure Trade Off," *Peasant Studies News Letter* 1, no. 2 (1972): 48.

33. J. D. Chambers, "Enclosure and Labour Supply in the Industrial Revolution," *Economic History Review*, vol. 6 (1953).

34. Joan W. Scott and Louise A. Tilly, "Women's Work and the Family in 19th Century Europe," *Comparative Studies in Society and History* 17, no. 1 (1975): 51–55.

35. Svend Aage Hansen, *Økonomisk Vaekst i Danmark*, vol. 1 (Copenhagen: Gads Forlag, 1972), p. 162, table VIII, 6.

36. Landes, "Japan and Europe," p. 155.

37. Chaianov, *Theory of Peasant Economy*, pp. 107 ff.

38. Thomas McKeown, R. G. Brown, and R. C. Recard, "An Interpretation of the Modern Rise of Population in Europe," *Population Studies* 26, no. 3 (1972): 381.

39. Ibid.

40. Michael Drake, ed., *Population in Industrialization* (London: Methuen, 1969), p. 5.

41. P. E. Razzel, "An Interpretation of the Modern Rise of Population in Europe: A Critique," *Population Studies* 28, no. 1 (1974).

42. P. E. Razzel, "Population Change in 18th Century England: A Reappraisal," in Drake, ed., *Population in Industrialization*. P. E. Razzel, "Population Growth and Economic Change in 18th Century and Early 19th Century England and Ireland," in E. L. Jones and G. E. Mingay, eds., *Land, Labour and Population in the Industrial Revolution* (London: Edward Arnold, 1967).

43. McKeown, et al., "Interpretation of the Modern Rise of Population," p. 349.

44. Ladurie, "Zero Population Growth," p. 62.

45. Moeller, "Population and Society."

46. Hall, "Military Technology," p. 374.

47. André Armengaud, "Population in Europe, 1700–1914," in *Fontana Economic History of Europe*, vol. 3, p. 42.

48. Russel, "Population in Europe," pp. 42–45.

49. Armengaud, "Population in Europe," p. 48. Dominique Tabutin, "La Mortalité Féminine en Europe avant 1940," *Population* 33, no. 1 (1976).

50. Aldo de Maddalena, "Rural Europe, 1500–1700," in *Fontana Economic History of Europe*, vol. 2, pp. 332–34.

51. Razzel, "Population Change."

52. Razzel, "Interpretation," pp. 13–17.

53. Landes, "Japan and Europe," pp. 128, 155.

54. H. J. Habakkuk, *Population Growth and Economic Development since 1750* (Leicester: Leicester University Press, 1972), pp. 35–48.

55. Robert McC. Netting and Wekter S. Elias, "Balancing on an Alp: Population Stability and Change in a Swiss Village," in Priscilla Copeland Reining and Barbara Lenkard, eds., Village Viability in Contemporary Society (Washington, D.C.: AAAS, 1980).

56. United Nations and Food and Agriculture Organization, *European Agriculture: A Statement of Problems* (Geneva: United Nations and FAO, 1954), pp. 15–19.

57. Ibid., pp. 37–40, 66–68.

CHAPTER ELEVEN

1. L. Girard, "Transport," in *Cambridge Economic History of Europe*, vol. 6.

2. Ibid., pp. 229, 238.

3. United Nations, *Determinants and Consequences*, vol. 1, pp. 183–93.

4. Heckscher, *Svensk Arbete och Liv*, p. 283.

5. Hall, "The Rise of the West," p. 709.

6. Kuznets, *Modern Economic Growth*, p. 52.

7. Youngson, "The Opening up of New Territories," pp. 198–99.

8. Douglass C. North, "Industrialization in the United States," in *Cambridge Economic History of Europe*, vol. 6, p. 678.

9. Youngson, "The Opening up of New Territories," pp. 139 ff.

10. Preston Holder, *The Hoe and the Horse on the Plains* (Lincoln: University of Nebraska Press, 1970).

11. Youngson, "The Opening up of New Territories," pp. 192–94.

12. Nathan Rosenberg, *Perspectives on Technology* (Cambridge: Cambridge University Press, 1976), pp. 42 ff. Erik P. Eckholm, *The Other Energy Crisis, Firewood* (Washington, D.C.: Worldwatch Institute, 1975), p. 17.

13. North, "Industrialization," p. 678.

14. Temin, "A New Look," p. 278.

15. North, "Industrialization," p. 702.

16. Ibid.

17. Frank Thistlewaite, "Migration from Europe to Overseas in the 19th and 20th Centuries," in Moeller, ed., *Population Movements in Modern European History*.

18. Borchardt, "Industrial Revolution in Germany," pp. 123–24.

19. Kuznets, *Modern Economic Growth*, pp. 52–55.

20. United Nations, *Determinants and Consequences*, vol. 1, p. 314.

21. Paul David, "The Mechanization of Reaping in the Ante-Bellum Mid-West," in Rosenberg, ed., *The Economics of Technological Change*, p. 257.

22. North, "Industrialization," pp. 691–92.

23. Youngson, "The Opening up of New Territories," pp. 191–94.

CHAPTER TWELVE

1. D. S. Neumark, *Foreign Trade and Economic Development in Africa* (Stanford: Food Research Institute, 1964), pp. 149 ff.

2. Ibid., pp. 51–52.

3. J. N. Boeke, *Economics and Economic Policy in Dual Societies* (Harlem: Institute of Pacific Relations, 1953).

4. J. S. Furnival, *Colonial Policy and Practice* (Cambridge: University Press, 1967).

5. W. S. Morgan, "Peasant Agriculture in Tropical Africa," in H. F. Thomas and G. W. Whittington, eds., *Environment and Land Use in Africa* (London: Methuen, 1969), p. 246.

6. Boserup, *Woman's Role.*

7. D. R. F. Taylor, "Agricultural Change in Kikuyuland," in Thomas and Whittington, eds., *Environment and Land Use*, p. 488.

8. A. Baron Holmes, "The Gold Coast and Nigeria," in W. Arthur Lewis, ed., *Tropical Development*, pp. 164–65.

9. Neumark, *Foreign Trade*, p. 72.

10. Holmes, "Gold Coast and Nigeria," p. 152.

11. Morgan, "Peasant Agriculture," p. 268.

12. Neumark, *Foreign Trade*, p. 72.

13. Holmes, "Gold Coast and Nigeria," p. 161.

14. Audrey I. Richards, ed., *Economic Development and Tribal Change* (Cambridge: W. Helfer, 1954).

15. William Watson, *Tribal Cohesion in a Money Economy* (Manchester: Manchester University Press, 1958), p. 34.

16. J. van Velsen, "Labour Migration as a Positive Factor in the Continuity of Tonga Traditional Society," *Economic Development and Cultural Change* vol. 8 (1960), pp. 266 ff.

17. Audrey I. Richards, *Land, Labour and Diet in Northern Rhodesia* (Oxford: International Institute of African Languages and Culture, 1939), pp. 298, 404–5. A. W. Southall, "Alur Migrants," in Richards, ed., *Economic Development and Tribal Change.*

18. Boserup, *Woman's Role*, pp. 76–79.

19. Holmes, "Gold Coast and Nigeria," p. 165.

20. Ester Boserup, "The Impact of Population Growth on Agricultural Output," *Quarterly Journal of Economics* 89 (1975): 260–65.

21. Lewis, ed., *Tropical Development*, p. 13.

22. Boserup, *Woman's Role*, p. 149.

23. Taylor, "Agricultural Change," pp. 485–92.

24. Boserup, *Woman's Role*, pp. 92–95.

25. The other two were Zaire, as mentioned above, and Swaziland. The latter was unindustrialized but was at medium technological levels, due to remittals of wages from migrant labor.

26. The seven densely populated, unindustrialized countries were India, Bangladesh, Nepal, Vietnam, Burundi, Rwanda, and Haiti.

CHAPTER THIRTEEN

1. G. C. Allen, "The Industrialization of the Far East," in *Cambridge Economic History of Europe*, vol. 6, p. 911.

2. Landes, "Japan and Europe."

3. Irene Tauber, *The Population of Japan* (Princeton: Princeton University Press, 1958).

4. Susan B. Hanley and Kozo Yamamura, "Population Trends and Economic Growth in Pre-Industrial Japan," in Glass and Revelle, eds., *Population and Social Change*, p. 463.

5. Girard, "Transport," p. 259.

6. Ssu-yu Teng and John King Fairbank, *China's Response to the West* (Cambridge, Mass: Harvard University Press, 1954), pp. 116 ff.

7. Michelle Burge McAlpin, "Railroads, Prices and Peasant Rationality: India, 1860–1900," *Journal of Economic History* 34 (1974).

8. Girard, "Transport," pp. 231, 238. International Union of Railways, *International Railway Statistics* (Paris: IUR, 1972).

9. Lewis, ed., *Tropical Development*, p. 19.

10. Allen, "Industrialization," p. 881.

11. International Road Federation, *World Road Statistics* (Geneva-Washington, D.C.: IRF, 1973).

12. Allen, "Industrialization," p. 909.

13. Allen, ibid., pp. 875–76. Landes, "Japan and Europe," pp. 111 ff.

14. Teng and Fairbank, *China's Response*.

15. James J. Nakamura, *Agricultural Production and the Economic Development of Japan, 1873–1922* (Princeton: Princeton University Press, 1966), pp. 82–83.

16. Kazushi Ohkawa and Bruce F. Johnston, "The Transferability of the Japanese Pattern of Modernizing Traditional Agriculture," in Erik Thorbecke, ed., *The Role of Agriculture in Economic Development* (New York: Columbia University Press, 1969), pp. 282–84.

17. Kazushi Ohkawa, "Phases of Agricultural Development and Economic Growth," in Kazushi Ohkawa, Bruce F. Johnston, and Hiromitsu Kaneda, eds., *Agriculture and Economic Growth* (Princeton: Princeton University Press, 1970), pp. 21–26.

18. Shigeru Ishikawa, *Economic Development in Asian Perspective* (Tokyo: Kinokuniya Bookstore, 1967), pp. 98.

19. Arlon R. Tussing, "The Labor Force in Meiji Economic Growth," In Ohkawa, Johnston, and Kaneda, eds., *Agriculture and Economic Growth*, pp. 199 ff.

20. Boserup, *Conditions*, p. 61. Thomas C. Smith, *The Agrarian Origins of Modern Japan* (Stanford: Stanford University Press, 1959).

21. Ishikawa, *Factors Affecting China's Agriculture*.

22. Ohkawa and Johnston, "Transferability of Japanese Pattern," pp. 288–89.

23. Dalrymple, *Survey of Multiple Cropping*, pp. 12, 18–19.

24. Shujiro Sawada, "Technological Change in Japanese Agriculture," in Ohkawa, Johnston, and Kaneda, eds., *Agriculture and Economic Growth*.

25. Hayami and Ruttan, *Agricultural Development*, pp. 154–55.

26. Ishikawa, *Factors Affecting China's Agriculture*, p. 62.

27. Ishikawa, *Economic Development*, pp. 245–46n.

28. Kenzo Hemmi, "Primary Product, Exports and Economic Development: The Case of Silk," in Ohkawa, Johnston, and Kaneda, eds., *Agriculture and Economic Growth*, p. 320.

29. Hayami and Ruttan, *Agricultural Development*, p. 301.

30. Yukio Masiu, "The Supply Price of Labor from Family Workers," in Ohkawa, Johnston, and Kaneda, eds., *Agriculture and Economic Growth*.

31. Sawada, "Technological Change," p. 150.

32. Ishikawa, *Economic Development*, pp. 222 ff.

33. Mataji Umemura, "Agriculture and Labor Supply in the Meiji Era," in Ohkawa, Johnston, and Kaneda, eds., *Agriculture and Economic Growth*, p. 194–95.

34. Landes, "Japan and Europe," pp. 115–16.

35. Allen, "Industrialization," p. 898.

36. Susan J. Pharr, "Japan: Historical and Temporary Perspectives," in Janet Zollinger Giele and Audrey Chapman Smock, eds., *Women: Role and Status in Eight Countries* (New York: Wiley, 1977), pp. 228–29.

37. Tussing, "Labor Force," p. 211.

38. Allen, "Industrialization," p. 899.

39. Ibid., pp. 881–82.

40. Ohkawa, "Phases," pp. 27 ff.

41. Bruce F. Johnston, *Agriculture and Economic Development* (Stanford: Food Research Institute, 1966), p. 265.

42. R. P. Dore, "Agricultural Improvement in Japan 1870–1900," in Jones and Woolf, eds., *Agrarian Change*, p. 109.

43. Hayami and Ruttan, *Agricultural Development*, p. 159.

44. Yujiro Hayami and Vernon W. Ruttan, "Korean Rice, Taiwan Rice and Japanese Agricultural Stagnation," *Quarterly Journal of Economics* 84 (1970): 562–89.

45. Kuznets, *Modern Economic Growth*, p. 117.

46. Saburo Okita, *Causes and Problems of Rapid Growth in Postwar Japan* (Tokyo: Japan Economic Research Institute, 1967), p. 24.

47. Shinzo Kiuchi, "Population Pressure in Japan," in Zelinski, Kosinski, and Prothero, eds., *Geography and a Crowding World*.

48. Yujiro Hayami, "Technological Progress in Agriculture" in Lawrence Klein and Kazushi Ohkawa, eds., *Economic Growth* (Homewood, Ill.: R. D. Irwin, 1968), p. 145.

49. Boserup, *Woman's Role*, pp. 15–36.

50. Ishikawa, *Factors Affecting China's Agriculture*, pp. 4–5.

51. Boserup, *Conditions*, pp. 98–101.

52. Ibid., p. 40. Ishikawa, *Economic Development*, pp. 226 ff.

CHAPTER FOURTEEN

1. R. A. Easterlin, "The Effects of Population Growth on the Economic Growth of Developing Countries," *Annals of the American Academy of Political and Social Sciences* 369 (1967). Julian J. Simon, *The Economics of Population Growth* (Princeton: Princeton University Press, 1977), pp. 137 ff.

2. George J. Stolnitz, "International Mortality Trends," in United Nations, ed., *The Population Debate* (New York: United Nations, 1975), vol. 1, pp. 220–36.

3. Thomas McKeown, *The Modern Rise of Population* (New York: Academic Press, 1976).

4. Robert S. Desowitz, "Epidemiologic-Ecological Interaction in the Tropical Savanna," in Harris, ed., *Human Ecology in Savanna Environments*.

5. World Health Organization, "Malaria Control: A Reoriented Strategy," *WHO Chronicle* 32 (1978): 226–30.

6. Remy Clairin, "Evaluation de la mortalité infantile et juvénile d'après les données disponibles en Afrique," in Caldwell and Okonjo, eds., *Population in Tropical Africa*.

7. Coale, "Demographic Transition," pp. 354–55.

8. Nadia H. Youssef, "Women's Status and Fertility in Muslim Countries of the Middle East and Africa." Paper delivered at Symposium on Women's Status and Fertility, American Psychological Association, New Orleans, 1974.

9. Boserup, *Conditions*, pp. 88–94.

10. Boserup, *Woman's Role*, pp. 37–52.

11. John C. Caldwell, "Toward a Restatement of Demographic Transition Theory," *Population and Development Review* 2, nos. 3–4 (1976): 341.

12. Romaniuk, "Infertility in Tropical Africa."

13. Richard A. Easterlin, "The Conflict between Aspirations and Resources," *Population and Development Review* 2, nos. 3–4 (1976): 422.

14. Coale, "Demographic Transition," pp. 348–49.

15. Habakkuk, *Population Growth*, p. 98.

16. J. Barrington Moore, *Social Origins of Dictatorship and Democracy* (Harmondsworth: Penguin, 1967), pp. 211–13.

17. Boserup, *Woman's Role*, pp. 48–50.

18. Preus, "Biomedical Techniques."

19. Moore, *Social Origins*, pp. 20 ff.

20. Chambers and Mingay, *Agricultural Revolution*.

21. Amy Ong Tsui and Donald J. Bogue, "Declining World Fertility," *Population Bulletin* 33, no. 4 (1978): 46. See, however, Paul Demeny, "On the End of the Population Explosion," *Population and Development Review* 5, no. 1 (1979), for a critical evaluation of the estimates by Tsui and Bogue.

22. Tauber, *Population of Japan*, pp. 29–32.

23. Kuichi, "Population Pressure," p. 488.

24. Deborah Oakley, "American-Japanese Interaction in the Development of Population Policy in Japan, 1945–52," *Population and Development Review* 4, no. 4 (1978): 622 ff.

25. K. Srinivasan, "Application of Methods of Measuring the Impact of Family Planning Programmes on Fertility," in United Nations, ed., *Methods of Measuring the Impact of Family Planning* (New York: United Nations, 1978), pp. 45–47.

26. Mogens Boserup, "Europe's New Fertility Pattern: Facts, Causes, Perspectives," in Scandinavian Demographic Society, ed., *The Fertility Decline in the Nordic Countries* (Copenhagen: Scandinavian Demographic Society, 1978), pp. 11–30.

27. Bruce Stokes, "Filling Family Planning Gaps," *Population Reports*, series i, no. 20 (1978), p. 373.

28. United Nations, *Report of the United Nations's World Population Conference* (New York: United Nations, 1975).

29. Stokes, "Family Planning." Ronald Freedman, "Summary of Research Findings on Asian Population Programmes," *Population Reports*, series i, no. 20, pp. 380–81.

30. Stokes, "Family Planning," p. 386.

31. United Nations, *The World Population Situation in 1977* (New York: United Nations, 1979).

CHAPTER FIFTEEN

1. Leon F. Bouvier, Henry S. Shryock, and Henry W. Henderson, "International Migration: Yesterday, Today and Tomorrow," *Population Bulletin* 32, no. 4 (1977).

2. Willard W. Cochrane, "The Impact of Different Forms of Foreign Assistance on Agricultural Development," in *Proceedings of the World Food Conference of 1976* (Ames: Iowa State University Press, 1977), pp. 183–93.

3. Boserup, "Impact of Population Growth."

4. W. Arthur Lewis, *Aspects of Tropical Trade, 1863–1965: Wicksell Lectures 1969* (Stockholm: Almquist, 1970).

5. United Nations, "Industrialization and Development," *Journal of Development Planning*, no. 8 (1975).

6. United Nations, "Development Trends since 1960 and Their Implications for a New Development Strategy," *Journal of Development Planning*, no. 13 (1978), p. 162.

7. United Nations Industrial Development Organization, *Industrial Development Survey* (New York: United Nations, 1970).

8. United Nations, *World Economic Survey*, pt. 1 (New York: United Nations, 1974).

9. Calculated from estimates in International Labour Organization, *1950–2000 Labour Force*, vols. 1–4 (2d ed., Geneva: ILO, 1977), table 5.

10. United Nations Research Institute for Social Development, *Data Bank of Development Indicators*, vol. 3, p. 88.

11. United Nations, "Foreign Aid and Development Needs," *Journal of Development Planning* 10 (1976).

12. Bouvier, et al., "International Migration."

13. United Nations, *The Impact of Multinational Corporations on Development and on International Operations* (New York: United Nations, 1974). United Nations, *The Transnational Corporations in World Development: A Reexamination* (New York: United Nations, 1978).

14. United Nations, "Salient Features of Economic Cooperation among Developing Countries," *Journal of Development Planning* 13 (1978).

CHAPTER SIXTEEN

1. Hans P. Binswanger and Vernon W. Ruttan, *Induced Innovation, Technology, Institutions and Development* (Baltimore: Johns Hopkins, 1978), p. 49.

2. Food and Agriculture Organization, "Population, Food Supply, and Agricultural Development," in United Nations, ed., *The Population Debate*, vol. 1 (New York: United Nations, 1976), p. 494–97.

3. Ibid., pp. 494–97.

4. International Union of Railways, *International Railway Statistics*.

5. International Road Federation, *World Road Statistics*.

6. United Nations Research Institute for Social Development, *Data Bank of Development Indicators*, vol. 1, p. 56.

7. J. N. Sinha, "Population and Agriculture," in Leon Tabah, ed., *Population Growth and Economic Development in the Third World*, vol. 1 (Dolhain: Ordina IUSSP, n.d.), pp. 298–300.

8. Ibid. Simon, *Economics of Population Growth*, pp. 265–68.

9. H. A. Oluwaseanmi, "Socio-Economic Aspects of Feeding People," in *Proceedings of the World Food Conference of 1976*, pp. 96–97.

10. Kumar, *Population and Land Use*, annex table 6.

11. Dalrymple, *Survey of Multiple Cropping*.

12. Mario Valderrama and Edgardo Moscardi, "Current Policies Affecting Food Production: The Case of Wheat in the Andean Region," in *Proceedings of the World Food Conference of 1976*, pp. 219–32.

13. Boserup, *Woman's Role*, pp. 15 ff.

14. Food and Agriculture Organization, *Regional Food Plan for Africa* (Rome: FAO, 1978).

15. T. H. Lee, "Food Supply and Population Growth in Developing Countries: Case Study of Taiwan," in Nurul Islam, ed., *Agricultural Policy in Developing Countries*, p. 179.

16. Chukuko Okonjo, "Population Dynamics and Nigerian Development," paper delivered at African Population Conference in Accra, 1971, p. 13.

17. United Nations, *Implementation of the International Development Strategy*, vol. 1 (New York: United Nations, 1973), pp. 78–80.

18. Ashish Bose, "Migration Streams in India," in Sydney Conference (Sydney: IUSSP, 1967).

19. United Nations, *Poverty, Unemployment and Development Policy: A Case Study of Kerala* (New York: United Nations, 1975), p. 28.

20. Ester Boserup, "Population and Agricultural Productivity," in United Nations, ed., *The Population Debate*, vol. 1, p. 500.

21. United Nations, *Poverty, Unemployment*, pp. 21–23.

22. Boserup, "Population and Agricultural Productivity," p. 500.

23. Oded Stark, *Technological Change and Rural-to-Urban Migration of Labour* (Liege: IUSSP, 1978).

24. Hans P. Binswanger, *The Economics of Tractors in South Asia* (New York: Agricultural Development Council, 1978).

BIBLIOGRAPHY

Adams, Robert McC. "Early Civilization, Subsistence and Environment." In Carl H. Kraeling and Robert McC. Adams, eds., *City Invincible*. Chicago: University of Chicago Press, 1960.

Adams, Robert McC. *The Evolution of Urban Society: Early Mesopotamia and Pre-Hispanic Mexico*. London: Weidenfeld and Nicolson, 1966

Adams, Robert McC. *Land behind Baghdad*. Chicago: University of Chicago Press, 1965.

Adams, Robert McC., and Nissen, Hans J. *The Uruk Countryside*. Chicago: University of Chicago Press, 1976.

Allen, G. C. "The Industrialization of the Far East." In *Cambridge Economic History of Europe*. Vol. 6. Cambridge: University Press, 1965.

Ames, E., and Rosenberg, N. "Changing Technological Leadership and Industrial Growth." In Nathan Rosenberg, ed., *The Economics of Technological Change*. Harmondsworth: Penguin, 1971.

Angel, Lawrence J. "Paleoecology, Paleodemography and Health." In Steven Polger, ed., *Population, Ecology and Social Evolution*. The Hague: Mouton, 1975.

Armengaud, André. "Population in Europe 1700–1914." In *Fontana Economic History of Europe*. Vol. 3. Glasgow: Collins, 1973.

Bairoch, Paul. *Révolution industrielle et sous-développement*. Paris: SEDES, 1969.

Barrington Moore, J. *Social Origins of Dictatorship and Democracy*. Harmondsworth: Penguin, 1967.

Bernard, Jacques. "Traders and Finance in the Middle Ages, 900–1500." In *Fontana Economic History of Europe*. Vol. 1. Glasgow: Collins, 1972.

Binford, Sally R. B., and Binford, Lewis R. *New Perspectives in Archeology*. Chicago: Aldine, 1963.

Binswanger, Hans P. *The Economics of Tractors in South Asia*. New York: Agricultural Development Council, 1978.

Binswanger, Hans P., and Ruttan, Vernon W. *Induced Innovation, Technology, Institutions and Development*. Baltimore: Johns Hopkins, 1978.

Boeke, J. N. *Economics and Economic Policy in Dual Societies*. Harlem: Institute of Pacific Relations, 1953.

Borchardt, Knut. "The Industrial Revolution in Germany." In *Fontana Economic History of Europe*. Vol. 4. Glasgow: Collins, 1973.

Bose, Ashish. "Migration Streams in India." In *Sydney Conference*. Sydney: IUSSP, 1967.

Boserup, Ester. *The Conditions of Agricultural Growth*. London: Allen and Unwin, 1965.

Boserup, Ester. "Food Supply and Population in Developing Countries." In Nurul Islam, ed., *Agricultural Policy in Developing Countries*. London: Macmillan, 1974.

Boserup, Ester. "The Impact of Population Growth on Agricultural Output." *Quarterly Journal of Economics* 89 (1975).

Boserup, Ester. "Population and Agricultural Productivity." In United Nations, ed., *The Population Debate*. Vol. 1. New York: United Nations, 1975.

Boserup, Ester. "Present and Potential Food Production in Developing Countries." In Wilbur Zelinzky; Leszeh A. Kosinski; and Mansel R. Prothero, eds., *Geography and a Crowding World.* New York: Columbia University Press, 1970.

Boserup, Ester. *Woman's Role in Economic Development.* New York: St. Martin's, 1970.

Boserup, Mogens. "Europe's New Fertility Pattern: Facts, Causes, Perspectives." In Scandinavian Demographic Society, ed., *The Fertility Decline in the Nordic Countries.* Copenhagen: Scandinavian Demographic Society, 1978.

Bouvier, Leon F.; Shryock, Henry S.; and Henderson, Henry W. "International Migration: Yesterday, Today and Tomorrow." *Population Bulletin* 32, no. 4 (1977).

Brunt, P. A. *Social Conflicts in the Roman Republic.* London: Chatto and Windus, 1971.

Buck, John Lossing. *Land Utilization in China.* Nanking: University of Nanking Press, 1937.

Butzer, Karl W. *Early Hydraulic Civilization in Egypt.* Chicago: University of Chicago Press, 1976.

Cafagna, Luciene. "The Industrial Revolution in Italy 1830–1914." In *Fontana Economic History of Europe.* Vol. 4. Glasgow: Collins, 1973.

Caldwell, John C. "Toward a Restatement of Demographic Transition Theory." *Population and Development Review* 2, nos. 3–4 (1976).

Carneiro, Robert L. "The Measurement of Cultural Development in the Ancient Near East and in Anglo Saxon England." *Transactions of the New York Academy of Sciences* 31, no. 8 (1969).

Carneiro, Robert L. "Slash and Burn Cultivation among the Kuikuru." *Anthropologica.* Caracas, 1961.

Carneiro, Robert L. "A Theory of the Origin of the State." *Science* 169 (1970).

Chaianov, A. V. *The Theory of Peasant Economy.* Homewood: Irwin, 1966.

Chambers, J. D. "Enclosure and Labour Supply in the Industrial Revolution." *Economic History Review* 5 (1953).

Chambers, J. D., and Mingay, G. E. *The Agrarian Revolution 1750–1880.* London: Batsford, 1966.

Childe, Gordon V. *New Light on the Most Ancient East.* London: Routledge and Kegan Paul, 1952.

Childe, Gordon V. *The Prehistory of European Society.* London: Cassell, 1962.

Cipolla, Carlo. *The Economic History of World Population.* Harmondsworth: Penguin, 1962.

Clairin, Remy. "Evaluation de la mortalité infantile et juvénile d'après les données disponibles en Afrique." In Caldwell and Okonjo, eds., *Population in Tropical Africa.* New York: Population Council, 1968.

Clark, Colin. *Population Growth and Land Use.* London: Macmillan, 1968.

Clark, Colin, and Hasswell, Margaret. *The Economics of Subsistence Agriculture.* 4th ed. rev. London: Macmillan, 1970.

Clark, Desmond J. "Early Human Occupation of African Savanna Environments." In David E. Harris, ed., *Human Ecology in Savanna Environments.* London: Academic Press, 1980.

Coale, Ansley J. "The Demographic Transition." In United Nations, ed., *The Population Debate.* Vol. 1. New York: United Nations, 1975.

Cochrane, Willard W. "The Impact of Different Forms of Foreign Assistance on Agricultural Development." In *Proceedings of the World Food Conference 1976*. Ames: Iowa State University Press, 1977.

Coe, Michael D., and Flannery, Kent V. *Early Cultures and Human Ecology in South Coastal Guatemala*. Washington, D.C.: Smithsonian Institution Press, 1967.

Cohen, Mark N. *The Food Crisis in Prehistory*. New Haven: Yale University Press, 1977.

Cohen, Mark N. "Population Pressure and the Origin of Agriculture." In Steven Polger, ed., *Population, Ecology and Social Evolution*. The Hague: Mouton, 1975.

Cowgill, George L. "On Causes and Consequences of Ancient and Modern Population Changes." *American Anthropologist* 77, no. 3 (1975).

Dalrymple, Dana G. *Survey of Multiple Cropping in Less Developed Nations*. Washington, D.C.: Department of Agriculture, 1971.

Das Gupta, Ajit. "Study of the Historical Demography of India." In D. V. Glass and Roger Revelle, eds., *Population and Social Change*. London: Arnold, 1972.

David, Paul. "The Mechanization of Reaping in the Ante-Bellum Mid-West." In Nathan Rosenberg, ed., *The Economics of Technological Change*. Harmondsworth: Penguin, 1971.

Davis, Kingsley. "The Origin and Growth of Urbanization in the World." *American Journal of Sociology* 60 (1955).

Deane, Phyllis. "The Industrial Revolution in Great Britain." In *Fontana Economic History of Europe*. Vol. 4. Pt. 1. Glasgow: Collins, 1973.

Deane, Phyllis, and Cole, W. A. "British Growth 1868–1959." In *Cambridge Economic History of Europe*. Vol. 6. Cambridge: University Press, 1965.

Demeny, Paul. "On the End of the Population Explosion." *Population and Development Review* 5, no. 1 (1979).

Desowitz, Robert S. "Epidemiologic-Ecological Interaction in the Tropical Savanna." In David R. Harris, ed., *Human Ecology in Savanna Environments*. London: Academic Press, 1980.

de Vries, Jan. "Labor/Leisure Trade Off." *Peasant Studies Newsletter* 1, no. 2 (1972).

Diop, Majhamout. *Histoire des classes sociales dans l'Afrique de l'Ouest*. Paris: Maspero, 1971.

Dore, R. P. "Agricultural Improvement in Japan 1870–1900." In E. L. Jones and S. J. Woolf, eds., *Agrarian Change and Economic Development*. London: Methuen, 1969.

Dovering, Folke. "The Transformation of European Agriculture." In *Cambridge Economic History of Europe*. Vol. 6. Cambridge: University Press, 1965.

Drake, Michael. *Population in Industrialization*. London: Methuen, 1969.

Duby, Georges. "Medieval Agriculture 500–1500." In *Fontana Economic History of Europe*. Vol. 1. Glasgow: Collins, 1972.

Dumond, Don E. "The Limitation of Human Population." *Science* 187 (1975).

Dumond, Don E. "Population Growth and Political Centralization." In Brian Spooner, ed., *Population Growth: Anthropological Implications*. Cambridge: MIT Press, 1972.

Duncan-Jones, Richard. *The Economy of the Roman Empire*. Cambridge: University Press, 1974.

Durand, John D. "Historical Estimates of World Population." *Population and Development Review* 3, no. 3 (1977).

Easterlin, R. A. "The Conflict between Aspirations and Resources." *Population and Development Review* 2, nos. 3–4 (1976).

Easterlin, R. A. "The Effects of Population Growth on the Economic Growth of Developing Countries." *Annals of the American Academy of Political and Social Sciences* 369 (1967).

Eckholm, Erik P. *The Other Energy Crisis: Firewood.* Washington, D.C.: Worldwatch Institute, 1975.

Ekvall, Robert E. "Demographic Aspects of Tibetan Nomadic Pastoralism." In Brian Spooner, ed., *Population Growth: Anthropological Implications.* Cambridge: MIT Press, 1972.

Finley, M. I. *The Ancient Economy.* London: Chatto and Windus, 1973.

Flannery, Kent V. "Origin and Ecological Effects of Early Domestication." In Peter J. Ucko and G. N. Dimbleby, eds., *The Domestication and Exploitation of Plants and Animals.* London: Duckworth, 1969.

Fohlen, Claude. "The Industrial Revolution in France 1700–1914." In *Fontana Economic History of Europe.* Vol. 4. Pt. 1. Glasgow: Collins, 1973.

Food and Agriculture Organization (FAO). "Population, Food Supply and Agricultural Development." In United Nations, ed., *The Population Debate.* Vol. 1. New York: United Nations, 1975.

Food and Agriculture Organization (FAO). *Production Yearbook.* Rome: FAO, 1972.

Food and Agriculture Organization (FAO). *Regional Food Plan for Africa.* Rome: FAO, 1978.

Forbes, R. J. "Food and Drink." In Charles Singer; E. J. Holmyard; A. R. Hall; and Trevor L. Williams, eds., *A History of Technology.* Vol. 3. Oxford: Clarendon Press, 1957.

Fourastie, Jean. *L'Evaluation des prix à long terme.* Paris: Presses Universitaires de France, 1969.

Freedman, Ronald. "Summary of Research Findings on Asian Population Programmes." *Population Reports* 1, no. 20 (1978).

Furnival, J. S. *Colonial Policy and Practice.* Cambridge: University Press, 1967.

Girard, L. "Transport." In *Cambridge Economic History of Europe.* Vol. 6. Cambridge: University Press, 1965.

Habakkuk, H. J. *Population Growth and Economic Development since 1750.* Leicester: University Press, 1972.

Hall, A. R. "Military Technology." In Charles Singer, et al., eds., *A History of Technology.* Vol. 3. Oxford: Clarendon Press, 1957.

Hall, A. R. "The Rise of the West." In Charles Singer, et al., eds., *A History of Technology.* Vol. 3. Oxford: Clarendon Press, 1957.

Hanley, Susan B., and Yamamura, Kozo. "Population Trends and Economic Growth in Pre-Industrial Japan." In D. V. Glass and Roger Revelle, eds., *Population and Social Change.* London: Arnold, 1972.

Hansen, Svend Aage. *Økonomisk Vaekst i Danmark.* Vol. 1. Copenhagen: Gads Forlag, 1972.

Harris, David R. "Alternative Pathways toward Agriculture." In Charles A. Reid, ed., *Origins of Agriculture.* The Hague: Mouton, 1977.

Harris, David R. *Human Ecology in Savanna Environments.* London: Academic Press, 1980.

Hassan, Fekri. "Determination of the Size, Density and Growth Rate of Hunting Gathering Populations." In Steven Polger, ed., *Population, Ecology and Social Evolution.* The Hague: Mouton, 1975.

Hayami, Yujiro. "Technological Progress in Agriculture." In Lawrence Klein and Kazushi Ohkawa, eds., *Economic Growth.* Homewood: Irwin, 1968.

Hayami, Yujiro, and Ruttan, Vernon W. *Agricultural Development.* Baltimore: Johns Hopkins, 1971.

Hayami, Yujiro, and Ruttan, Vernon W. "Korean Rice, Taiwan Rice and Japanese Agricultural Stagnation." *Quarterly Journal of Economics* 84 (1970).

Heckscher, Eli F. *Svensk Arbete och Liv.* Stockholm: Aldus Bonnier, 1969.

Hemmi, Kenzo. "Primary Production, Exports and Economic Development: The Case of Silk." In Kazushi Ohkawa; Bruce F. Johnston; and Hiromitsu Kaneda, eds., *Agriculture and Economic Growth.* Princeton: University Press, 1970.

Hoffman, Richard. "Medieval Origin of the Common Fields." In W. N. Parker and Eric L. Jones, eds., *European Peasants and Their Markets.* Princeton: University Press, 1975.

Holder, Preston. *The Horse and the Hoe in the Great Plains.* Lincoln: University of Nebraska Press, 1970.

Holmes, A. Baron. "The Gold Coast and Nigeria." In W. Arthur Lewis, ed., *Tropical Development 1880–1913.* London: Allen and Unwin, 1970.

Houdaille, Jacques. "Les Méchanismes régulateurs de la fécondité dans les sociétés traditionelles." In *International Population Conference: Mexico.* Vol. 3. Dolhain: IUSSP, 1977.

International Labor Organization (ILO). *1950–2000 Labour Force.* Vols. 1–4. 2d ed. Geneva: ILO, 1977.

International Road Federation. *World Road Statistics.* Geneva-Washington: IRF, 1973.

International Union of Railways. *International Railway Statistics.* Paris: IUR, 1972.

Ishikawa, Shigeru. *Economic Development in Asian Perspective.* Tokyo: Kinokuniya Bookshop Co., 1967.

Ishikawa, Shigeru. *Factors Affecting China's Agriculture in the Coming Decade.* Tokyo: Institute for Asian Economic Affairs, 1967.

Johnston, Bruce F. *Agriculture and Economic Development.* Stanford: Food Research Institute, 1966.

Jones, E. L., and Woolf, S. J. *Agrarian Change and Economic Development.* London: Methuen, 1969.

Jones, Rhys. "Hunters in the Austrilian Tropical Savanna." In David R. Harris, ed., *Human Ecology in Savanna Environments.* London: Academic Press, 1980.

Kellenbenz, Hermann. "Technology in the Age of the Scientific Revolution." In *Fontana Economic History of Europe.* Vol. 2. Glasgow: Collins, 1974.

Kiuchi, Shinzo. "Population Pressure in Japan." In Wilbur Zelinsky, et al., eds., *Geography and a Crowding World.* New York: Columbia University Press, 1970.

Kumar, Joginder. *Population and Land in World Agriculture.* Berkeley: University of California Population Monograph Series 12, 1973.

Kuznets, Simon. *Modern Economic Growth: Rates, Structure and Spread.* New Haven: Yale University Press, 1966.

Kuznets, Simon. "Population Trends and Modern Economic Growth." In United Nations, ed., *The Population Debate.* Vol. 1. New York: United Nations, 1975.

Landes, David S. "Japan and Europe." In William W. Lockwood, ed., *The State and Economic Enterprise in Japan.* Princeton: University Press, 1965.

Landes, David S. "Technological Change and Development in Western Europe 1750–1914." In *Cambridge Economic History of Europe.* Vol. 6. Cambridge: University Press, 1965.

Landes, David S. *The Unbound Prometheus.* Cambridge: University Press, 1969.

Lee, Richard B. "Population Growth and the Beginnings of Sedentary Life among the Kung Bushmen." In Brian Spooner, ed., *Population Growth: Anthropological Implications*. Cambridge: MIT Press, 1972.

Lee, Richard B., and de Vore, Irven, eds. *Man the Hunter*. Chicago: Aldine, 1968.

Lee, T. H. "Food Supply and Population Growth in Developing Countries: Case Study of Taiwan." In Nurul Islam, ed., *Agricultural Policy in Developing Countries*. London: Macmillan, 1974.

Le Roi Ladurie, Emmanuel. "Zero Population Growth and Subsistence in 16th Century Rural France." *Peasant Studies Newsletter* 1, no. 2 (1972).

Lewis, W. Arthur, *Aspects of Tropical Trade 1863–1965: Wicksell Lectures 1969*. Stockholm: Almquist, 1970.

Lewis, W. Arthur. *Tropical Development 1880–1913*. London: Allen and Unwin, 1970.

Lilley, Samuel. "Technological Progress and the Industrial Revolution." In *Fontana Economic History of Europe*. Vol. 3. Glasgow: Collins, 1973.

McAlpin, Michelle Burge. "Railroads, Prices and Peasant Rationality: India 1860–1900." *Journal of Economic History* 34 (1974).

McKeown, Thomas. *The Modern Rise of Population*. New York: Academic Press, 1976.

McKeown, Thomas; Brown, R. G.; and Recard, R. C. "An Interpretation of the Modern Rise of Population in Europe." *Population Studies* 26, no. 3 (1972).

McNeill, William H. *Plagues and Peoples*. Oxford: Blackwell, 1977.

Maddalena, Aldo de. "Rural Europe 1500–1700." In *Fontana Economic History of Europe*. Vol. 2. Glasgow: Collins, 1974.

Maity, Sachindra Kumar. *The Economic Life of Northern India in Gupta Period*. Calcutta: World Press, 1957.

Masiu, Yukio. "The Supply Price of Labor from Family Workers." In Kazushi Ohkawa, et al., eds., *Agriculture and Economic Growth*. Princeton: University Press, 1970.

Mathias, Peter. *The First Industrial Nation*. London: Methuen, 1969.

Mauldin, W. Parker, and Berelson, Bernhard. "Conditions of Fertility Decline in Developing Countries 1965–75." *Studies in Family Planning* 9, no. 5 (1978).

Minchinton, Walter. "Pattern and Structure of Demand 1500–1750." In *Fontana Economic History of Europe*. Vol. 2. Glasgow: Collins, 1974.

Ministry of Agriculture. *Selected Economic Indicators Relating to Agriculture*. Tokyo: Ministry of Agriculture, March 1971.

Moeller, Herbert. "Population and Society during the Old Regime 1640 to 1770." In Herbert Moeller, ed., *Population Movements in Modern European History*. London: M:acmillan, 1964.

Morgan, W. S. "Peasant Agriculture in Tropical Africa." In H. F. Thomas and G. W. Whittington, eds., *Environment and Land Use in Africa*. London: Methuen, 1969.

Nakamura, James J. *Agricultural Production and the Economic Development of Japan 1873–1922*. Princeton: University Press, 1966.

Needham, Joseph. *Clerks and Craftsmen in China and the West*. Cambridge: University Press, 1970.

Needham, Joseph. *Science and Civilization in China*. Cambridge: University Press, 1961–.

Nef, J. V. "Coal Mining and Utilization." In Charles Singer, et al., eds., *A History of Technology*. Vol. 3. Oxford: Clarendon Press, 1957.

Netting, Robert McC. *Cultural Ecology.* Menlo Park: Cummings, 1977.

Netting, Robert McC. *Hill Farmers of Nigeria.* Seattle: University of Washington Press, 1969.

Netting, Robert McC. "Sacred Power and Centralization." In Brian Spooner, ed., *Population Growth: Anthropological Implications.* Cambridge: MIT Press, 1972.

Netting, Robert McC., and Elias, Wekter S. "Balancing on an Alp: Population Stability and Change in a Swiss Peasant Village." In Priscilla Copeland Reining and Barbara Zenkera, eds., *Village Viability in Contemporary Society.* Washington, D.C.: AAAS, 1980.

Neumark, D. S. *Foreign Trade and Economic Development in Africa.* Stanford: Food Research Institute, 1964.

North, Douglass C. "Industrialization in the United States." In *Cambridge Economic History of Europe.* Vol. 6. Cambridge: University Press, 1965.

Oakley, Deborah. "American-Japanese Interaction in the Development of Population Policy in Japan 1945–52." *Population and Development Review* 4, no. 4 (1978).

Ohkawa, Kazushi. "Phases of Agricultural Development and Economic Growth." In Kazushi Ohkawa, et al., eds., *Agriculture and Economic Growth.* Princeton: University Press, 1970.

Ohkawa, Kazushi, and Johnston, Bruce F. "The Transferability of the Japanese Pattern of Modernizing Traditional Agriculture." In Erik Thorbecke, ed., *The Role of Agriculture in Economic Development.* New York: Columbia University Press, 1969.

Okita, Saburo. *Causes and Problems of Rapid Growth in Postwar Japan.* Tokyo: Japan Economic Research Institute, 1967.

Okonjo, Chukuko. "Population Dynamics and Nigerian Development." Paper delivered at African Population Conference in Accra, 1971.

Olson, Gerald W. "Some Pedological Observations of Soils in Maya Areas in Relation to Archeology." Presentation Statement at Meeting of Society for American Archeology, Tucson, 1978.

Oluwaseanmi, H. A. "Socio-Economic Aspects of Feeding People." In *Proceedings of the World Food Conference 1976.* Ames: Iowa State University Press, 1977.

Pharr, Susan J. "Japan: Historical and Temporary Perspectives." In Janet Zollinger Giele and Audrey Chapman Smock, eds., *Women: Role and Status in Eight Countries.* New York: Wiley, 1977.

Piggott, Stuart. *Ancient Europe.* Edinburgh: University Press, 1965.

Preus, Anthony. "Biomedical Techniques for Influencing Human Reproduction in the Fourth Century B.C." *Arethusa* 8, no. 2 (1975).

Price, Derek J. "The Manufacture of Scientific Instruments from c. 1500 to c. 1700." In Charles Singer, et al., eds., *A History of Technology.* Vol. 3. Oxford: Clarendon Press, 1957.

Puleston, Dennis E. "Terracing, Raised Fields and Tree Cropping in the Maya Lowlands." In Peter D. Harrison and B. L. Turner, eds., *Pre-Hispanic Maya Agriculture.* Albuquerque: University of New Mexico Press, 1978.

Razzel, P. E. "An Interpretation of the Modern Rise of Population in Europe: A Critique." *Population Studies* 28, no. 1 (1974).

Razzel, P. E. "Population Change in 18th Century England: A Reappraisal." In Michael Drake, ed., *Population in Industrialization.* London: Methuen, 1969.

Razzel, P. E. "Population Growth and Economic Change in 18th Century and Early 19th Century England and Ireland." In E. L. Jones and G. E. Mingay, eds., *Land, Labour and Population in the Industrial Revolution*. London: Arnold, 1967.

Redfield, Robert. *The Primitive World and Its Transformation*. Harmondsworth: Penguin, 1968. Orig. pub., 1953.

Reinhard, Marcel R.; Armengaud, André; and Dupaquier, Jacques. *Histoire générale de la population mondiale*. Paris: Montchrestien, 1968.

Rice, Don S. "Population Growth and Subsistence Alternatives in a Tropical Lacustrian Environment." In Peter D. Harrison and B. L. Turner, eds., *Pre-Hispanic Maya Agriculture*. Albuquerque: University of New Mexico Press, 1978.

Richards, Audrey I. *Economic Development and Tribal Change*. Cambridge: Heffer, 1954.

Richards, Audrey I. *Land, Labour and Diet in Northern Rhodesia*. Oxford: International Institute of African Languages and Culture, 1939.

Roehl, Richard. "Patterns and Structure of Demand 1000–1500." In *Fontana Economic History of Europe*. Vol. 1. Glasgow: Collins, 1972.

Romaniuk, A. "Infertility in Tropical Africa." In John C. Caldwell and Chukuku Okonjo, eds., *Population in Tropical Africa*. New York: Columbia University Press, 1968.

Rosenberg, Nathan. *Perspectives on Technology*. Cambridge: University Press, 1976.

Russel, J. C. "Population in Europe 500–1500." In *Fontana Economic History of Europe*. Vol. 1. Glasgow: Collins, 1972.

Sanders, William T. "The Fon of Bahut and the Classical Maya." *Actes du XLII Congrès International des Américanistes*. Vol. 8. Paris: Société des Américanistes, 1976.

Sanders, William T. "Population, Agricultural History and Societal Evolution in Mesoamerica." In Brian Spooner, ed., *Population Growth: Anthropoligical Implications*. Cambridge: MIT Press, 1972.

Sanders, William T., and Price, Barbara J. *Mesoamerica: The Evolution of a Civilization*. New York: Random House, 1968.

Sawada, Shujiro. "Technological Change in Japanese Agriculture." In Kazushi Ohkawa, et al., eds., *Agriculture and Economic Growth*. Princeton: University Press, 1970.

Schultz, T. W. *Transforming Traditional Agriculture*. New Haven: Yale University Press, 1964.

Scott, Joan W., and Tilly, Louise A. "Women's Work and the Family in 19th Century Europe." *Comparative Studies in Society and History* 17, no. 1 (1975).

Sella, Domenico. "European Industries 1500–1700." In *Fontana Economic History of Europe*. Vol. 2. Glasgow: Collins, 1974.

Simon, Julian J. *The Economics of Population Growth*. Princeton: University Press, 1977.

Sinha, J. N. "Population and Agriculture." In Leon Tabah, ed., *Population Growth and Economic Development in the Third World*. Vol. 1. Dolhain: Ordina IUSSP, n.d.

Skempton, A. W. "Canals and River Navigations before 1750." In Charles Singer, et al., eds., *A History of Technology*. Oxford: Clarendon Press, 1957.

Skovgaard-Petersen, Inge. "Oldtid og Vikingetid." In Inge Skovgaard-Petersen; Aksel E. Christensen; and H. Paludan, eds., *Danmarks Historie*. Vol. 1. Copenhagen: Gyldendal, 1977.

Slicher van Bath, B. H. *The Agrarian History of Western Europe*, A.D. 500–1500. New York: St. Martin's, 1963.

Slicher van Bath, B. H. "The Rise of Intensive Husbandry in the Low Countries." In Charles K. Warner, ed., *Agrarian Conditions in Modern European History*. London: Macmillan, 1966.

Smith, Cyril Stanley, and Forbes, R. J. "Metallurgy and Assaying." In Charles Singer, et al., eds., *A History of Technology*. Oxford: Clarendon Press, 1957.

Smith, Philip E. L. "Changes in Population Pressure in Archeological Explanation." *World Archeology* 4, no. 1 (1972).

Smith, Philip E. L. *The Consequences of Food Production*. Reading: Addison Wesley, 1972.

Smith, Philip E. L., and Young, T. Cuyler. "The Evolution of Early Agriculture and Culture in Greater Mesopotamia." In Brian Spooner, ed., *Population Growth: Anthropological Implications*. Cambridge: MIT Press, 1972.

Smith, Thomas C. *The Agrarian Origins of Modern Japan*. Stanford: University Press, 1959.

Southall, A. W. "Alur Migrants." In Audrey I. Richards, ed., *Economic Development and Tribal Change*. Cambridge: Heffer, 1954.

Sprandel, Rolf. "La Production du fer au moyen age." *Annales* 24 (1969).

Srinivasan, K. "Application of Methods of Measuring the Impact of Family Planning Programmes on Fertility." In United Nations, ed., *Methods of Measuring the Impact of Family Planning*. New York: United Nations, 1978.

Stark, Oded. *Technological Change and Rural-to-Urban Migration of Labour*. Liege: IUSSP, 1978.

Stokes, Bruce. "Filling Family Planning Gaps." *Population Reports* 1, no. 20 (1978).

Stolnitz, George J. "International Mortality Trends." In United Nations, ed., *The Population Debate*. Vol. 1. New York: United Nations, 1975.

Tabutin, Dominique. "La Mortalité féminine en Europe avant 1940." *Population* 33, no. 1 (1976).

Tauber, Irene. *The Population of Japan*. Princeton: University Press, 1958.

Taylor, D. R. F. "Agricultural Change in Kikuyuland." In H. F. Thomas and G. W. Whittington, eds., *Environment and Land Use in Africa*. London: Methuen, 1969.

Temin, Peter. "A New Look at Hunter's Hypothesis about the Ante-Bellum Iron Industry." In Nathan Rosenberg, ed., *The Economics of Technological Change*. Harmondsworth: Penguin, 1971.

Teng, S'su-yu, and Fairbank, John King. *China's Response to the West*. Cambridge: Harvard University Press, 1954.

Thistlewaite, Frank. "Migration from Europe to Overseas in the 19th and 20th Centuries." In Herbert Moeller, ed., *Population Movements in Modern European History*. London: Macmillan, 1964.

Thrupp, Sylvia. "Medieval Industry 1000–1500." In *Fontana Economic History of Europe*. Vol. 1. Glasgow: Collins, 1972.

Tilly, Louise. "La Révolte frumentaire: Forme de conflit politique en France." *Annales* 27, no. 3 (1972).

Tracy, Michel. "Agriculture in Western Europe: The Great Depression 1880–1900." In Charles K. Warner, ed., *Agrarian Conditions in Modern European History*. London: Macmillan, 1966.

Tsui, Amy Ong, and Bogue, Donald J. "Declining World Fertility." *Population Bulletin* 33, no. 4 (1978).

Turner, B. L. "Ancient Agricultural Land Use in the Central Maya Lowlands."
   In Peter D. Harrison and B. L. Turner, eds., *Pre-Hispanic Maya Agriculture*.
   Albuquerque: University of New Mexico Press, 1978.
Turner, B. L.; Hanham, Robert Q.; and Portararo, Anthony V. "Population Pres-
   sure and Agricultural Intensity." *Annals of the Association of American Geographers*
   67, no. 3 (1977).
Tussing, Arlon R. "The Labor Force in Meiji Economic Growth." In Kazushi
   Ohkawa, et al., eds., *Agriculture and Economic Growth*. Princeton: University
   Press, 1970.
Umemura, Matari. "Agriculture and Labor Supply in the Meiji Era." In Kazushi
   Ohkawa, et al., eds., *Agriculture and Economic Growth*. Princeton: University
   Press, 1970.
United Nations. *The Determinants and Consequences of Population Trends*. New York:
   United Nations, 1973.
United Nations. *Developing Countries and Level of Development*. E/AC 54/L 81 Annex
   2. New York: United Nations, 1975.
United Nations. "Development Trends since 1960 and Their Implications for a
   New Development Strategy." *Journal of Development Planning* 13 (1978).
United Nations. "Foreign Aid and Development Needs." *Journal of Development
   Planning* 10 (1976).
United Nations. *The Impact of Multinational Corporations on Development and on
   International Operations*. New York: United Nations, 1974.
United Nations. *Implementation of the International Development Strategy*. Vol. 1.
   New York: United Nations, 1973.
United Nations. "Industrialization and Development." *Journal of Development
   Planning* 8 (1975).
United Nations. *Poverty, Unemployment and Development Policy: A Case Study of
   Kerala*. New York: United Nations, 1975.
United Nations. *Report of the United Nations' World Population Conference*. New
   York: United Nations, 1975.
United Nations. "Salient Features of Economic Cooperation among Developing
   Countries." *Journal of Development Planning* 13 (1978).
United Nations. *The Transnational Corporations in World Development: A Reexami-
   nation*. New York: United Nations, 1978.
United Nations. *World Economic Survey*. Pt. 1. New York: United Nations, 1974.
United Nations. *The World Population Situation in 1977*. New York: United Nations,
   1979.
United Nations and Food and Agriculture Organization (FAO). *European Agri-
   culture: A Statement of Problems*. Geneva: United Nations and FAO, 1954.
United Nations Industrial Development Organization (UNIDO). *Industrial De-
   velopment Survey*. New York: United Nations, 1970.
United Nations Research Institute for Social Development (UNRISD). *Data Bank
   of Development Indicators*. Vol. 1. Geneva: UNRISD, 1976.
Valderrama, Mario, and Moscardi, Edgardo. "Current Policies affecting Food
   Production: The Case of Wheat in the Andean Region." In *Proceedings of the
   World Food Conference 1976*. Ames: Iowa State University Press, 1977.
van Velsen, J. "Labour Migration as a Positive Factor in the Continuity of Tonga
   Traditional Society." *Economic Development and Cultural Change* 8 (1960).

Wailes, B. "The Origins of Settled Farming in Temperate Europe." In George Cardena; Henry H. Hoeningswald; and Alfred Senn, eds., *Indo Europe and Indo Europeans*. Philadelphia: University of Pennsylvania Press, 1970.

Wailes, B. "Plow and Population in Temperate Europe." In Brian Spooner, ed., *Population Growth: Anthropological Implications*. Cambridge: MIT Press, 1972.

Wallerstein, Immanuel. *The Modern World-System*. New York: Academic Press, 1974.

Warming, Jens. *Danmarks Erhvervs og Samfundsliv*. Vol. 3. Copenhagen: Gads Forlag, 1939.

Warner, Charles K. *Agrarian Conditions in Modern European History*. London: Macmillan, 1966.

Watson, William. *Tribal Cohesion in a Money Economy*. Manchester: University Press, 1958.

White, Lynn, Jr. "The Expansion of Technology 500–1500." In *Fontana Economic History of Europe*. Vol. 1. Glasgow: Collins, 1972.

Wilken, Gene C. "Food Producing Systems Available to the Ancient Mayas." *American Antiquity* 36, no. 4 (1971).

Wittfogel, Karl A. *Oriental Despotism*. New Haven: Yale University Press, 1957.

Wolf, Eric R. *Sons of the Shaking Earth*. Chicago: University of Chicago Press, 1959.

Wolf, Eric R., and Palerm, Angel. "Irrigation in the Old Acolhua Domain." *Southwestern Journal of Anthropology* 11, no. 3 (1955).

World Bank. *The World Bank Report 1978*. Washington, D.C.: World Bank, 1978.

World Health Organization (WHO). "Malaria Control: A Reoriented Strategy." *WHO Chronicle* 32 (1978).

Wrigley, E. A. *Industrial Growth and Population Change*. Cambridge: University Press, 1961.

Wrigley, E. A. *Population and History*. London: Weidenfeld and Nicolson, 1969.

Wrigley, E. A. "The Supply of Raw Materials in the Industrial Revolution." *Economic History Review* 15, no. 1 (1962).

Youngson, A. J. "The Opening Up of New Territories." In *Cambridge Economic History of Europe*. Vol. 6. Cambridge: University Press, 1965.

Youssef, Nadia H. "Women's Status and Fertility in Muslim Countries of the Middle East and Africa." Paper delivered at Symposium on Women's Status and Fertility. New Orleans: American Psychological Association, 1974.

Zangheri, R. "The Historical Relationship between Agricultural and Economic Development in Italy." In E. L. Jones and S. J. Woolf, eds., *Agrarian Change and Economic Development*. London: Methuen, 1969.

INDEX

Abortion: induced, 34, 37–39, 84, 183–85, 187; involuntary, 37–38,180
Adams, Robert McC., 44, 52–54, 61, 74, 82
Administrative technology: in ancient world, 72, 77, 86; in Europe, 99, 102; in Japan, 162–63, 171; in Third World, 210–11
Africa, 144–57; agriculture, 145–48, 180, 206–7; fertility, 178, 180–81, 186–87; industrialization, 153–57; urbanization, 151–54. *See also* Arab region; *and names of individual countries*
Age of death, 37, 85
Agricultural Revolution: first, in England, 113–16; first, in Japan, 164–66, 168; second, in England, 116–17; second, in Japan, 168–70
Agriculture: definition of intensive, 18–20; modernization, 191–93, 201–4, 206; number of operations, 44–46, 49, 60, 81, 121–23, 164–66; traditional, 15, 204–6. *See also* Cash crops; Fallow; Food; Food supply system; Output; Subsidies; Taxation; *and names of individual countries and regions*
Aid, international: distribution, 196–97, 199, 203; to family planning, 184–86; to food imports, 191–92, 202; medical, 177
Airports, 129
Ancient world: agriculture, 43–62; breakdown of, 84–88; urbanization, 63–90
Andean region, 55–56, 69–70, 73, 80–81, 205–6
Animal draft power, 24, 48–50; in ancient world, 52, 53, 55–56, 65, 67, 79, 86; in Europe, 57–62, 96, 101; in Third World, 201
Animal husbandry, 17–18, 22–24, 95–96, 103, 115–16, 121–23. *See also*

Food supply system; Meat; Milk; Prices
Annual cropping (AC), 18–20, 22–23; in ancient world, 86; in Europe, 114–17, 121–23; in India, 171–72; in Japan, 164–65, 169–70
Arab region: agriculture, 201–2, 208; definition, 13; fertility, 178–79, 187; industrialization, 155–56, 158. *See also names of individual countries*
Area: agricultural per inhabitant, 52–53, 69, 170–71; agricultural per worker, 26–28, 138–39, 159, 166; arable, 17–18, 26–27; arctic, 16; definition of, 16
Argentina, 138
Army, role of: in ancient world, 81–84, 87; in Europe, 98–100, 108. *See also* Military sector
Artificial islands, 55
Asia, 40–41, 158–72. *See also* Arab region; Mesopotamia; *and names of individual countries*
Australia. *See* Oceania

Baltic. *See* Northern Europe
Bangladesh, 194
Belgium. *See* Low Countries
Bengal, 158
Black Death, 94–96, 100
Boeke, J. N., 146
Bombay, 158
Breast-feeding, 38, 125, 178
Bricks, 78–79, 107
Broad spectrum period, 34
Bubonic plague, 85
Bush fallow (BF), 19–23, 44–45; in Africa, 147; in America, 54–55, 135; in Europe, 57–58, 95. *See also* Long fallow
Bushmen, 33

Calorie loss by transformation, 18, 49, 118
Canada. *See* North America